SUCCESS STRATEGIES
FOR ADJUNCT FACULTY

RICHARD E. LYONS

Faculty Development Associates

Boston ■ New York ■ San Francisco
Mexico City ■ Montreal ■ Toronto ■ London ■ Madrid ■ Munich ■ Paris
Hong Kong ■ Singapore ■ Tokyo ■ Cape Town ■ Sydney

To Mikhayla, Rebekah, Alisa, and Merica

Executive Editor and Publisher: Stephen D. Dragin
Senior Series Editorial Assistant: Barbara Strickland
Manufacturing Buyer: Andrew Turso
Executive Marketing Manager: Amy Cronin Jordan
Cover Designer: Suzanne Harbison
Production Coordinator: Pat Torelli Publishing Services
Editorial-Production Service: Argosy Publishing
Electronic Composition: Argosy Publishing

For related titles and support materials, visit our online catalog at www.ablongman.com.

Portions of this book first appeared in *Teaching College in an Age of Accountability* (Lyons, R., McIntosh, M., & Kysilka, M.) and *The Adjunct Professor's Guide to Success* (Lyons, R., Kysilka, M., & Pawlas, G.). Copyright ©2003 and 1999 (respectively) by Allyn and Bacon.

To obtain permission(s) to use material from this work, please submit a written request to Allyn and Bacon, Permissions Department, 75 Arlington Street, Boston, MA 02116, or fax your request to 617-848-7320.

Library of Congress Cataloguing-in-Publication Data
Lyons, Richard E.
    Success strategies for adjunct faculty / Richard E. Lyons.
        p.cm.
    Includes bibliographical references and index.
    ISBN 0-205-36017-3 (pbk. : alk. paper)
        1. College teachers, Part-time—United States. 2. College teaching—United States. I. Title

LB2331.72.L96 2004
378.1'2—dc21

                                                                            2003054937
Printed in the United States of America

9 8 7 6 5 4 3 2   07 06

CHAPTER 9

Infusing Technology into Your Teaching   159

CHAPTER 10

Managing the Examination Process   177

CHAPTER 11

Alternative Methods of Assessing Student Learning   199

CHAPTER 12

Bringing Your Course to an Effective Conclusion   219

CHAPTER 13

Evaluating the Effectiveness of Your Teaching   231

CHAPTER 14

Managing Your Adjunct Career   249

Bibliography   267

Index   274

■ ■ ■ ■ ■

A little more than a decade ago, research on part-time instructors employed in North American colleges and universities was difficult to find, and there was no indication that the increasingly critical issue was being widely discussed by institutional leaders. Through their 1993 breakthrough study published as *The Invisible Faculty*, Judith Gappa and David Leslie were successful in putting an array of issues surrounding adjunct faculty onto the agendas of instructional leaders. Their work triggered additional studies, articles, and books that have since trickled into the academic literature.

My first co-authored book for part-time instructors, *The Adjunct Professor's Guide to Success* (Allyn and Bacon, 1999), quickly became the leading title among the dozen or so titles that had by that time been published, and has maintained its standing since. It has provided aspiring and newly appointed instructors insights for obtaining their early teaching assignments, a better understanding of the higher education culture, and a toolkit of teaching and classroom management ideas for surviving and thriving in their initial teaching assignments. While employing a similar sequential approach to the issues adjunct professors typically encounter, *Success Strategies for Adjunct Faculty* addresses the needs of those who have already launched their part-time teaching careers and want to improve their teaching effectiveness and course management efficiency. Besides that intensified focus throughout, it adds a chapter on infusing technology into the reader's teaching and a richer set of tools located in the appendix of most chapters.

In addition to these new features, *Success Strategies for Adjunct Faculty* leverages feedback from hundreds of readers of *The Adjunct Professor's Guide to Success*, many of whom completed one of the dozen sections of a course especially designed for adjunct faculty, which I have taught since 1996. Additional feedback generated at workshops delivered at a wide array of institutions throughout North America, input from instructional leaders especially tuned in to adjunct faculty issues, and recent research findings with special appeal to adjunct professors have enabled me to broaden the scope and increase the depth of the content.

ORGANIZATION

Each chapter of *Success Strategies for Adjunct Faculty* opens with a testimonial from a successful adjunct professor that frames the chapter content to follow. These contributors and their colleagues whose testimonials close each chapter average 14 years teaching experience and are employed by land-grant universities, large and moderate-size public universities, private liberal arts colleges, for-profit universities, and community colleges in Canada and throughout the United States.

Chapter 1 opens by providing readers with a comprehensive view of the internal and external factors influencing part-time teaching today, including the increasingly critical accountability initiatives that mandate improved student recruitment, retention, and degree completion.

The second chapter provides coaching for developing a successful master strategy, based on the reader's self-analysis of personal strengths, limitations, and beliefs about learning, which should guide all aspects of his or her teaching.

Especially well-received by participants in my workshops and courses for adjunct faculty members, the material in Chapter 3 will provide invaluable insights into today's students. These insights enable the adjunct professor to orchestrate more grounded learning, as well as improved accountability outcomes.

Chapter 4 focuses on the critical factors inherent in effective course planning, many of which are not part of the adjunct professor's orientation to the initial teaching assignment at most institutions. It encourages the development of a comprehensive syllabus that serves as a contract with students, the formulation of strategic teaching practices, and the gathering of student feedback throughout the term.

Focused exclusively on the first retention milepost within the course, Chapter 5 details proven strategies for launching a new course. Its mastery ensures that the ever vulnerable adjunct professor and students establish common ground from the outset and foster a learning community that maximizes course completers.

Chapter 6 outlines strategies for organizing your materials and yourself to achieve the objectives of your course plan. It includes proven strategies for managing large classes and the term's second retention milepost, the first examination or submission of the first major assignment, as well as other critical but often overlooked issues.

Chapters 7 and 8 focus on opposite ends of the teaching methods continuum—the former on instructor-directed methods and the latter on those that are largely driven by students themselves. Bulleted tips for achieving improved student learning and more accountable results for instructional leaders are provided for each of a wide array of methods.

Chapter 9 provides the adjunct professor with strategies for integrating popular technology into teaching, again to improve student learning and to improve the retention of students through the end of the term.

Chapters 10 and 11 focus on the increasingly critical area of evaluating student learning with the former focusing on examinations and the latter on alternative forms of assessment. These two chapters provide especially useful exercises in their appendices for ensuring mastery of the overall evaluation process.

Chapter 12 helps the adjunct professor master strategies for bringing each course to a successful close, including those that help energize the classroom and help students more effectively manage their time and project completion.

Chapter 13 provides strategies for more effectively managing the evaluation of your teaching. It emphasizes regular "informal" methods of evaluation, before the administration of student ratings and observations by instructional administrators.

The final chapter equips adjunct professors to more effectively manage their teaching careers, including those who aspire to teach full time. Among its strategies are detailed tips for building strong mentoring relationships, both as a *protégé* and mentor.

Closing each chapter are two recurring components, designed to help ground the reader's mastery of its content: a summary of key points and the testimonials from the highly experienced adjunct professors mentioned earlier. In addition, most chapters include an appendix of tools for implementing the strategies included therein.

Success Strategies for Adjunct Faculty is designed to be a book you will carry in your briefcase and refer to often and in which you highlight or flag content that is especially critical to your needs. To ensure its currency is maintained, an array of resources are posted at the author's website, http://www.developfaculty.com, including teaching tips each week and a comprehensive list of links to an array of online resources. Please make the author aware through that site how your success might be further supported.

ACKNOWLEDGMENTS

Besides the resources listed throughout, this book would not have been possible without the input of a number of special educators. Foremost is Marcella Kysilka, who served as chair on my dissertation, which focused on adjunct faculty development, and as co-author on two of my previous books and who is a legend at the University of Central Florida. Meggin McIntosh, who has directed the Excellence in Teaching Program at the University of Nevada, Reno, and served as co-author on *Teaching College in an Age of Accountability,* contributed an array of valuable insights. George Pawlas, of the University of Central Florida and co-author of *The Adjunct Professor's Guide to Success,* contributed his wise counsel on a number of critical issues. Also deserving recognition for an array of reasons are Betsy Price of Westminster College; Susan Wambach of Montcalm Community College; Violeta Mutafova-Yamboli of the University of Nevada, Reno; Mike Wambach and Joy Harrison of Davenport University; Richard France of Cuyahoga Community College; and Dottie Vandergrift and Pat Profeta of Indian River Community College. I also thank members of the National Council for Staff, Program and Organizational Development and the Professional and Organizational Development Network in Higher Education, whose thought-provoking conferences and postings on organizational listservs stirred deeper investigation and provided useful insights. Finally, I thank the twenty-nine adjunct professors whose reflections open and close each chapter for enriching the book far beyond anything a single author could ever orchestrate.

Using Technology in Learner-Centered Education: Proven Strategies for Teaching and Learning
David G. Brown, Gordon McCray, Craig Runde, and Heidi Schweizer
ISBN: 0-205-35580-3

Faculty Work and Public Trust: Restoring the Value of Teaching and Public Service in American Academic Life
James S. Fairweather
ISBN: 0-205-17948-7

Emblems of Quality in Higher Education: Developing and Sustaining High-Quality Programs
Jennifer Grant Haworth and Clifton F. Conrad
ISBN: 0-205-19546-6

Grant Writing in Higher Education: A Step-by-Step Guide
Kenneth T. Henson
ISBN: 0-205-38919-8

Learner-Centered Assessment on College Campuses: Shifting the Focus from Teaching to Learning
Mary E. Huba and Jann E. Freed
ISBN: 0-205-28738-7

The Adjunct Professor's Guide to Success: Surviving and Thriving in the College Classroom
Richard E. Lyons, Marcella L. Kysilka, and George E. Pawlas
ISBN: 0-205-28774-3

Teaching College in an Age of Accountability
Richard E. Lyons, Meggin McIntosh, and Marcella L. Kysilka
ISBN: 0-205-35315-0

An Introduction to Interactive Multimedia
Stephen J. Misovich, Jerome Katrichis, David Demers, and William B. Sanders
ISBN: 0-205-34373-2

Teaching Tips for College and University Instructors: A Practical Guide
David Royse
ISBN: 0-205-29839-7

Creating Learning-Centered Courses for the World Wide Web
William B. Sanders
ISBN: 0-205-31513-5

Designing and Teaching an On-Line Course: Spinning Your Web Classroom
Heidi Schweizer
ISBN: 0-205-30321-8

Faculty of Color in Academe: Bittersweet Success
Caroline Sotello Viernes Turner and Samuel L. Myers Jr.
ISBN: 0-205-27849-3

The Effective, Efficient Professor: Teaching, Scholarship and Service
Phillip C. Wankat
ISBN: 0-205-33711-2

The Online Teaching Guide: A Handbook of Attitudes, Strategies, and Techniques for the Virtual Classroom
Ken W. White and Bob H. Weight
ISBN: 0-205-29531-2

For further information on these and other related titles, contact:
College Division
ALLYN AND BACON
75 Arlington Street, Suite 300
Boston, MA 02116
www.ablongman.com

CHAPTER 1

A CURRENT PERSPECTIVE ON ADJUNCT TEACHING

"One of the best classes in my program was in my sophomore year. It was team-taught by a full-time professor and an adjunct, who was a writer for the local newspaper. She arrived at class straight from reporting a story, with lots of passion, as well as practical tips. Believe me—all of us cared a lot more about the opinions of the adjunct instructor than the full-time theoretician, because she was giving us the straight talk on what it was really like in the profession."

—Caralee Adams, freelance writer, Bethesda, Maryland

FOCUS QUESTIONS

- What factors have contributed to the increased employment of adjunct professors?
- How does the accountability movement influence those who teach part time?
- What are the characteristics of today's adjunct professors?
- What do instructional leaders look for in the adjunct professors they hire?

Not so long ago, academia—with its trappings of ivy-covered halls and rich, colorful traditions—was perceived from both inside and outside as quite removed from the rest of society. Its unique ambiance provided a magical allure to students but perhaps an even stronger attraction to those who found something fascinating about working within its culture. Some were driven to spend their careers there—researching, engaging in conversation with brilliant colleagues, and mentoring the development of thirsty young minds—and are feeling rewarded in their efforts. Others were content to make academia a small, but continuing part of their lifestyles, while they pursued another career that provided what was perceived as more desirable rewards. Still others, perhaps encouraged by an academic mentor, wanted a full-time career but encountered an array of challenges that made them settle for something disappointingly less, at least in the short-run. Today, nearly a half million members of the latter two groups teach regularly in North American college and university classrooms (Almanac 2003, *Chronicle of Higher Education*).

   In recent years, a number of factors have signaled that an interesting (some traditionalists would say alarming) shift has occurred in academia. Like the business world that so many academics disdain, higher education has increasingly employed such strategies as targeting successful adults as their primary "market," using the Internet and other technology to deliver its primary "product," promoting its core and subsidiary products through savvy advertising, responding aggressively to stakeholders' growing consumer mindset, and assigning its President such chief executive officer (CEO) duties as developing new "markets" and building coalitions with once seemingly unlikely partners. Like many business organizations that rely increasingly on consultants, outsourcing, and temporary and part-time workers, nearly all colleges and universities have also come to rely on a growing body of contingent workers—primarily adjunct faculty—to mitigate spikes and troughs in its core business and to help curtail rising costs and decreased revenues. Although the term *adjunct* connotes a range of meanings at colleges and universities whose missions and governance structures vary greatly, I will use it throughout this book to refer to all who teach part time, or on a temporary contract, at any post-secondary institution.

HIGHER EDUCATION'S CHANGING ENVIRONMENT

Historically, North American colleges and universities have embraced the traditions of the British and German models, including "academic freedom" that has empowered professors to pursue their research interests freely, and the tenure system that has protected instructors' ability to work long term in what many have regarded as an ivory tower immune from external checks and balances. They established high standards for admission that focused on applicants' standardized tests scores, high school class rankings, and other "objective" predictors of student success. The integrity of their practices was regularly confirmed through their own internal reviews, as well as through assessments by their peers at other institutions through the regional and discipline-specific accrediting bodies. While establishing a culture of quality in the minds of internal stakeholders, many potentially outstanding students came to perceive these practices as rigid and exclusionary, and lacking the support resources to reduce their barriers to admission, they did not try to pursue their educations immediately after high school.

   Beginning nearly a century ago with John Dewey (1916), an initially small but courageous number of educators challenged the higher education community to extend the full potential of a democratic system by serving a larger share of those within our society. They lobbied extensively to change the goal of admissions "gate-keeping" from one of *exclusion* to one of *inclusion*, arguing that colleges should employ a wider range of admissions criteria that did not penalize "late bloomers," those from working-class families, or others who did not meet the "standard." The first community colleges, which from their infancy largely served marginalized students, were an outgrowth of their efforts. After the victorious close of World War II, military veterans used the GI Bill to be the first from their families to kick open college and university doors, and in the process, they established themselves as role models for others who had been bypassed by higher education, as well as for their own children. As the first wave of veterans completed their degrees, they left college and university doors ajar for those empowered through the civil rights movement—minorities, women pursuing nontraditional careers, recent immigrants, and others—to stream through in increasingly larger numbers.

In recent years, the historical chasm between academia and our mainstream society has eroded markedly. It is now commonplace for esteemed professors to appear on television news shows to provide perspective in political debates and to discuss other matters of concern to an increasingly informed populace. In the process, they often promote their latest books, private consulting practices, or latest research projects. Meanwhile, institutions began to promote their sports teams widely to broaden support among the general population and to attract upscale *niche* markets to on-campus theatrical and musical productions. They also developed and promoted more intellectually oriented activities such as professor-accompanied tours of foreign countries and Elderhostel programs. Each of these initiatives was undertaken, in part, as a strategy for increasing institutional prestige but also to boost student enrollments and to mitigate declining public funding for quality enhancement initiatives.

As a college degree has become more widely valued as a ticket to upward mobility, enrollments have increased significantly, and much of the mystique of the ivory tower has evaporated. To meet the demand for courses by those fully employed by day, an increasing number of colleges and universities have expanded their course schedules into evenings and weekends—hours during which many full-time faculty members do not prefer to teach. Although many institutions have employed a small number of adjunct instructors through the years, as well as some of their staff members (e.g., the college attorney), to teach a few highly specialized courses per term, the expansion of course offerings into nontraditional hours dramatically drove the increased employment of part-time instructors. Because evening and weekend students are largely part time, a common bond has developed between the "new" students and their adjunct instructors that has fueled further growth in part-time enrollments (Lyons, Kysilka, & Pawlas, 1999).

More recently, powerful external stakeholder groups, followed by proactive citizens, have imposed a template of college-as-business-enterprise on higher education. The increasing number of college presidents hired from outside academia (Basinger, 2002), the growing number of closings and mergers of less profitable institutions (Van Der Werf, 2002), and other factors reinforce this paradigm. Although significant differences between higher education and business enterprises (Birnbaum, 2000) will always remain, this public perception parallels that imposed on other societal institutions (e.g., health care, organized religion, and philanthropic organizations), which historically seemed insulated from society. As with other entities, the higher-education-as-business-enterprise paradigm invited society's consumer mind-set into academia. Students, as well as their parents and employers who reimbursed their tuitions, began to demand increased value from their investments, and most institutions installed student ratings of faculty and courses. Since student ratings have an especially significant impact on adjunct instructors, they will be addressed in greater detail in Chapter 13.

Once reserved for instructional decision makers, student ratings information has become increasingly more widely disseminated, in both official and unofficial print versions, and more recently online to increasingly technology-savvy student-consumers. For a number of years, *U.S. News and World Report* and others have published highly popular guides that rank institutions on such critical factors as percentages of classes with fewer than 20 students and retention rates of freshmen. Although many highly rated institutions and their faculty members initially resisted consumer-driven incursions into their cultures, an increasing number now embrace such comparative evaluations for their own benefit. One need not look far to see *U.S. News'* ratings featured in institutions' print and online marketing efforts, with the objective of differentiating their "product" from those of others in the increasingly competitive higher education marketplace.

Over the past few years, for-profit institutions have begun to have a dramatic effect on the delivery of higher education. Employing a "skimming" strategy, they typically target the most lucrative market segment—the increasing numbers of bright working professionals who are older than traditional students and who are willing to juggle an array of responsibilities as they pursue degrees in highly popular disciplines such as business, technology, and health care. The more successful for-profit institutions have developed "campuses" in suburban office parks, where they offer classes, often in an accelerated format that students interested in rapid achievement perceive as more convenient and manageable. Courses of the for-profits are typically highly standardized and display few gaps or overlaps in content from one course in each curriculum to the next—thus reducing the instructor's preparation time and achieving other productivity gains.

Classes at the for-profits are facilitated overwhelmingly by adjunct professors, most employed full time in their areas of specialization, a factor that most of their student-client view as an advantage over traditional institutions. The for-profits typically invest heavily in developing the instructional skills of their part-time instructors, unlike many traditional institutions, which often play down their numbers of adjunct faculty members, and have been very slow to invest in the development of their teaching and classroom management skills. Students at for-profits typically expect their courses to mirror the fields in which they work or aspire to work more closely than courses at traditional institutions do. Learning from instructors who were "on the firing line" earlier in the day helps fulfill that expectation. Because of the high regard in which they are held, ongoing professional development, and nature of the students, many adjunct instructors have come to prefer the environment of the for-profits to that of traditional institutions (Lyons, McIntosh, & Kysilka, 2003).

The success of the highly competitive for-profits, especially measured by student enrollment in the most popular degree programs, has been nothing short of phenomenal (Borrego, 2001). Many traditional institutions have benchmarked their marketing and course delivery strategies, including the employment of highly qualified adjunct faculty. In addition more than 2,000 businesses—largely dissatisfied with the applicability of coursework available to their employees, whose tuition reimbursement represents a significant investment of company resources—have established *corporate universities* (Meister, 2001). As the for-profits, corporate universities rely on those most current with the best practices of business (adjunct instructors) to deliver the majority of their courses.

As other products and services in the economy have become available 24/7, demand for quality college instruction that can be delivered to time- and place-bound students has also increased. Many institutions, led by the for-profits, have responded with a variety of distance education initiatives, all of which require faculty facilitators. One of the largest for-profits, The University of Phoenix, employs 7,000 adjunct instructors to deliver its online courses alone, and has expanded the number of students it serves by tenfold over the past five years (Olsen, 2002).

Prodded by their constituents armed with data on such wasteful practices as high dropout rates in expensive programs and excessive credit hours accumulated by students (Lovitts and Nelson, 2000), state legislators and institutional boards of trustees are being increasingly asked to justify tuition increases, to provide more effectively taught classes and more comprehensive student support services, and to improve articulation practices between institutions (Ewell & Jones, 1994). The legislatures of more than thirty states have implemented significant accountability measures, including "performance-based budgeting," into their public higher education systems (Schmidt, 2002). More recently, the Federal Department of Education has begun demanding that colleges and universities whose students draw federally supported financial aid retain and graduate students in a more effective and timely fashion with the tacit message being that their eligibility to continue awarding student financial aid hinges on their improving their performance (Burd, 2002). Although varied in their approaches, the measures mandated by state governments tend to focus on the following objectives:

1. Increasing accessibility to higher education to all citizens who can benefit from it, as a strategy for expanding the tax base and reducing the costs of social services (Waller, et al., 2000)
2. Improving productivity by limiting students' accumulation of excessive credit hours, through more effective advising and "seamless" articulation between institutions and though improving student retention, graduation, and placement rates (Selingo, 2001)
3. Dovetailing higher education funding and review processes with state economic development objectives, especially workforce development (Schmidt, 2001)
4. Deregulating public higher education by strengthening consumer information about factors of institutional performance (Wellman, 2001)

Among private colleges and universities, members of the boards of trustees, especially those with business backgrounds, have become more active in their institutions' decision making, with the objective of promoting standards of accountability for their alumni, benefactors, parents, and other stakeholders. Increasingly, private colleges and universities are scrutinizing investments of institutional resources that were once rubber-stamped. In their increasingly visible roles, trustees seek to ensure the achievement of their institutions' widely communicated missions and to reinforce their institutions' image among their especially demanding stakeholders (Ehrenberg, 2000).

Lastly, the regional accrediting associations—the entities that confirm overall institutional quality—have ratcheted up their role. With so much riding on the results (e.g., students' ability to get financial aid to pay rising tuition costs, students' ability to transfer credits earned to other accredited institutions, and institutional prestige, among others), accreditation processes are instituting an array of changes to foster institutional effectiveness and accountability. These include a shift in primary focus from "inputs" and "must statements" relative to educational processes such as the academic preparation of professors, number of resources in campus libraries, and so on toward a focus on student outcomes and related indicators of quality within their specific missions. The accrediting associations are thus playing perhaps the leading role in defining *institutional effectiveness* (Eaton, 2001) and are therefore examining more closely than before institutions' policies toward employment and development of their adjunct faculty members.

The widening circle of external stakeholders in higher education appear fully committed to win out over traditionalists who seek to hold on to those arcane practices that appear to benefit only those on the inside. In the process, we are likely to see a reduction in the bifurcation between full- and part-time faculty that has historically plagued many colleges and universities and contributed to so much angst for part-timers (Gappa & Leslie, 1993).

INSTITUTIONAL EFFECTIVENESS

Although many traditionalists decry the motives and strategies of accountability, as well as the employment of adjunct instructors (Ohmann, 2000), a growing number within higher education are tuning in to the message of their legislators, trustees, and regional accrediting commissions, as well as the voices in the marketplace. In short, they are initiating processes that reflect the concerns of those paying the bills, including a more proactive effort to integrate part-time faculty members into their institutions' cultures. Interestingly, the success of higher education in North America in comparison with systems in other parts of the world is often a hindrance to convincing many to embrace a more inclusive, global, technology-enhanced paradigm.

In a larger sense, increased effectiveness is a valid expectation for the stakeholders in any major societal organization. Most stakeholders in higher education currently define effectiveness in terms of student recruitment and retention rates, rates of program and degree completion, and placement of graduating students into the workplace or graduate education programs. Institutional effectiveness has become the mantra of both accrediting commissions and of a growing number of institutional administrators throughout the nation. The focus on institutional effectiveness is evident not only in the actions of state legislatures and the federal government, but also in those of individual institutions. For example, Ohio State University has initiated a "tax" on all its instructional programs to reward those departments, which, as recognized by faculty, most effectively support the university's master strategy to achieve truly exemplary programs in critical areas (Wilson, 2001).

Calls for increased institutional effectiveness, increasingly driven by "performance-based funding" mechanisms, originated with politically powerful external stakeholders. Administrators responded through such initiatives as "first-year experience" programs that address the historically severe freshman retention problem, developing tutoring centers for those having difficulty in core academic courses, and creating more inviting space in student unions that contributes to fostering bonds between students of diverse backgrounds. Although other creative, "intrapreneurial" practices are no doubt on the way, administrators are increasingly recognizing that they can do little to foster pro-gram reputation, which most influences the recruitment of new students. Additionally, administrators have even less ability to orchestrate classroom experiences that influence the thornier issues of student retention, degree completion, and graduate placement. Further complicating the issue of insti-tutional effectiveness is the rather common perception that improving student retention somehow necessitates the lowering of academic standards. Although the research in this area is limited, studies indicate that "dumbing down" the curriculum and lowering grade standards are not effective strategies for improving student retention. On the other hand, improving the effectiveness of instruction and quality of relations with each student is significant. Only a dedicated faculty comprised of a rich blend of full-time academics overseeing the curriculum and part-time faculty connected to their communities, both employing strategies such as those outlined in this book, will in the end improve institutional quality and the relevance of students' education (Lyons, McIntosh, & Kysilka, 2003).

Entrenched in their research and teaching, full-time faculty members have often steered clear publicly of the discussion regarding their institutions' employment of adjunct faculty. Increasingly, insightful leaders among them are acknowledging that the long-held belief that part-time instructors are a threat to their self-interest is bogus. Many are beginning to view the instruction that part-timers deliver as a critical, enriching component of their curricula, a means of providing flexibility during times of shifting enrollments, and a network for an array of potential synergies.

Swimming in the cross-currents of market, institutional, and political pressures—often with no safety line—adjunct professors play an increasingly critical role in the effectiveness of many institutions of higher education. Those who survive and thrive in their journeys will develop strong instincts and alternative navigation systems that include proactive networking with their peers and linkage to one or more advocates who work full-time at their employing institutions. Although the role of adjunct instructors has historically been underappreciated and sometimes even criticized by some misinformed stakeholders in higher education, enlightened instructional leaders are increasingly appreciating their contributions and dedicating resources toward assimilating their efforts into an enriched learning environment for students.

A PROFILE OF TODAY'S ADJUNCT PROFESSORS

Although there has been far less research on adjunct faculty issues than many would like, the most reliable data indicates that the approximately half million individuals teaching part time in North American colleges and universities will grow well into the future. Many decry the employment of part-time professors in such numbers, and their voices are published widely in an array of media. Others cite research, showing there is no significant difference in the quality of instruction delivered by part-timers and ask why increasingly scarce dollars should be used unnecessarily for additional full-time positions (Roueche, Roueche, & Milliron, 1995). The most rapidly growing sector of higher education—for-profit institutions such as the University of Phoenix—rely on part-time instructors nearly exclusively and in the process attain very positive student satisfaction ratings. One might ask how there could be such widespread disparity of opinion on an issue so critical to the future of higher education. Perhaps much could be gained through a more grounded understanding of the very different motivations that bring such an eclectic group of professionals to the front of college classrooms.

Only a few major studies have been undertaken to illuminate the backgrounds and motivation of part-time faculty members. The first, published in 1978 by Howard Tuckman, surveyed 3,700 respondents from all levels of higher education, to establish baseline information on what was even then being seen as a significant trend. Tuckman's findings delineated seven rather tightly defined categories of adjunct instructors (e.g., *full-mooners,* defined as individuals who held another primary job of at least thirty-five hours per week). A subsequent study, conducted by Judith Gappa and David Leslie and published in 1993 as *The Invisible Faculty,* built on Tuckman's work and a study of 2,000 part-timers conducted by the National Center for Education Statistics in 1988 to examine the myths, issues, and problems associated with the employment of adjunct faculty members. Gappa and Leslie analyzed the perspectives of instructional deans, department chairs, full-time faculty, and 240 adjunct instructors at eighteen U.S. and Canadian public and private colleges and universities. Although it replicated many of Tuckman's findings, *The Invisible Faculty* collapsed his groupings into a typology of four looser categories, predicated on the employment situation, lifestyle, and motivation to teach of those they studied. The typology yielded by their study, in which adjunct instructors are identified as *aspiring academics, freelancers, specialists, experts, or professionals,* and *career enders,* has become the most widely accepted in the increasingly widespread discussion of adjunct faculty issues.

The Invisible Faculty identified aspiring academics as those who teach part time while developing their credentials and teaching and research skills in preparation for an anticipated full-time teaching career. Many have earned a terminal degree, whereas others are completing its final requirements. Aspiring academics typically juggle research, writing, and family duties while seeking to earn a standing with academic leaders to whom they will sooner or later present their *curriculum vitae.* Although they constitute well less than half of the total of all adjunct instructors overall, aspiring academics do, at some institutions, represent a majority of those in the humanities, English, and foreign languages (Stephens & Wright, 1999). The ratio of aspiring academics is often high across disciplines at colleges and universities located in large metropolitan areas where there are many institutions of higher education, and/or in areas served by one or more graduate-degree granting institutions. Some full-time academics, especially those who taught as an adjunct instructor for some period and identify so personally with their lifestyles and challenges, have come to assume mistakenly that aspiring academics comprise the largest ratio of the adjunct instructor population (Dubson, 2001). Their widespread willingness to build a track record through teaching concurrently at more than one institution has increased their visibility in the media, where they are sometimes dubbed *academic gypsies, freeway flyers*, or *roads scholars*. Such stories have no doubt further reinforced the perception by many of aspiring academics as the dominant adjunct profile.

Given their dependence on teaching salaries as their only means of financial support and their need to repay often hefty educational loans and regular living expenses, aspiring academics have been the most vocal over the low salaries paid to adjunct professors by many colleges and universities. In some states, aspiring academics have joined collective bargaining groups, participated in public demonstrations, lobbied state legislatures, and achieved some improvements in salaries, modest benefits, and employment security (Longmate & Cosco, 2002). Those with the most comprehensive view of higher education funding trends however see a continued decline in the number of full-time, tenure track positions to which those in this category of adjunct professors aspire. We have hit the tipping point where the traditional paradigm of faculty employment has been overwhelmed by the market and accountability concerns of external stakeholders. Privy to growing accounts of institutions choosing not to replace retiring full-time faculty positions in spite of the upward trend in student enrollment, aspiring academics are increasingly realizing that their chances of attaining a full-time position like they once envisioned are declining severely. In *How to Survive as an Adjunct Lecturer* (2001), Jill Carroll encourages aspiring academics to face this fact, give up their feelings of being victimized, identify the benefit of not having to attend boring meetings and other undesirable aspects of full-time teaching, and focus their academic energy on teaching alone, by embracing a strategy of entrepreneurship. More detailed career development strategies for those who would like to teach in a more stable environment are addressed in Chapters 2 and 14.

Gappa and Leslie called their second category of adjunct instructors "freelancers," because they, by choice, maintain more than one part-time employment position, including a regular teaching assignment. One common example of freelancers is professional musicians who perhaps cobble together a chair in an orchestra with giving some private lessons, and writing some music or playing some special gigs, with teaching one or two courses in the school of fine arts. For many, this arrangement achieves a rewarding, financially viable lifestyle while providing independence and flexibility. Other artists, as well as consultants, owners of specialized small businesses, and others, employ a similar strategy. Some "soccer moms and dads" do the same while focusing much of their attention on rearing a child and/or caring for an infirm family member. Freelancers, like other categories of adjunct instructors, are likely from time to time to move from one of Gappa and Leslie's categories to another, depending on shifts in their lifestyle factors.

Overall half of part-time college teachers were found by Gappa and Leslie to be those fully employed in a career directly related to their teaching assignments, a category they termed *specialist, expert, or professional*. Many members of this category teach primarily for the ability to network themselves into their communities (sometimes one to which they had recently moved), facilitating their own professional development, the growth of their full-time careers, and the establishment of social contacts. Few have any immediate intention to teach full time, but some do entertain the thought as a long-term goal. Although the percentages of *specialist, expert, or professional* were found to be highest at private doctoral-granting institutions and lowest at liberal arts colleges, the extensive growth of for-profit institutions and corporate universities since the Gappa and Leslie research was conducted may have contributed to a shift in these figures. Because many adjunct instructors in this category capped their formal educations with a master's degree, their numbers are also high at community colleges, where the expectation of professors to have earned a doctoral degree is not as critical. Probably the most immune from financial issues, members of this category seldom have their perspective articulated in the larger discussions of adjunct faculty issues. Some creative professionals have attained "a best of both worlds" by obtaining a full-time, benefits-granting position in a quasi-academic situation such as museums or philanthropic foundations, which, coupled with part-time teaching, fosters a truly synergistic intellectual career.

The final category of adjunct professors identified in *The Invisible Faculty* is *career enders*—those who are about to retire from full-time work or already have done so. These individuals often possess career and other experiences rich with learning opportunities for today's students. Career enders are typically motivated to teach and/or to serve as paid members of graduate student committees, as a way to give something of themselves back to the communities in which they have established their careers, or to which they have moved to retire, and to keep themselves intellectually stimulated (Lyons, Kysilka, & Pawlas, 1999). As Baby Boomers rush toward retirement, often at earlier ages than has been the previous norm, we can probably expect marked growth among adjunct instructors within the career ender category.

YOUR ROLE AS AN ADJUNCT INSTRUCTOR

Like adjunct professors themselves, those who make decisions that directly affect part-time instructors operate daily at the confluence of the market, financial, accreditation, and internal and external political pressures identified earlier. Increasingly, they seem to be realizing how vital adjunct professors are to their instructional units. When grounded in the full range of their responsibilities, instructional leaders have come to rely on adjunct instructors for these inherent advantages:

- The ability to staff specialized courses (often on short lead time) with an instructor who has up-to-date expertise in areas in which the knowledge of full-time faculty might not be sufficient and/or current

- Flexibility in mitigating spikes in student enrollment that might not be sustained over a long period and therefore do not financially justify the hiring of additional permanent faculty
- Reduced instructional costs attained through a reduction in fringe benefits and course salaries *vis-à-vis* those mandated to full-time faculty members, especially critical during a period of reduced funding
- The ability to provide real-world perspectives and up-to-date information in the increasing ratio of courses with a career orientation
- The potential to provide linkages to the real world that many full-time faculty members have yet to develop, through field trips, guest speakers, internship opportunities, and the like
- The ability to offer rich learning experiences for introductory students that veteran full-time faculty members have lost the desire to deliver
- The potential to offer courses in times and places that are inconvenient or undesirable for full-time faculty members
- The ability to add passion for the subject matter that has been fostered through a lifetime of rich experiences

Depending on the discipline, and the institution's culture, mission, and competitive situation, additional advantages for employing part-time faculty members might emerge. In an age when we all need to be prepared to defend our views, you would be wise to remain familiar with the most critical issues in the debate over use of adjunct faculty, including the findings of several studies that indicate that the quality of instruction delivered by part-time instructors has been found to be equal to that of full-time faculty members (Leslie & Gappa, 2002). Although very few institutions have cut back on their employment of adjunct instructors and created more full-time positions, most appear to be poised to increase their employment of part-time faculty members well into the future.

Those who make the direct decision of assigning particular adjunct instructors to course sections, faced with the growing array of challenges described earlier, prefer to hire those who:

- Demonstrate a genuine mastery of theory and applications related to the courses they might be assigned
- Project an affinity for most students they encounter, regardless of age, gender, ethnicity, motivational level, academic preparedness, or personality type
- Accept that significant out-of-class preparation and effective grading are required to perform their duties effectively
- Are poised to "think on their feet" in challenging situations
- Demonstrate a warm sense of humor and a consistently positive attitude
- Present a professional image and demeanor, without seeming "stuffy"

- Invest out-of-class time to talk with and facilitate the success of individual students
- Display high regard for the institution, department, and the subject matter
- Regularly recruit a few students from their sphere of influences
- Submit final grades and reports in a timely fashion and adhere to institutional policies conservatively and consistently

Be aware that most discipline leaders have received some negative feedback or had to deal with unpleasant situations involving adjunct instructors and are likely to dread employing those who:

- Spend inordinate amounts of class time relaying stories that students do not regard as relevant to the topic or to overly promoting their own accomplishments
- Read extensively to students from the textbook or their notes
- Arrive late to class, excuse the class early, or otherwise misuse scheduled class time
- Fail to meet or have an acceptable substitute meet their class for every scheduled session
- Make insensitive comments of a racial, gender, political, or other nature
- Administer examinations that include material not appropriately addressed in class, contain ambiguous questions, or have other problems
- Assign projects or papers that are perceived as inconsistent with course objectives, lack clarity of criteria, and/or are scored ineffectively
- Award grades, either high or low, that are abnormal when compared with those assigned by others teaching the same courses (Lyons, Kysilka, & Pawlas, 1999)

The remainder of this book is focused largely on helping readers develop the strategies to master the standards expected by instructional leaders, students, and external stakeholders and to avoid the undesirable behaviors above. The following chapter encourages you, whether new to teaching or a seasoned adjunct instructor, to invest some time in deepening your understanding of your talents and limitations so that you can develop a master strategy that will increase your teaching success and maximize the personal rewards that you can derive from your teaching.

SUMMARY OF KEY POINTS

- The cultural gap between higher education and other societal institutions has closed markedly.

- Emphasis has shifted from excluding students with less-than-exemplary records to including all those with a legitimate chance to benefit from higher education.
- Higher education is being increasingly influenced by external stakeholders including the marketplace, government, business, accrediting associations, and taxpayers.
- Today's mantra in higher education is for greater accountability and institutional effectiveness.
- Adjunct professors are staffing more course sections than ever before.
- Based on motivations to teach and lifestyle factors, adjunct professors are commonly categorized as aspiring academics, freelancers, employed specialists or professionals, or career enders.
- The employment of adjunct faculty members offers colleges and universities many advantages, above and beyond cost savings.
- Colleges and universities rely on adjunct professors to improve student recruitment, retention, and program/degree completion.

THE FINAL WORD

"After 31 years as a chief executive officer (twenty-four in Europe and the last seven with a subsidiary of a Japanese corporation in the United States) I walked out of the executive suite and into a classroom as Adjunct Professor in International Business. The preparation time for each of the two roles is very similar, when one is driven to do an exemplary job developing a program that embraces the dynamic developments within international business. The rewards from teaching are fully as exhilarating as managing an innovation that yields profits far above projections. And I discovered a new kind of bonus—classroom discussions during the last third of that first semester, which demonstrated that students, like younger members of my former executive teams, are truly invested in thinking critically. As a manager, I know that universities require sufficient full-time faculty to conduct most of the curriculum planning and related work, but there is much to be gained from the disciplines and insights of adjunct faculty provided by their experience in a market economy. In addition, employing an optimal ratio of part-timers provides the university flexibility with regards to short terms needs."

—William Streeter, St. Louis, Missouri

CHAPTER 2

FORMULATING A MASTER STRATEGY

"When I was called to jury duty, all candidates were asked to stand and announce their job titles. As others called out 'elementary school teacher,' 'plumber,' and the like, I struggled with the term that would define my job. I'm only a professor to my students and not a real professor to the powers that be, so I blurted out 'adjunct professor'! As questioning eyes turned my way, I heard one guy yell, 'What the hell is an adjunct professor?' That experience told me I could either let others define me, or I could define myself in others' eyes."

—Peggy Roche, Monroeville, Pennsylvania

FOCUS QUESTIONS

- Why must an adjunct instructor develop a master strategy for their teaching career?
- How can you assess your readiness to infuse accountability into your teaching?
- What are some proven guidelines for improving student outcomes?
- How can you effectively manage the key accountability objectives?

Three of the fifteen or so books published previously on adjunct faculty issues bear compelling, yet rather ominous titles: *The Invisible Faculty* (Gappa & Leslie, 1993), *Strangers in Their Own Land* (Roueche, Roueche, & Milliron, 1995), and *Ghosts in the Classroom* (Dubson, 2001). Two others, including my first book, feature a form of the verb *survive* in their titles (Lyons, Kysilka, & Pawlas, 1999; Carroll, 2001). Although each makes a significant contribution to the body of research on a topic in great need of study, the perception of their messages among adjunct professors who read them, or simply hear their titles, might well reinforce negative paradigms and contribute to self-fulfilling prophecies of marginalization and victimization. Undoubtedly many who have taught part time have been mistreated by the colleges and universities employing them. In spite of the heretofore lack of widespread leadership on this issue, however, many adjunct professors, like those whose quotes open and close each of this book's chapters, have long recognized that, on balance, there are far more positive rewards for most part-time instructors than there are negative consequences. As in most any endeavor, success in adjunct teaching is largely a matter of developing an accurate set of expectations that are grounded in sound data and broad experiences, then assessing for oneself if success, as that individual defines it, is realistically attainable (Lyons, 1999b). This chapter is dedicated to helping you achieve those two objectives.

Several of the books mentioned above were written primarily for instructional leaders and justifiably criticize the poor preparation most colleges and universities have up until now provided their newly hired adjunct instructors. The esteem in which those are held and the articles written in response provide evidence that their message was heard. A review of college and university websites indicates a shift among some to improve the orientation, training, and support provided to part-time faculty. However, adjunct professors should not assume that such wise, professional practices are yet in place at most institutions. To promote teaching success and peace of mind, it is therefore critical that each adjunct professor develop a personalized master strategy for achieving success, as he or she defines it. Like the strategic plan of a well-managed business, such a master strategy will provide you focus and direction and help you avoid obstacles that have the potential to frustrate and deter your teaching success. After all, tens of thousands of other adjunct professors have relished their experiences, so it can be done. This chapter is designed to lead you through the process to develop your own master strategy.

GROUNDING YOUR MASTER STRATEGY

Experts universally agree that the first component of a strategic plan is the formulation of a succinct, future-oriented mission statement, which provides focus and supplies energy and clarity to your remaining planning activities. You would be wise to invest a few moments in crafting a one- or two-sentence statement that captures the essence of why you are pursuing part-time teaching. The mission statement of a "specialist, expert, or professional," who is fully employed as a hospital administrator and recently relocated to a new city, might read:

> *I teach to deepen and broaden my understanding of my profession, through discussions with those not as insulated in their view of the industry as I, as well as future professionals in my field. I value the opportunity to network with community resources that provide synergistic opportunities for facilitating my own career success.*

For an "aspiring academic," whose dissertation was recently defended but who has significant financial obligations and few resources, the mission statement could read:

I teach in the short-run to supplement more generous salary and modest benefits that can be achieved from other employment related to my education and to develop a network of long-term colleagues on which I can slowly build my teaching career.

The mission statement should be brief enough that it can easily be committed to memory and rich enough in its wording that it evokes emotional energy for moving you toward its fulfillment. Once drafted, your mission statement might be shared with your mentor and instructional leader to gauge its plausibility within the context in which you operate and to confirm your commitment to teaching in his or her eyes.

After finalizing a mission statement, the strategic adjunct professor should be focused to identify and clarify the factors that influence his or her potential as a facilitator of learning—the *raison d'etre* of an adjunct professor. In doing so, it is critical to not be limited by such factors as research skills and publication record, whose correlation with teaching effectiveness has been shown to be far less than many traditionalists assume (Feldman, 1987). Another commonly cited factor, *teacher's knowledge of subject,* was found in another major study to be the ninth most important dimension in both student achievement and student satisfaction ratings. Among more significant factors were teacher's clarity, stimulation of interest, openness to opinions, and sensitivity to class progress—each largely functions of emotional intelligence (Feldman, 1998). To provide an accurate picture of one's potential, a structured self-assessment should be employed to help you better understand the dimensions of your own teaching and learning practices. A proven process includes (1) an analysis of the personal strengths, weaknesses, opportunities, and threats (SWOT) that affect your teaching; (2) the development of a personal philosophy of teaching and learning that flows naturally from your mission statement; and (3) an assessment of your personal learning and teaching styles.

To conduct a personal SWOT analysis (a form is provided in Appendix 2.1 to facilitate your work), focus first on your own natural talents, learned skills, and formal and informal educational experiences to identify your personal teaching strengths and weaknesses. Strengths and weaknesses are both internal factors that include your values, beliefs, knowledge of teaching and learning theory, and communications skills. After thoroughly illuminating these, focus next on the external factors affecting your teaching—your institutional and departmental culture, the students about to arrive in your classroom, the current political climate in which education operates, and other such factors—to identify the opportunities and threats imposed on your teaching. Although they influence your teaching, these environmental factors are generally beyond your control. I suggest you complete the SWOT analysis in these two steps, allowing at least several hours between identifying your strengths and weaknesses and clarifying your opportunities and threats. Analyzing the results of this exercise is very likely to provide you with insights that would otherwise have gone unnoticed—factors that could have a powerful impact on your teaching effectiveness.

A valuable second activity is to develop a personal philosophy of teaching and learning. If you have already crafted such a philosophy, revisit, update, and refine it. As you do so, you might want to review the example in Appendix 2.2. Conducting this exercise will enable you to ground your approach to teaching in your beliefs about students, learning, and other essential factors and will likely help you determine potential new directions and strategies that you might consider for your teaching (Haugen, 2000).

A tool that has proven useful to a number of analytically minded users is the assessment of your personal teaching and learning style (see Appendix 2.3). It engenders a deeper understanding of your course planning, instructional delivery, classroom management, and student evaluation practices. The self-reflection that it fosters can lead to potentially extensive gains in your teaching effectiveness.

Together, these three exercises, conducted over a period of several days, should provide you with a comprehensive perspective of your unique qualities as a facilitator of learning. By doing so, you will identify potential barriers to success and be better able to establish objectives for orchestrating a sound course plan and course management strategies, in addition to identifying some individual areas of self-improvement. Beginning your assigned courses more deeply grounded in your own strengths and sound teaching strategies will unquestionably foster self-confidence and approachability to students.

THE SEVEN HABITS OF HIGHLY EFFECTIVE ADJUNCT PROFESSORS

When a system of individual effectiveness proves itself hugely successful with millions of proponents, we owe it to ourselves to consider fully its potential for implementation in our careers. Developed especially for strategic, accountability-minded thinkers, *The Seven Habits of Highly Effective People* (1989), written by Dr. Stephen Covey, himself a professor and consultant, has done just that. Its structure, approach, and easy-to-remember guidelines provide a practical foundation on which to build successful teaching and course management strategies. I will leave some of Covey's concepts, such as the "circle of concern, circle of influence" and the "emotional bank account," for you to explore through the numerous materials developed by Dr. Covey and his colleagues but will look closely at the potential of the seven habits themselves to improve our effectiveness.

Habit 1: Be Proactive

Unfortunately, many adjunct professors have viewed themselves as less influential on the education of their students than they have often actually been (see Chapter 1's opening quote). One of the most satisfying rewards of part-time teaching is developing relationships with a manageable number of new students each term. Proactively fostering those relationships from the very first class meeting (see Chapter 5) not only increases the effect of your teaching on your students but enables you to anticipate and manage challenges that commonly occur later in the term. In addition, your proactive strategies will likely lead to improved retention of students, which, as noted in Chapter 1, is an increasing concern of instructional leaders.

To be proactive, adjunct professors should:

- Anticipate challenges students are likely to face and plan for their solution.
- Initiate a dialogue with as many students as possible, at the first class meeting.
- Gather sufficient information from students to meet their needs.
- Orchestrate a rich initial class meeting that achieves multiple objectives.
- Follow up promptly on student inquiries for information and on absenteeism.
- Use e-mail to update students weekly on course developments.

Habit 2: Begin with the End in Mind

Having formulated a mission statement for your teaching and conducted a thorough personal analysis of your teaching potential, you have probably already begun to clarify the results you expect at the end of the term. Because an adjunct professor's teaching contract is typically open to renegotiation at the end of each term, it is critical that you provide learning opportunities that fit the needs of the particular group of students in each class that you are assigned. Chapter 3 will sensitize you to today's college and university students, who are far more likely than yesterday's to attend classes part time while working full time, to be older, and to have family responsibilities (in child-rearing, caring for aging parents, or both).

To begin with the end in mind, adjunct professors should integrate the following tactics into their teaching:

- Prior to beginning your course planning, obtain documents (e.g., course outlines, departmental syllabi) that specify the learning objectives for each course you are assigned.
- Develop rich assignments that lead to students' achievement of these objectives and are likely to be perceived by students as relevant to their lives.

- Develop a detailed, eye-appealing syllabus that clearly explains course objectives, strategies, and guidelines, and refer back to it openly and often.
- Develop examination and other assessment tools before course material is addressed.
- Clarify throughout the term the objectives communicated in the course syllabus.

Habit 3: Put First Things First

With an effective course plan in place and the persistence to follow through on it, you are likely to avoid the trap that has ensnarled many adjunct professors—procrastination. Becoming and staying organized and disciplining yourself to divide weekly planning into two distinct steps—prompt evaluation and analysis of the previous class meeting—and a separate planning session that looks ahead to the following meeting—will pay many dividends. Within the class meeting itself, effective professors must manage their class meeting time to address the most critical concepts when students are physiologically receptive and to regularly connect activities and assignments to the course objectives.

To put first things first, the most successful adjunct professors will employ the following tactics:

- Evaluate and compartmentalize the last class meeting.
- Develop a detailed agenda for each class meeting that includes time parameters.
- Address critical learning objectives early in the class meeting while students are most fresh and receptive.
- Develop assignments and examinations that foster students' mastery of the most critical content of the course.
- Dedicate the majority of class time to content on which students will be evaluated.
- Provide an overview of the following class meeting that enables students to organize their thinking in advance of new instruction.
- Communicate regularly with students through e-mail to provide reinforcement and clarification of upcoming course events.

Habit 4: Think Win/Win

In his book, Covey details the common strategies that individuals bring to their dealings with others, or what he calls the "six paradigms of human interactions." They are "lose/win" (i.e., I will lose and help you win), "lose/lose" (i.e., because I will likely lose, you are going to lose also), "win" (i.e., I am going to make sure that I win, you are on your own), "win/lose," "win/win," and "win/win or no deal." Covey believes that most highly effective people employ the latter two strategies regularly. Often professors are perceived by students to employ "win" and "win/lose" strategies in their interactions with them. Such interactions commonly lead to outcomes that are increasingly undesirable in today's higher education environment, such as student detachment or de-motivation. Although we have all likely seen an argument between a professor and student, we might ask whether any professor ever really "won" such an exchange. Using a "win/win" approach will allow professors and students to achieve mutual success. Students who see the professor as a caring human being truly invested in their well-being will typically extend themselves to meet higher expectations, and also begin to internalize high standards for subsequent performance.

In addition to their teaching, adjunct professors are often asked by instructional leaders to perform an extra favor related to their area of expertise, such as help organize a new initiative. Hoping that the favor will lead to something more, many part-timers volunteer many hours, often to discover afterward that for them, the arrangement achieved a lose/win outcome. Such situations not only foster short-term disappointment but can establish the expectation in the instructional leader's mind that you will volunteer additional time in the future, which contributes to anger and burnout. When you are offered such an arrangement, be certain to evaluate the invitation for its ability to offer a meaningful reward, (i.e., if it offers the opportunity to learn something of value or to benefit your students). If necessary, negotiate and arrive at a "win/win or no deal" arrangement before taking on extra duties, remembering that your success with students is your greatest security (Carroll, 2002).

Sensitized professors who think "win/win" will regularly employ the following tactics:

- Provide positive feedback to students in front of their peers.
- Encourage flexibility on assignments to enhance students' mastery of course learning objectives.
- Prepare students thoroughly for examinations, especially the first one in the course.
- Foster students' performance by providing and reviewing the scoring rubric for each assignment as it is being made.
- Provide prompt, individualized feedback on scored examinations and assignments.
- Talk regularly with students, before and after class meetings and via e-mail between classes, about their progress toward their personal learning goals.

Habit 5: Seek First to Understand, Then to Be Understood

Perhaps none of the seven habits resonates with more significance for the adjunct professor than "seek first to understand, then to be understood." Invest the time and emotional energy to understand fully the perspective of the instructional leader making class assignments; the institution's policies on an array of issues influencing teaching; and most critically, the students who enroll in your course sections. Chapter 1 sought to provide you critical information on the first two perspectives, including the importance of student recruitment and retention and timely completion of degrees, and Chapter 3 will provide insights into today's students, with whom we will invest the greatest ratio of our teaching time and energy. When we reflect on it, most of us would readily acknowledge that those who have had the greatest effect on our lives first listened to us unconditionally, or to use Covey's word, *empathically,* before explaining their perspective in detail. They took the initiative and invested the necessary time to truly understand us, before expecting us to listen intently to their view of the world. Effective professors have learned that they do not "teach a discipline" so much as they teach students, who have the potential to grow well beyond the multiple challenges they bring with them to the classroom. Such professors will say that the most rewarding aspect of their profession is to see the lights come on in the eyes of their students. It will always be so.

Seeking first to understand and then to be understood is facilitated by employing the following tactics:

- Employ a student profile form such as the one in the appendix of Chapter 5 to gather useful information on each student at the first class meeting.
- Update the form throughout the term to note key points that surface in student conferences and other critical events and have it handy when talking with the individual student.
- View students' various characteristics, experiences, and attitudes as potential enriching factors to the classroom experience, for other students and you.
- Demonstrate awareness of the popular culture and use vocabulary and examples to which your students can relate easily.
- Solicit "informal" feedback from students throughout the term.

Habit 6: Synergize

Synergy is popularly defined as *an interaction or situation in which the whole attains more than the sum of its individual parts.* Stephen Covey refers to synergy as *creative cooperation.* A professor who works toward synergy believes that a particular course should be more than the sum of its assignments, examination results, and classroom interactions, and thus thrives on the diversity that today's students offer. Each course section and class session should truly enrich the lives of students by giving them a foundation on which to build an understanding of subsequent academic work, life experiences, and personal insights. You can probably recall a few special courses that achieved great synergy between the students and professors and unfortunately many others that did not. Achieving synergy in your teaching requires embracing Covey's first five habits to draw students in and make the course an individualized learning event, and then trusting students to develop the insights and courage to take their learning a step further.

To synergize, professors should employ the following tactics:

- Promptly review student profiles closely to identify strengths of individual students.
- During discussions, draw out students' experiences that relate to classroom topics.
- Link course assignments and discussions to students' real-world lives.
- Encourage students individually to contribute more of themselves to the class as a whole.
- Employ small groups of students to focus on learning goals more effectively.
- Orchestrate out-of-class study groups.
- Actively build a classroom community that celebrates the unique nature of learning.

Habit 7: Sharpen the Saw

In *The Seven Habits of Highly Effective People,* Covey relays a number of parables, including one about watching a man while he is sawing down a tree. The man admits to being at the task for more than five hours. When asked why he didn't stop to sharpen the saw, he exhaustedly exclaims, "I don't have time. I'm too busy sawing." Many adjunct professors become frustrated when their "tried and true" techniques fail with a particular group of students. Like the man sawing, many do not take the time to sharpen their tools. Citing the whimsical definition of insanity, they seem to expect a different result from doing things the same way they have done them a hundred times before.

In the last few years, research that employs technology to record brain functioning of humans while performing critical tasks has revealed some truly fascinating insights into how learning occurs. As professionals, we should invest the time to become familiar with at least some of this research and assess its ramifications on teaching and learning methodologies.

Adjunct professors who seek to continuously "sharpen the saw" might employ the following tactics:

- Establish mentoring relationships with effective veteran instructors.
- Mentor a novice adjunct professor, regularly discussing effective teaching strategies (Zachary, 2000).
- Annually extend beyond a single discipline to read a well-received book on teaching and learning practices.

- Make use of on-campus workshops, discussion groups, and related resources, which are often sponsored by one of the growing number of teaching and learning centers.
- Access on-line resources, including *www.developfaculty.com.*

The Seven Habits of Highly Effective People is a practical philosophy for facilitating greater success in your part-time teaching, which, when integrated into an adjunct professor's regular practices, will pay huge dividends. Consider delving further into its potential to affect your teaching, and you will be rewarded many times over.

MANAGING THE MILEPOSTS OF THE TERM

Adjunct professors are increasingly being viewed by students, instructional leaders, and other stakeholders in higher education as facilitators of learning and course managers, rather than simply dispensers of information. To achieve the degree of success you desire, it is wise to benchmark the strategies of the best in their fields and then fine-tune them to your specific needs most effectively.

Successful managers in many arenas commonly embrace a strategy called the *Pareto Rule,* also known as the 20/80 or the 80/20 rule. In short, it postulates that 80 percent of the success (or failure) of a particular endeavor is derived from roughly 20 percent of its contributing factors. For example, 80 percent of the business of a particular restaurant (or any other business) is generated by roughly 20 percent of its customers. Roughly 80 percent of the complaints an organization receives are generated by 20 percent of the reasons why their clients or customers complain. The payoff of using the Pareto Rule is clear: manage the key 20 percent of any issue effectively and the overwhelming majority of your job is done. In the context of teaching, adjunct professors are likely to see many applications of the Pareto Rule, such as that 80 percent of all crisis management time is spent on only 20 percent of their students. Returning to one of our biggest challenges—the need to manage student retention more effectively—we are likely to see that 20 percent of our class meetings correlate with 80 percent of student dropouts. Further analysis would likely tell us that the critical 20 percent of class meetings include the initial meeting, the one at which the first examination is administered or major assignment is submitted, and the midterm meeting. Therefore, if we manage those 20 percent of meetings effectively, about 80 percent of the course retention problems should be solved.

Initial class meetings are critical times for adjunct instructors, but Covey's Habit 5 (seek first to understand, then to be understood) should tell you that it is also a challenging time for students. Typically confronted by a very brief "drop-add" period, students must quickly decide whether a given course is a wise investment of their time, money, and self-esteem. Experience has led me to reject the idea that most students are truly looking for "an easy A" and instead say that most students are in fact searching for an experience that is rewarding and relevant but also allows them to pursue other critical activities in their lives. To play an active role in attaining sufficient numbers of properly prepared students at the first class meeting, professors can promote courses in advance to previous classes and individual students outside of class. They must then ensure that students attending the first class meeting perceive that they can be trusted to orchestrate a rewarding, relevant learning experience throughout the term. Students who encounter such professors will not only be more likely to return for the second meeting of the class but will also recruit their peers during the drop-add period. Chapter 5 provides a comprehensive plan for launching your courses effectively.

The second (and in most cases even more significant) milepost is the first examination or the submission date of the first major assignment such as a written paper or oral presentation. To reduce the chances of students' stumbling (and possibly withdrawing) at this milepost, the professor would be wise to communicate precisely the content and approach of the examination or the performance standards of the assignment. Professors should preview examination content in a manner students can assimilate, whether through a study guide, an oral review, the completion of practice tests, or some other means. Chapter 10 provides details on managing the examination process. For other assignments, the most critical key is the design and thorough explanation of a scoring rubric that will be employed to evaluate it. Chapter 11 addresses that issue in detail.

Within the context of a single course, the third key retention milepost is typically at the midpoint of the term. Although the midterm meeting often coincides with a second examination or the submission of a major assignment, the most significant factor at this juncture seems to be students' weighing of the resources they are required to invest against the outcomes they expect. Energizing the midterm class meetings, talking individually with students before or after class meetings, communicating encouragement and study tips by e-mail, and other proactive measures usually help students pass this milepost and complete the course. Chapter 6 provides additional information on managing the context of your course.

When the focus shifts from the completion of a single course to the completion of an entire degree program, the last class meeting typically supplants the midterm meeting as the third most critical retention milepost. Chapter 12 addresses tactics for closing the course effectively to maximize more accountable and personally rewarding outcomes.

CONCEIVING STUDENTS AS CLIENTS

As relayed in Chapter 1, higher education now displays elements of a competitive marketplace, driven by students whose tuition dollars are sought by many providers. In this environment, increasingly influenced by the practices of for-profit providers, more is expected from all professors. Many adjunct professors, whose teaching effectiveness has often been evaluated solely on the basis of student evaluations, understandably question the influence of such a single, often flawed activity. Still other professors of all status and disciplines bristle at any discussion of students being consumers, customers, or clients, citing reasons such as the following:

- Our college (or university) is not a business. We teach, not "train," and therefore we should not "service." We are not a factory that turns out products.
- The legislature (or the trustees) and parents pay the bills; therefore, if we have any clients, it is them.
- Knowledge is not a product to be sold.
- If I treat students like clients, then I will have to lower my standards, give them grades they do not deserve, entertain them, resist challenging their existing beliefs, or otherwise compromise my values.
- The business/client model is an insult to which I will not even respond (Slaughter, 2001).

At the opposite end of the continuum are those who support the paradigm of students being clients and who suggest the following:

- A college (or university) has both fixed and variable expenses that must be offset through sufficient tuition revenues. Such revenues can be generated only by meeting the expectations of those who register for our classes.
- Like any revenue-producing organization, colleges and universities have an array of clients, but the most critical are those who register for its classes. When they are not pleased with the quality of the product or service they receive, they will make that fact known to internal and external stakeholders who will likely come to their support.
- Physicians, architects, engineers, attorneys, writers, and other professionals market their knowledge to clients with the expectation of receiving prestige and financial rewards in return. Professors today are not significantly different.
- The quality movement in business has demonstrated that retaining customers over the long term requires raising standards rather than lowering them.
- Although, admittedly, there are some unsavory businesses, much of the success of our society is attributable to the entrepreneurial, profit-achieving strategies of businesses, each of which is predicated on the requirement to meet or exceed their clients' expectations.

By tradition, college teaching is a fiercely independent profession, and professors, regardless of part- or full-time status, discipline, and institutional type, thrive on intellectual challenges (Bowen, 2001). Somewhere between the two polarized positions outlined above is a place where you can articulate for yourself what will enable you to achieve consistency in your approach to students while also satisfying other stakeholders (Lyons, McIntosh, & Kysilka, 2003).

Many professors have never before looked at their students as clients, and change is difficult for some. However, when successful institutions fundamentally change the way the higher education is delivered, competition dictates that others must adapt. As Spencer Johnson stated in his best-selling book *Who Moved My Cheese?* (1999), "If you do not change, you could become extinct" (p. 46).

SUMMARY OF KEY POINTS

- Most books and articles on adjunct faculty issues have focused on negatives that may have fed a self-fulfilling prophecy for many choosing to teach part time.
- Achieving success in part-time teaching is facilitated by a personalized mission statement and master strategy grounded in accurate analysis.
- Conducting a personal SWOT analysis and developing a personal philosophy of teaching and learning will help focus your instructional energy and decision making.
- Stephen Covey's *The Seven Habits of Highly Effective People* is a valuable tool for adjunct guiding professors in the continuous improvement of their teaching effectiveness.
- Adjunct professors can markedly influence student retention rates by actively managing the key mileposts of the term.
- Students are clients, albeit of a special type.

THE FINAL WORD

"The critical element of my teaching is the type of love for students that I learned in the spring of 1982, while a student at Memorial University of Newfoundland. I was a good student, but I was shy. Morbidly so. One of my professors, a Mr. Rolf Hattenauer (God rest his soul!) was a man who held great respect among his students. He was tough of mind, and, some thought, of heart. Yet somehow, we knew he cared. I did not realize how much until, one day, it was my long-avoided turn to report my analysis of a current event. Like a scared rabbit, I had indeed avoided this inevitability like the plague. Still, it was near the end of the term, and I had not yet offered my contribution.

When Mr. Hattenauer said, in his notable German accent, 'Mr. Green, it is your turn,' I looked down at my newspaper article and notes and then looked up. Moments crept by. I looked down and then up again. Still nothing would leave my 22-year-old lips. I looked down a third time and thought, 'Maybe I should check to see if anyone is looking.' I did. They were. Terror!

Mr. Hattenauer sensed my 'discomfort.' I can only guess what went through his head at that moment, but I know now that it had something to do with love. He could have let me off with it there and then. He could have ridiculed and mocked me. He could have dug in and harshly dragged me through this 'hell.' Instead, he quietly walked over, sat on the desk in front of me, and with a firm but gentle voice, asked while pointing, 'Mr. Green, what is that word?' 'The,' I said. He responded with ' . . . and that word?' I replied, looking up for approval, 'airlines?' This happened with maybe five words. As I started to string them together on my own, he discreetly rose and walked to the front of the room, leaving me to lead the class in a discussion of 'my' topic.

I left that class that day, exhausted from the horror but understanding that I could survive. More importantly, I had a glimpse of my own potential. Somewhat later, I realized that Mr. Hattenauer perceived that potential first, and he did it with love. I love my students, every one of them. Education starts with love. I know because Mr. Hattenauer taught me so."

—Barry Green, St. John's, Newfoundland

TEACHING AND LEARNING SWOT ANALYSIS

Strengths	Weaknesses
Opportunities	**Threats**

PERSONAL PHILOSOPHY OF TEACHING AND LEARNING (EXAMPLE)

BELIEFS ABOUT STUDENTS

- Students should be held accountable for their own learning.
- Students have legitimate differences in their learning styles and other factors that influence their learning effectiveness.
- Students should come to class prepared to learn.
- Students should help others when possible and never infringe on anyone else's learning.
- Students should derive an array of rewards from learning.

BELIEFS ABOUT PROFESSORS

- Professors should be held accountable for facilitating learning in their students.
- Professors should be active participants in a learning community with colleagues.
- Professors should adapt their teaching styles to the learning styles of students.
- Professors should evaluate students' work according to consistently high standards.
- Professors should seek to regularly update and improve their teaching skills.

BELIEFS ABOUT THE LEARNING ENVIRONMENT

- Expectations of the environment should be formed with input from students.

- The environment should be interactive and should validate diverse perspectives.
- The environment should protect the dignity of all its participants.
- A nonthreatening environment facilitates learning.

BELIEFS ABOUT THE SUBJECT MATTER

- All disciplines recognized by the institution are worthy of study and, where appropriate, connections should be made between or among them.
- Content should be regularly examined for accuracy, currency, and appropriateness.
- The content of each course should dovetail with that of other courses in the curriculum.
- Course content should be driven by the needs of students and other stakeholders.
- Students' existing base in the subject matter should be assessed before teaching and factored into instructional practices.

BELIEFS ABOUT LEARNING

- Learning goals should be challenging yet achievable.
- Effective learning can occur in a wide variety of environments, in and out of school.
- No method of learning is effective for all students all of the time.
- Appropriate, frequent feedback is essential to effective learning.
- All students are motivated to learn, but their motivations differ in style and intensity.

TEACHING STYLE SELF-ASSESSMENT

Directions: This instrument is designed to provide insights into your individual teaching style. For each of the following sections, indicate the priority of your decisions or actions relative to each factor, by allocating a total of 100 points among those identified.

My instructional planning *is driven by:*

____ **1.** An accrediting association, department of education, or other external standards

____ **2.** Recommendations of the entire faculty within my department

____ **3.** My perceptions from past experiences of the needs of the class as a whole

____ **4.** My assessment of external stakeholders (e.g., employers or transfer institutions)

____ **5.** Content of the course textbook and its ancillary materials

____ **6.** Students' individual characteristics, including their learning styles

____ **7.** My personal strengths, experiences, interests, and time availability

____ **8.** Other: _____

100   TOTAL

My instructional delivery practices *are driven by:*

____ **9.** Standard procedures agreed upon by faculty within my department

____ **10.** My personal strengths and interests, including my learning style

____ **11.** The need to address the course material in the time allocated

____ **12.** The need to keep the class as a whole focused on course objectives

____ **13.** The characteristics of individual students in each section

____ **14.** The need to provide students with an enjoyable experience

____ **15.** How I have been taught as a student

____ **16.** Other: _____

100   TOTAL

The instructional environment *of my courses is driven by:*

____ **17.** The furniture, equipment, size, and other aspects of classrooms in which I teach

___**18.** The needs of students to accommodate their abilities and learning styles
___**19.** My need to maintain control of the whole class
___**20.** My desire to maximize overall class outcomes, (e.g., passing rates)
___**21.** My desire to foster an accepting and enjoyable environment
___**22.** My desire to maximize learning for individual students
___**23.** Other: _____
100 TOTAL

The process of evaluating student achievement *within my courses is driven by:*
___**24.** Externally mandated standards (e.g., licensing examinations, transfer requirements)
___**25.** Practices agreed on by all faculty within my department
___**26.** My own time availability for developing and scoring assessments of student learning
___**27.** My own experiences as a student
___**28.** The need to defend grades to instructional leaders, students, and others
___**29.** My comfort level with alternative methods of assessment
___**30.** Other: _____
100 TOTAL

Follow-Up: Because of differences within disciplines, institutional missions, and other factors, there are no target scores on the factors within this self-evaluation. The value comes in pondering and writing a private written response to each of the following questions—and perhaps others that might enter your own mind— then reviewing your responses with a trusted colleague now or revisiting your responses alone at an appropriate milepost in the future:

1. Does your instructional planning take into account all relevant perspectives?
2. In what ways might your instructional delivery practices become more effective?
3. How can you manage your instructional environment to increase student learning?
4. Do your evaluation methods improve the quality and quantity of student learning?
5. What preexisting perceptions did this exercise confirm?
6. What additional insights did this exercise provide?
7. What other specific changes might you consider making to improve student learning?
8. Who should be consulted in your decision making? Why?
9. How will you test your recommendations?

CHAPTER 3

TODAY'S COLLEGE STUDENTS

"The greatest reward of teaching is in watching students who had struggled with a concept suddenly light up as they realized they finally 'got it'."

—Tonya Schuler, Reno, Nevada

FOCUS QUESTIONS

- What are the significant characteristics of today's college students?
- How have perceptions toward attending college changed in the last generation?
- How should professors structure their teaching to meet the needs of today's students?
- How might knowledge of multiple intelligences and learning styles improve outcomes?

Oftentimes adjunct faculty members are amazed at how much students have changed since their days in college. Over the last several decades, student populations at most colleges and universities have become increasingly diverse—in age, gender, ethnicity, working status, and other significant factors. To be successful, a faculty member must understand this new student population in terms not only of its demographic makeup but also of its social conditioning and values. This chapter helps you understand the dimensions of the increased diversity of undergraduate students and suggests ways you can address varying student backgrounds, attitudes, and approaches to learning.

According to the National Center for Educational Statistics (2001), enrollment at U.S. colleges and universities increased from 12.2 million in 1985 to 14.6 million in 1998, a 20 percent increase. The projected college enrollment in 2010 is 17.5 million, an additional 20 percent. Much of this increase has been and will continue to be the result of growing numbers of part-time students, who now comprise nearly half of the total college enrollment. By the end of this decade, women are expected to comprise 58 percent of the total college-going population, furthering the stake as the majority gender they have had since the mid-1980s. The late twentieth century also saw a huge increase in the number of older students, especially among those attending part time. This situation is quite different from what existed up through the early 1980s, when even the occasional twenty-four-year-old classmate seemed somewhat exotic. Although a great deal of common ground exists between students of any age, it is critical for adjunct professors to understand some of the key differences between younger and older students.

In recent years, much has been written and spoken of a generational gulf within our society—an inability or unwillingness of those in one generation to understand and value how those of markedly different ages perceive and react to the world. An ineffective professor will accept the gulf as a given and fail to see how it can contribute to the development of a fragmented classroom environment in which individuals work at cross-purposes. The enlightened professor will proactively manage the classroom so that, regardless of the course or discipline, students will learn to work cooperatively and, in the process, create a synergy that intensifies the class experience for both students and professor. This chapter examines the array of factors that you are likely to see influence the students in your classrooms, often all at the same time!

AGE FACTORS INFLUENCING TODAY'S STUDENTS

As we more closely examine the age factor among the students you will increasingly see in your classrooms, let us define the widely used terms *traditional* and *nontraditional* students and explain why their focus may no longer be as appropriate as it once was. *Traditional* students are considered by most to be recent high school graduates who attend full time, reside on or near campus, limit their work to on- or near-campus positions, belong to campus-based social and political groups, and have yet to start families. *Nontraditional* students are usually defined as those older than twenty-two, who typically reside off campus and work part time or full time to support themselves. They may have already launched their chosen careers, started families, and/or begun to participate in the full array of adult activities.

Although approximately half of students (by virtue of their ages) still fall into the *traditional* category overall, evidence indicates other determinants of their traditional status no longer fit the definition and that their ratio of enrollment on many campuses is falling. At the same time the size of the cohort group graduating high school in the next few years is expected to grow, and the number of students age eighteen to twenty-four is expected to rise to 10.5 million by 2010, an increase of 25 percent from 1998 (*Chronicle Almanac*, 2002). Younger students however typically comprise a low ratio of those in the evening and weekend classes so often taught by adjunct professors. Because the terms *traditional* and *nontraditional* are no longer as illuminating as they once perhaps were, this chapter will describe student age groups that we are likely to encounter through the more precise paradigm of *generations*.

Employing four critical criteria, (1) historical events during their formative years that have largely shaped their views of the world, (2) the family and societal dynamics that influenced the social development of most within the generation, (3) the significant technologies that came into common use, and (4) the resulting values developed by the critical mass of generational members (see complete matrix in Figure 3.1), we can illuminate key differences between students belonging to the Baby Boomers, the 13th Generation (called *Generation X* by many), and the Millennial Generation. Although no analysis of this type can accurately explain all members of a particular cohort group, the generalizations will help us more clearly see why the critical mass of students within an age cohort approach life quite differently from those a generation older or younger. This analysis also hopefully sensitizes you to the very human tendency to view "my (or our) way" as "*the* way" and to refrain from too quickly faulting the paradigms of those of different ages and life experiences. The discussion of each generation will conclude with how each generation's common values should be taken into account to foster more grounded learning.

THE BABY BOOM GENERATION

Although demographers disagree somewhat on the beginning and ending dates of each generation, Howe and Strauss (2000) identify 1943 and 1961 as the birth parameters of the oldest students you are likely to encounter in your classes today—the Baby Boom Generation. The generation's name, which was co-opted later as the "boomlet" when their children began college, is derived from the population explosion that occurred shortly after the first wave of veterans returned from World War II. Baby Boom adjunct professors tended to start college shortly after completing high school (or right after discharge from the armed forces during the Vietnam War), when the paradigm of full-time student who resided near campus was still very strong. For many reasons, attending college at age twenty is very different from doing so at age forty-five or fifty. Even though Baby Boom adjunct professors share many values with many of their older students, they may find it challenging to identify with the full range of these students' lifestyle pressures.

Overall Baby Boom students have seen their ranks grow dramatically in recent years, especially in the evening and weekend classes that adjunct faculty members are increasingly expected to teach. Looking deeper, their enrollment tends to increase when the economy is in downturn and they are motivated to improve their career potential. Although a disproportionate number of evening students are single mothers, many others are single men, and both often have child-rearing duties. Still others care for grandchildren or invalid parents. Some of these students lack a support system, whereas others have in place a strong system of family and longtime friends. Although their employers might have a policy of supporting their education financially, their co-workers sometimes resent their leaving work early or arriving late to pursue their college education.

FIGURE 3.1   Analysis of Student Generations (Adapted from Howe, N., and W. Strauss. *Millennials Rising*. New York: Vintage, 2000.)

	Baby Boom Generation Born: 1943 – 1961	13th Generation (Gen X) Born: 1962 – 1981	Millennial Generation Born: 1982 – 2002
What historical events shaped most members of the generation?	Launch of Sputnik, "Cold War," Cuban missile crisis Vietnam War Assassinations: John F. and Robert F. Kennedy, Martin Luther King, Malcolm X, and John Lennon Anti-war protests, Woodstock Civil Rights movement Space program, man's landing on moon Women's movement	Watergate scandal, Nixon resignation Three Mile Island, Chernobyl, and Challenger disasters Fall of communism AIDS epidemic Stock market downturn (1987) Desert Storm Deaths of John Belushi and Kurt Cobain	Decade of economic success Oklahoma City bombing, Columbine Princess Diana's death Clinton scandal and impeachment O.J. Simpson trial, Rodney King riots Impact of Title IX Attack on World Trade Center, Pentagon, and its aftermath, terrorism Wars in Afghanistan & Iraq Enron, WorldCom, and related scandals
What social dynamics influenced most of the generation?	2 to 3 children per family Families moved away from small towns and big cities, but revisited often Beginning of suburbia Mom's work was supplemental income Growth in illicit drug use Neighborhood schools, consolidation Major role of religion in family life	1 to 2 children per family 50 percent divorce rate, Child custody issues Mom's work essential family income Latchkey children common, "blended" families Single heads of households Rise of European Union and Pacific Rim economies Downsizing of corporations	1 planned child per family Soccer moms, and detailed planning of children's futures Fully integrated schools Falling divorce, abortion, child abuses and crime rates Increased security measures in schools, airports, and public venues
Which new technologies affected this generation?	Automobiles in middle-class homes The birth control pill Mainframe computers Television in most homes, plastics Shopping malls	Calculators, transistors Computer games Color, cable television, remote control Push-button telephones Personal computers, the Internet	CNN, MTV, and other *niche* channels DNA testing, cloning Electronic security devices Cellular phones, beepers, etc. Artificial intelligence
What values are shared?	Rebellious, challenge status quo, get on with changes, question authority	Disconnected, fragmented, freelancers, inwardly focused, importance of personal benefits, delayed emotional development	Values-conscious, team-oriented, respect for authority, race and gender neutral
What are the ramifications for teaching and learning?	Show respect for their strong opinions by listening intently and reassuring; avoid "hot button" words/phrases; give latitude in assign-ments; explain difficult concepts through stories from real life	Provide structure and support resources; use charts, diagrams, and other visuals, including Internet; "sell" them on the personal benefits of your point of view; use popular personalities as examples	Lecture only to establish parameters, then listen intently; infuse technology whenever possible, e.g., e-mail, Internet; stress the ethical aspects of your point of view; use service learning strategies

Older students who are attending college after a long hiatus or for the first time often doubt their ability to succeed. Other time-consuming life challenges often prevent them from preparing as adequately for class as they would like or from attending class as regularly as they would choose. These students commonly display test anxiety, a lack of confidence in their writing and mathematics skills, and hesitancy in using computers and other forms of technology.

On the upside, many older students somehow make it all work. Thirsty for the knowledge, prestige, and resulting self-efficacy they did not attain when they might have, they overcome the initial obstacles of attending college, achieve a measure of success, and become very self-directed. They are motivated first to just pass but then to achieve high grades that are deeply internalized. Older adult learners often become overachievers who will rewrite entire term papers to gain an extra few points. Although younger students sometimes expect special privileges, many older students will not ask for any extra consideration (e.g., to submit a project a day late.)

As their successes grow, older students often become highly motivated to serve as role models for their children or grandchildren, who may be struggling in school. They often speak of posting their successful examinations and assignments on the family refrigerator to serve as a motivator. Although many younger students have become astute at masking their disappointments behind a blank countenance, older students tend to display their successes and disappointments on their faces and in their voices. Older students are far more likely to stay after class to share their frustrations with an empathetic instructor, to discuss stimulating concepts from the course material, or to share obstacles from home or work. In the process, it is not uncommon for them to develop emotional reliance, or even a crush, on the professor—a situation that requires careful handling.

Many older students learn best by doing—that is, by applying the theory of textbooks to the rich set of experiences they have accumulated over the years and to the reality of tomorrow at work. They have a great deal they want to share, and they usually do when their perspectives are shown respect in a safe, informal environment. In the process, they make connections for themselves with the learning goals of the course and for other students in the class who may not have anywhere near the experience that these older students do. Baby Boomers tend to be problem-centered, rather than content-centered, and will often lose focus with an instructor who is intent merely on getting through the material. Adult learners, recalling the classrooms of their childhood, tend to respond most effectively when the classroom environment is organized and relatively quiet, and when they perceive they have ready access to the instructor, even though they might not take advantage of that access (Lyons, McIntosh, & Kysilka, 2003).

THE 13TH GENERATION

Instead of the derisive term *Generation X*, I prefer to use the term *13th Generation*—that is, the thirteenth generation since 1776—to refer to the age cohort that followed the rebellious Baby Boomers (Howe & Strauss, 2000). Members of this generation typically stay close to home to attend college while working full or part time. Many have been at least partially supporting themselves for several years and have accumulated significant debt due to tuition costs that have been rising at rates faster than the inflation rate or the purchase of items that were once considered luxuries but are now seen as necessities for students (cars, electronic equipment, and so on).

13th Generation students are more likely than students of previous generations to come from families that do not conform to the nuclear pattern (two parents, married, and two or more children at home). Their parents may have divorced one or more times, remarried, and/or formed blended families. Other students are the children of parents who have never been married. Such situations may have contributed to the stifling of psychological and academic development during the student's most formative years, residually affecting their college-age performance.

The Baby Boomer, or young Silent Generation parents of students in this age cohort, are likely to have been employed under the unsettling circumstances of corporate downsizing and to have changed jobs and residences. As a result, 13th Generation children changed elementary and secondary schools far more often than was the custom only a few decades ago. Such students often exhibit socialization problems throughout their college years, isolating themselves, becoming clinically depressed, and sometimes turning to unhealthy lifestyles. Many 13th Generation students were *latch-key kids* and may have been entertained often by television programs and videos with violent and otherwise negative themes. Their parents, exhausted when they arrived home after working long hours and traveling an extended commute, often did not read to them nor provide coaching for homework assignments during their early years.

Likely to have worked part-time while in high school—often well past what most would consider reasonable hours—many of today's twenty- to thirty-something college students have not been as focused on school success as Baby Boomers. Because of their employment, they are less likely than their predecessors to have played organized sports or been involved in other constructive school activities. When they were barely old enough to drive an automobile, some even maintained their own households, often cohabitating with equally unsophisticated peers. They may have engaged in other adult experiences for which they were insufficiently prepared and have developed extensive coping mechanisms for dealing with the challenges of their lives. Without structure and consistently communicated standards, many in this age cohort have not developed the self-discipline typically associated with success in higher education.

From another perspective, 13th Generation students have grown up in a society largely influenced by consumerism, materialism, increased demands for individual rights and decreased time horizons for nearly everything. One fast-food chain promised to deliver its products "your way," a theme that has been replicated in thousands of advertising messages that have inundated the minds of students in this age bracket. Conditioned by the Watergate, Three Mile Island, insider trading, and other high-profile business scandals, these students have developed cynicism and lack of respect for all authority figures, including, not surprisingly, college professors. Speaking spontaneously and angrily of the alleged misdeeds of others and lodging complaints and even lawsuits have become common behaviors. Students of this generation are quick to proclaim their rights. Some perceive professors as service providers, class attendance as a matter of individual choice, and grades as "pay" to which they are entitled for meeting what they perceive to be reasonable standards.

A litany of factors, including but not limited to depersonalized schools, teacher-turnover rates, and overemphasis on standardized tests, have contributed to a less than effective primary and/or secondary education for many students. A large number of 13th Generation students began college and required remediation in reading, writing, and mathematics skills (U.S. Department of Education, 2000). Conditioned by the hours they have spent surfing through MTV and dozens of other cable channels, playing computer games, and enjoying instantaneous access to the entire world through the Internet and other widespread technology, these students often exhibit extremely short attention spans and an affinity for color and rapid movement—qualities difficult to recreate in many traditional classrooms. For these reasons, they require structure and clear communications of expectations. These students have heard themselves identified as members of Generation X, perceiving the outside world as disliking them or, perhaps even worse, being unwilling to invest the time to understand them, so they have fulfilled the prophecy to be loners or under-achievers. The results are boredom, negativity, and lowered academic expectations that exhibit themselves in the classroom.

Many adjunct professors become frustrated when 13th Generation students do not appear as responsible and appreciative as they remember students of their generation to be. However, investing quality effort only with those students who display more conservative, traditional values is not a prescription for achieving learning success. Adjunct professors have a responsibility to all students—and to the profession—to accept all students where they are and to guide them toward an outcome that our highest standards indicate is appropriate. As you will recall from Chapter 2, Stephen Covey, himself a professor and author of *The Seven Habits of Highly Effective People,* encourages us to "seek first to understand, then to be understood." To achieve success with 13th Generation students, adjunct professors must sometimes work hard to practice this habit.

THE MILLENNIAL GENERATION

A very new age cohort of students is beginning to grace the doors of colleges and universities—the Millennial Generation. Neil Howe and William Strauss, authors of *Millennials Rising: The Next Great Generation* (2000), have described this generation as follows:

> As a group, Millennials are unlike any other youth generation in living memory. They are more numerous, more affluent, better educated, and more ethnically diverse. More important, they are beginning to manifest a wide array of positive social habits that older Americans no longer associate with youth, including a new focus on teamwork, achievement, modesty, and good conduct. (p. 4)

Students of this generation, born between 1982 and 2002, are making their presence known in the college classroom. Most do not want to be lumped in with the 13th Generation, whom they find to be negative, cynical, unfocused, rule-breaking slackers. Millennials are very clear on how different they are, and they want to be recognized as such.

The children and young adults of this generation typically feel more wanted than those of any previous generation. Their parents may have gone to great lengths to conceive them, and they have heard the media broadcast the fact that the United States is now a child-centered society. From the chief executive to individual parents, we are seeing an unprecedented focus on children and what is good for them.

Some of this focus has resulted in a generation that has been supervised more closely, has spent more time with parents, and has done more things that are family-oriented than some state-of-the-family pundits would have us believe. Compared with previous generations, Millennials tend to have a better sense of self and possibilities for the future. The Millennial Generation is more optimistic, not only about the future of society but also about themselves and what they can achieve. This certainly has potentially positive ramifications for the college classroom.

Millennials entering the college arena have grown up in an era of increased academic standards and high-stakes testing. Many are signing up for advanced placement or other types of intensive high school classes and are striving for high grades. In addition, students in this generation feel pressured about getting accepted to the college of their choice. We hear constantly about students who have already compiled an amazing curriculum vitae by the time they leave high school but still are not admitted to their schools of choice because of the intense competition. Therefore, depending on the college or university where you teach, you may have some students from this generation who are thrilled and thankful to be there and others who feel they had to settle for less and have a different attitude. (Leaders would be wise to be mindful of acceptance pressures as they admit their new classes so that all students are given the sense that they are fortunate to have been chosen and that the institution is proud to have them.)

In addition to being the largest generation (potentially 100 million when all is said and done and new immigrants are counted), Millennials are the most ethnically diverse generation. African Americans, who up to now had constituted the largest minority population, have been surpassed in number by Hispanics. Although professors may see the college classroom as becoming more diverse, Millennials may not see anything unusual or different. Large numbers of students have grown up in schools and neighborhoods that were populated by more than one race, and large numbers of Millennials are the result of unions between parents of more than one race.

As you prepare to teach increasing numbers of diverse students, be aware of the array of benefits that can arise from working in teams—an environment in which Millennials are especially likely to feel comfortable. Millennials also want to know the rules, not so they can break them but so they can follow them. Although they do not necessarily enjoy it, these students are used to feeling pressure and usually have the experience and drive that it takes to succeed. Having used technology since childhood, Millennials are likely to discount most courses that do not employ computers in some manner (see Chapter 9).

Although the mix will vary, each of your course sections will increasingly include members from each of the generations addressed here. Left to themselves, most students will gravitate toward those they perceive are "like me." Resist the path of least resistance and commit yourself to orchestrating an enriched classroom environment that expects students to address and work through the perspectives of those who are older or younger than them. At the end of the term, it will have been a "win-win" outcome for everybody!

COLLEGE STUDENTS WHO ARE OFTEN MARGINALIZED

In addition to greater age group diversity, other factors—some easily observable, others not—are increasingly reflected in the composition of college class enrollments. These factors have great potential to foster within students a sense of being marginalized from the mainstream, and often lead to isolation, lower success rates, and other challenges. On the other hand, they have potential for enriching the quality of education for all (Tatum, 1997). Adjunct professors who strive for success must understand the major marginalizing factors inherent at their institutions and formulate strategies for eliminating the impact of each.

The effort of colleges and universities to expand their proportion of minority students effectively has been the focus of countless news stories and legal actions in recent years. Since 1980, that effort has shown remarkable success as African-American enrollment has increased by 50 percent, Native-American enrollment by 75 percent, Hispanic enrollment by 200 percent, and Asian enrollment by 300 percent, as compared with a 5 percent increase in white enrollment (*Chronicle Almanac*, 2002). Today, nearly 25 percent of all college students are members of a minority group of some type. Dialogue on the somewhat heated issues of admissions criteria, targeted recruitment, and related factors that achieve the above enrollment increases is beyond the scope of this book. However achieving success with these more diverse students, who tend to enter higher education in the evening and weekend courses that are so often taught by adjunct professors, is a critical need for this book's readers. In many metropolitan colleges and universities, recent immigrants are an especially significant student population, whereas rural colleges often are charged with serving an indigenous population segment that historically has been underserved. Both cases and the myriad of other college cultures expand the range of issues on which adjunct professors must demonstrate sensitivity and effective strategies. Group values and beliefs, gender roles, and others each influence students' learning paradigms. The successful adjunct professor will begin to see these differences as an opportunity to enrich the learning of all, rather than an obstacle.

Looking ahead, the critical trends and issues that will affect your classrooms include the following:

- Over the next several decades, people of color, foreign-born residents, and children of foreign-born residents are projected to increase their proportion within the population of the United States and enrollments of colleges and universities (Howe & Strauss, 2000).
- Addressing the terrorism threat effectively will require us to leverage the foreign language skills and cultural perspectives of our diverse citizenry and the nurturing of those skills through higher education (Cox, 2002; Gedda, 2002).
- Only through the delegation of individual responsibility throughout the population—a basic tenet of the overall accountability movement—are we likely to improve the economic and social outlook for marginalized citizens (Banta & Borden, 1994).

Institutional initiatives that are driven by the accountability movement will continue to emerge and seek to address aspects of these issues. Remain apprised of each program's target groups and objectives, and leverage their resources to build "win-win" outcomes for students, administrators who must demonstrate results quickly, and yourself. At the same time however, remember that it will become incumbent on all professors, full and part time, to reach out more proactively to marginalized students to foster their academic and career success. Several groups of marginalized students deserve further analysis.

First-Generation Students

Those and their siblings who are the first from their families to attend college, commonly referred to as *first-generation* students, usually face formidable obstacles to success. Sandra Rodriguez (2002) studied first-generation students and discovered that their success in college allowed them to radically improve their social and economic tracks after graduation. In so doing, those students also positively affected the upward mobility of many others, by becoming activists who give back to society at a rate far above that of most college graduates. The forces that seem to have life-changing effects on first-generation students are "ascending cross-class identification" and "positive naming"—that is, someone of higher socioeconomic status often shows them the way to "switch the tracks" to become socially, economically, and politically enfranchised. Someone—often a professor—plays a transforming role in helping these students see capabilities that they had not previously realized.

Those who have at times felt marginalized by their institutions in teaching have a natural stake in helping first-generation students become more successful. Typically, first-generation students have arrived in our classrooms from environments that did not value higher education, schools whose resources did not foster their fullest development, and with little or no advisement that might help them formulate a clear path to success. Our sensitivity in recognizing these factors, mentoring such students, and ensuring that the gaps in their technology and other skills are closed, as early in their college careers as possible, can pay great dividends for their futures, our institutions' accountability scorecard, and our own success. First-generation and other marginalized students should be especially encouraged to participate in student organizations and other campus activities that help them adjust to college life more quickly and connect with those capable of contributing to academic success (Light, 2001). All professors can do an even better job with first-generation students by withholding judgment, listening to and genuinely understanding, connecting students more efficiently to campus resources, and modeling excellence.

Students with Disabilities

One of the most drastic changes on college and university campuses in recent years has been the influx of those with physical, mental, or psychological disabilities. Like other minority groups, students with disabilities and their families have become quite politically active and assertive and expect accountability from all faculty members and institutional support services. State and federal laws require colleges and universities to adopt policies that will guarantee full access to educational resources to all students who voluntarily disclose their disabilities. Depending on the student's situation, such services as note-taking, special seating arrangements, or changes in testing environment might be prescribed. Most sizeable colleges have created offices of disability services within their student services operations, developed detailed processes and documents, and taken other appropriate measures to ensure compliance. Adjunct instructors must be sensitive to this issue, understand exactly how to implement institutional policies, and take reasonable measures to ensure that those who have qualifying disabilities are made aware of self-disclosure procedures. There are several ways to do this without compromising students' desires.

First consider adding an appropriate section to each course syllabus, even if your institution is not yet among those requiring this action. Investigate and obtain suggested wording from the appropriate campus resource to ensure compliance with all rules. In addition, include a phrase on your student profile form (see Appendix 5.1 at the end of Chapter 5) that prompts students to share their needs with you privately. Asking the students to talk to you about their challenges during a private conversation will help you direct them to resources that can provide additional services and organize learning materials to accommodate their needs.

International Students

Over the past few years, stories of tragic conflicts between ethnic and religious groups throughout the world have punctuated nearly every television newscast and newspaper front page. Few readers of this book would deny that the root cause of these conflicts is a lack of understanding that can be addressed most effectively through education. Today there are 25 colleges and universities within the United States that count at least 3,000 international students among their student bodies and hundreds more whose foreign student enrollment was extensive (*Chronicle Almanac*, 2002). If you have yet to have an international student in your classes, there is a good chance that you soon will. Research indicates that international students are among those most marginalized on college campuses but, when empowered by their professors, can be among the highest achievers and most interesting to teach.

Differences in language, culture, religion, and values often manifest themselves in loneliness, loss of social status, and discrimination. In North America for only a few years, by nature, international students tend to feel in continuous transition and therefore hold on to their historic social networks rather than form new ones. Learning is fostered in a place perceived as safe by the learner, and it is incumbent on each professor to orchestrate such an environment (Lacina, 2002). Chapter 5 provides a number of suggestions that will help international students adapt more easily to your course, become comfortable with peers, and begin to achieve confidence in your course, and Chapter 8 focuses on teaching and learning strategies that emphasize learning in groups. The employment of these strategies should go a long way toward not only improving the success of international students but also helping your domestic students leverage the potential of their involvement.

Although we typically think in terms of teaching accounting, world religions, or some other course, or of teaching evening students, athletes, or some other group, those professors who derive the greatest reward from their teaching careers and demonstrate the greatest accountability to diverse stakeholders have adopted a different paradigm. They see their classrooms as mosaics made up of individuals, each with a unique background of academic, occupational, family, social, economic, military, recreational, and other experiences. In that sense, all students have some sort of "special needs." Such teachers are energized by students who are in the dark because they relish the challenge of helping these students turn on their light bulbs. Such professors view differences of opinions as adding depth to the classroom rather than challenging their authority. They view themselves as a facilitator of learning rather than "a sage on the stage."

INDIVIDUAL LEARNING STYLES

Over the past several decades, imaging technology that enables researchers to monitor the brain's functioning has generated some truly breakthrough findings. A number of researchers have theorized that students vary significantly in how they process new and difficult information and that each student has a distinct, definable learning style. Although much of the research into learning styles has focused on children, several models have proven useful with college students. Some academicians consider learning-styles research to be controversial, but for others, it seems to hold genuine potential for empowering students to manage their own learning and for increasing the quality of their mental engagement with material they perceive as difficult. From an accountability perspective, implementing learning styles strategies into course delivery methods offers potential for reducing the impact of learning bottlenecks—that is, situations in which students have difficulty mastering critical concepts—thus improving course retention and graduation rates. Three of the models most widely employed with adult learners are explained here.

The first, developed by David A. Kolb (1983), identifies four learning dimensions—concrete experience, reflective observation, abstract conceptualization, and active experimentation—and yields four types of learning behavior. Type I learners prefer to engage in "hands-on" learning, rely on intuition rather than logic, and enjoy applying learning to real-life situations. Type II learners prefer to look at issues from many points of view, create categories for information, and use imagination and personal sensitivity when learning. Type III learners enjoy solving problems, completing technical tasks, and finding practical solutions, but they shy away from interpersonal issues. Type IV learners are concise and logical; they thrive on abstract ideas and rational explanations. In recent years, Kolb's research has been supplemented by that of Anthony F. Gregorc (1986), who has modified the model into one that focuses on random (top-down, look at the whole task) and sequential (bottom-up, one step at a time) processing of information to yield four style types: concrete sequential, abstract sequential, abstract random, and concrete random (Kelly, 1997).

Richard Felder's model (Felder and Silverman, 1988) of individual learning styles focuses on the following five factors:

1. How students prefer to perceive information (i.e., by sensory or intuitive means)
2. Through which channel individuals perceive information most effectively (i.e., visual or auditory)
3. How students organize information most comfortably (i.e., inductively or deductively)
4. How students prefer to process information (i.e., actively or reflectively)
5. How students progress toward understanding of concepts (i.e., sequentially or holistically)

The third, and arguably most comprehensive model of learning styles was promulgated initially in 1971 by Rita Dunn and Kenneth Dunn, who have since continued to research and refine it. The Dunn and Dunn (1999) model postulates that a student's ability to learn and retain difficult information is a function of twenty factors, which are grouped into five categories. Physiological factors include light, background sound, temperature, and the degree of formality in the design of the learning environment. Emotional factors include motivation to learn, persistence, responsibility, and structure. Sociological factors include learning by oneself, in a pair, with peers, as a member of a team, under the direction of an authority figure, or through varied methods. Physiological factors include perceptual modality (i.e., visual, auditory, kinesthetic, or tactile), intake of food and drink during learning, time of day, and mobility while learning. Psychological factors are global versus analytic processors (similar to the random versus sequential Gregorc factors), and impulsive/reflective. The Dunn and Dunn model employs an assessment instrument that yields a continuum score on each factor for each learner. For any given learner, only four to twelve of the factors usually affect learning style significantly. The model states that by informing students of their individual strengths and providing them adequate sensitive support, professors can manage the learning environment to maximize each student's mental engagement and retention of material that is new and difficult to students (Dunn & Griggs, 2000).

The common elements of these and other learning styles models include the impact of perceptual modalities (e.g., visual, auditory, tactual, and kinesthetic learning preferences), and the role of mental processing styles (e.g., inductive versus deductive). Research indicates that professors who teach at levels through law school (Boyle & Dunn, 1998) and employ strategies grounded in these factors may not only reduce the impact of learning bottlenecks within their courses but also achieve higher levels of student success.

I suggest you delve a bit further, become comfortable with at least one of the learning style models, and complete at least one of the assessments. (There also may be resources on your campus through which you might complete one or more or find detailed information on other models.) My premise is that once you have revealed to yourself how you approach the learning of new, difficult material, it will sensitize you to the fact that all of your students have their own discrete ways of accomplishing the same objective. Since their learning styles are likely different from your own—and you, more than they, influence how material is introduced in your courses—you should consider modifying your instructional delivery methods as needed to achieve accountability objectives.

DEVELOPING A TEACHING STYLE THAT FITS STUDENTS' LEARNING STYLES

You have likely heard throughout your entire teaching career that people teach as they have been taught. I am not aware of specific research on this issue relative to professors, but I do not doubt the basic veracity of the statement. Digging a bit deeper, however, I am convinced that people derive much of their individual teaching styles from their individual learning styles—that is, people teach as they learn. You may think that what worked for you as a student would likely work for most students, but that may or may not be true (Wankat, 2002). Your SWOT analysis, the personal philosophy of teaching and learning, and the teaching styles self-assessment have helped you understand the impact of your primary talents, learned skills, abilities to respond to external forces, and core values on what has become your unique teaching style.

The strategic adjunct professor can ask which of two logical strategies is most likely to enhance students' learning effectiveness—that is, should we initially adapt to the preferred learning styles of students, or should we expect students to adapt to our preferred teaching methods? It is a highly complex issue with no instant answers, and each situation requires some study and individualized decisions to arrive at the "best" approach. Some professors can adapt quite effectively to the learning styles of students, whereas others would lose so much self-confidence in responding too quickly that they might become totally ineffective in the classroom. As in most any endeavor, the key is getting started.

When you identify gaps between desired and actual student retention rates or if the graduation rates from your program are not what you and other stakeholders expect, perhaps it is time to modify your teaching style. Accommodating students' learning styles is one logical strategy. I am convinced that the rather magical interchange that occurs between the professor and the student is the very heart of the accountability issue. When the interchange works well, retention, program completion, placement after graduation, and contract renewal often take care of themselves.

Richard Felder (1998) concludes that to address the issue of mismatches between the learning styles of students and their own dominant teaching styles, professors initially should do the following:

- Balance between concrete and abstract information.
- Make extensive use of visuals before, during, and after presenting verbal material.
- Conduct small group exercises in class regularly.

- Have students cooperate on homework assignments.
- Encourage creative solutions to problems, even "wrong" ones.

Research conducted by Rita and Kenneth Dunn (1999) indicates that the following tactics can improve learning outcomes of college students with diverse learning styles:

- Conduct a personal conference with each student to inform them of the critical dimensions of their individual learning style.
- Introduce new concepts with both "global" (deductive) and "analytical" (inductive) phrasing.
- Adapt classrooms with areas of varying light and both hard and soft seating.
- Attend to students' need for structure by employing agendas and other guides.
- Employ tactile and auditory materials and kinesthetic activities that introduce students with those dominant perceptual modalities to concepts that are likely difficult to them.

As evidence mounts on the benefits of employing learning styles strategies, institutions with an accountability paradigm are likely to fare well with them. Judging by research results, I believe the approach holds significant potential for enhancing students' ability to manage their own learning more effectively and for contributing to the attainment of retention and program-completion objectives.

MULTIPLE INTELLIGENCES

Research of recent years has provided us a final lens through which we can examine the diversity of learners. When professors accept only the traditional definition of the word *intelligence*, they foster an environment in which too many students are likely to fail. Seeking to broaden the scope of human potential beyond the traditional IQ score, Howard Gardner (1999), renowned for having developed the most well-known theory of multiple intelligences, defines *intelligence* as "a biopsychological potential to process information that can be activated in a cultural setting to solve problems or create products that are of value in a culture" (p. 34).

Gardner has challenged the validity of measuring intelligence by taking people out of their natural learning environments and asking them to complete isolated tasks they have never done before. His position that intelligence has more to do with solving problems and creating products in a context-rich environment has grown from his research, which now yields the following nine comprehensive categories:

1. *Verbal/linguistic intelligence:* The capacity to use words effectively (think Maya Angelou); students who possess this intelligence have generally been successful in school because their intelligence lends itself to traditional teaching.
2. *Logical/mathematical intelligence:* The capacity to reason and employ numbers effectively (think Milton Friedman); students who possess high logical/mathematical intelligence tend to do well in traditional classrooms where teaching is logically sequenced and students are asked to conform.
3. *Visual/spatial intelligence:* The ability to accurately manipulate mental representations of large or small spaces (think I.M. Pei); these learners like to see what is being talked about in order to understand.
4. *Bodily/kinesthetic intelligence:* Expertise in using the entire body to express ideas and feelings (think Tiger Woods); through their constant movement and expressive body language these students often give the professor every indication of what sort of intelligence they possess.
5. *Musical intelligence:* The capacity to perceive, discriminate, transform, and express musical forms effectively (think Wynton Marsalis); these learners use patterns, rhythms, instruments, and musical expression to represent their world.
6. *Interpersonal intelligence:* The ability to perceive and make distinctions in the moods, motivations, and feelings of other people (think Charlie Rose); these learners are noticeably people oriented and outgoing and do well working in groups or with a partner.
7. *Intrapersonal:* Self-knowledge and the ability to act adaptively on the basis of that knowledge (think Denzel Washington); these learners may tend to be more reserved, but they are actually quite intuitive about what they learn and how it relates to them.
8. *Naturalist:* Recognizing patterns in the living world (think Rachel Carson); a student possessing the naturalist intelligence demonstrates an ease in identifying and classifying living things.
9. *Existentialist:* A proclivity for asking the fundamental questions about life (think Pope John Paul II). This is Gardner's newest intelligence and one that is likely to be more extensively explored in the coming decade. Those with the existentialist intelligence ask questions like, "Why are we here?" and "What is our role in the world?"

It is likely that as you read through the brief descriptions listed above, you found yourself described by at least one, and it is also likely that you closely identified your academic field with one of the intelligences. For example, if you are a music professor, it would not be surprising if you believe that you possess musical intelligence and that your students (well, your best students) also possess this intelligence. Likewise, if you are working with graduate students who are preparing to be clinical psychologists, I hope you see evidence of both interpersonal and intrapersonal intelligence in them.

Some educators have taken the concept of multiple intelligences and made it into a cottage industry. A few have even promoted the teaching of every concept in a way that addresses all intelligence types, but Gardner himself has rejected such ideas. My intention here is not to introduce you to a complex concept in an oversimplified way but rather to alert you to the fact that you will have students whose talents and problem-solving abilities support their learning in a variety of ways. Your students' talents and abilities may or may not be well suited to the content and style of your teaching. If they are not, then both of you must put forth more effort in order for them to learn.

In the traditional paradigm, students either possess intelligence or they lack it. In Gardner's paradigm, students have more of, less of, or a wider variety of intelligences. In the process of helping all students in your class approach their fullest potential, not by imposing preconceived limitations but by proactively soliciting their individual input into learning decisions that have an impact on them, both your job and your perception of the human development process will become far more rewarding.

Understanding generational influences, diversity of students, multiple intelligences, and individual learning styles will help you see each student in front of you as unique. Get to know each one of your students as well as you can: welcome and get to know them at the first class meeting, review their completed student profile, and require them to visit you during office hours. Throughout the term, build an ongoing dialogue with individual students that will enhance your insights and foster students' willingness to approach you. I believe you will usually experience markedly improved motivation and attention levels, which will translate later into improved outcomes. One of the greatest rewards of teaching is allowing yourself to be sufficiently vulnerable so that you empower students to share their thoughts and feelings with you and their peers. It is critical that you regularly assess your values and predispositions and that you share discussions with both veteran and new instructors. Their feedback can help you deepen your own understanding markedly.

FOSTERING STUDENTS' RESPONSIBILITY FOR ACHIEVING LEARNING OUTCOMES

Accepting the mantle of accountability requires professors to commit to the continuous improvement of their teaching, learning, and classroom management practices, but it also engenders a concomitant obligation among learners. Giving students knowledge of their own individual learning styles has been shown to be an effective way of developing their sense of responsibility—that is, it empowers them to take control of their learning. Naysayers often tell us that students have become "slackers," yet exemplary teachers say that the majority of those who populate our classrooms are willing to produce at higher levels than those at which they are currently working. Our developing teaching styles and instructional strategies must energize these individuals and shift the paradigm toward learning rather than teaching.

Think about it—today's students are teaching themselves far more than we likely taught ourselves when we were their age. Many have taught themselves an array of technological skills on their home computers or in laboratories at their schools. Many were emotionally isolated by the significant adults in their lives yet taught themselves social skills—albeit sometimes ineffective ones—to survive in the resulting vacuum. Many have taught themselves occupational skills by working at fairly sophisticated part-time jobs (Howe & Strauss, 2000). An individual student's skill list can be quite extensive. Our challenge is to understand them for who they are, leverage their existing skills, and become a partner in moving them toward where they really want and need to be. Sometimes it requires tough love; at other times, quiet, nonjudgmental listening is the major requirement. For their long-term good and to meet accountability mandates, we must rise to the challenge if we are to call ourselves educators.

Developing a philosophy and style that improve students' learning requires a significant change in mind-set for many adjunct professors. Our minds and emotions are rich with an array of experiences that have influenced our approach and behavior as college instructors. But the common paradigm that is verbalized in the "look to your left, look to your right" exclamation that opened Chapter 1 is driven by inefficient, unaccountable considerations. While maintaining the high standards inherent in that statement, we need to become an emotionally intelligent link between our increasingly complex disciplines and students with varied and sometimes challenging learning systems.

Regardless of the demographic makeup of your institution's student body, you can consistently encourage self-direction and responsibility in all students. Our society seems to have instilled a sense of victimization among those who face challenges, and some students will judge your standards and procedures in that light. Be intellectually prepared and consistently willing to push students to turn out their best work. They may resist at first, but most will finish the term thanking you for helping them meet your high expectations.

Some students, especially those with low self-esteem or especially difficult backgrounds, may challenge your best-intended words as discriminatory. Following the suggestions in Chapter 5 for proactively building your understanding of your students early in the course will help with problems that arise later on. It is critical that in preparing each class meeting you think through your words on topics related to gender, race, politics, or any other potentially sensitive area. Doing so can help you prevent challenges or meet any that are raised. Common problems you can expect from students are tardiness, absenteeism, test anxiety, and lack of focus. Rather than becoming upset and taking punitive action, you should plan for these situations and build solutions into the design of your course. You can minimize the disruptions caused by tardy entry into your classroom, for example, by reserving a section of the room for late arrivers. Should you find several weeks into the course that the overwhelming majority of your students come in late, you might enlist the class's help in finding solutions that will allow everyone to experience the class fully and achieve the learning objectives. I believe that when the professor makes a concerted effort to foster a learning relationship with each student early in the term (see strategies in Chapter 5) and establishes an effective learning environment, then absences, motivation problems, inappropriate behavior, and other such problems will largely take care of themselves. Retention will improve incrementally. There will always be a handful of students whose behavior is inconsistent with your acceptable standards, but it is critical not to punish the entire group because of the actions of a few. The key is to uncover the root cause by listening actively. You can then address the problem in an objective, frank manner that preserves the dignity of the student. As in most other areas of like, ignoring the problem and hoping it will fix itself can only lead to unsatisfactory results. From the first class meeting, it is critical to demonstrate structure, establish your standards, reinforce those standards through consistent behavior, and take action promptly when warranted (McKeachie, 2001).

In an age of accountability, each professor is obligated to adopt a proactive posture toward potential extreme behavior than was previously required. Triggered by some of the factors identified in the discussion of generations earlier in the chapter, a very small minority of students may encounter emotional challenges, abuse substances, commit crimes, or even contemplate suicide. Become familiar with your campus resources so that when a student divulges troubling information during a conference, you are able to make an informed referral. Use the student profile forms you collected in the beginning to track patterns of behavior in case you need to refer to them later (Lyons, McIntosh, & Kysilka, 2003).

WHAT STUDENTS WANT FROM COLLEGE INSTRUCTORS

Although each student subgroup has particular characteristics that affect the dynamics of a college learning environment, what students need from their college instructors is fairly consistent among all groups and types. Students want instructors to do the following:

- Know them and care about them.
- Give clear, consistent expectations of student performance that are reasonable in quantity and quality.
- Be sensitive to the diverse demands on students and be flexible in accommodating them.
- Use class time effectively.
- Create a classroom environment that values student input into decisions and dialogue and protects their dignity.

- Present a classroom demeanor that includes humor and spontaneity.
- Design assessments that are clearly tied to the information addressed in class, appropriate to the level of the majority of students in the class, punctually graded and returned, and used fairly to determine final class grades.
- Consistently show positive treatment of individual students that includes being willing to spend extra time before or after class meetings to provide additional support as needed.

In *Making the Most of College: Students Speak their Minds* (2001), Richard Light reports students believe that they:

- Learn through extracurricular activities (this is vital and thus should be encouraged by professors).
- Learn more in classes that are highly structured with frequent assessment activities.
- Are more successful in their homework when they study with others rather than alone.
- Benefit markedly from mentoring opportunities with faculty.
- Learn much from their diverse peers when activities are effectively orchestrated.
- Benefit most when they are taught to manage their time to include opportunities for interaction focused on academic pursuits.
- Care about becoming better writers.
- Benefit from coaching in study skills.
- Are especially enthusiastic about literature and foreign-language study.

Although perhaps surprising in many ways, these findings show that adjunct professors can have a rich impact on the lives of today's students, who not only have high expectations but are also willing to invest of themselves to receive the fullest possible benefits from their college experiences.

SUMMARY OF KEY POINTS

- Today's college students are far more likely to be older and part time than were those of previous times.
- For very understandable reasons, many 13th Generation college students lack self-discipline and academic foundation.
- The newest generation of college students (the Millennials) are more eager to learn, to engage, and to make a difference.
- Students of whatever age or generation have challenges, issues, and constraints that affect their level of involvement in college.

- The concept of multiple intelligences is worth further study because it helps make us more sensitive to the variety of ways in which students process information
- More students with disabilities are enrolling in college. We have a responsibility to support their learning in appropriate ways.
- Professors should anticipate common student success problems before the class and design solutions into the course.

THE FINAL WORD

"As a student, I was very shy and introverted, but my brother, who was my father figure, told me I would be a great teacher because I had great empathy. It wasn't until I was presenting at a scientific meeting that I realized the meaning of empathy and its importance in being a good teacher. In his keynote, the late Carl Sagan mentioned, almost offhand, that to really explain a complicated concept, you must take yourself back to before you understood what it really meant. As I watch my students experience that first awareness, I am forever grateful for that insight and to be able to watch it again and again."

—Melodi Rodrigue, Reno, Nevada

CHAPTER 4

STRATEGIC COURSE PLANNING

"Each time I teach a course, I adjust and fine tune it—based on information I gather from students during the first meeting of the class. In defining the course goals, I integrate students' individual goals, their experience with the subject matter, and their learning styles. That dynamic type of planning ensures students' expectations are surpassed and that they succeed in my courses. It's an energizing process!"

—Lisa J. Sohl, M.S., C.A.C., Port Saint Lucie, Florida

FOCUS QUESTIONS

- How do you design quality into the course you will teach?
- Why is the syllabus critical to the success of your course?
- What elements and characteristics should an effective syllabus possess?
- What resources should you consider utilizing in your course design?

We can all recall being in a situation—at work, as a customer, or attending a social function—where there was a clearly formulated plan in evidence, and we can feel the security and confidence that it evoked in us. We can also probably remember a situation where there clearly was no plan developed and the sense of chaos and frustration that engendered in those seeking to coordinate their efforts. Within the first few minutes of each of your courses, your students will perceive the presence or absence of a sound plan and will either become energized about the exciting trip ahead or hold back on making a commitment. Some even respond by dropping the course immediately and finding what they consider a better opportunity. This chapter is designed to guide your preparation of a class plan that will provide students with an optimal learning experience within the context of the overall mission of the department and its established curriculum. The strategy underlying the planning of your next teaching assignment should maximize your strengths, identify the most effective learning resources, and minimize the impact of any weaknesses that you bring to the course. The time and energy you invest in the planning effort will pay both short- and long-term benefits, not the least of which is relieving much of the pressure to fulfill the expectations of students and other stakeholders.

DESIGNING AN EFFECTIVE COURSE

As an adjunct professor, your role in actual course design can vary between two extremes. If yours is a standard course within the curriculum, you might be provided a detailed outline, proven syllabus, carefully selected textbook, and other course materials so that you are required to do little more than embellish the course with your personal experiences and insights. Increasingly however, adjunct professors with recognized expertise in a critical field are being asked to design and deliver courses that have not previously been taught by the institution and/or which are incapable of being taught by anyone else on the faculty. Although the demands of designing a course "from scratch" may seem daunting, the rewards can be substantial. This might include extra course sections to teach—if you negotiate that into your deal initially—and developmental supplements that institutions are increasingly willing to pay.

Regardless of the point on that continuum where your next course assignment is positioned, it is critical to understand the basic course design process. Because it tends to have a long-term effect on the delivery of the course and student learning, understanding sound course design strategies repays the investment of the time and energy required (Stark & Lattucan, 1997; Diamond, 1998).

The foundation of the design of any college course must demonstrate an understanding of the concept of the three *learning domains.* The *affective domain* includes attitudes, character issues, appreciation of beauty, and the like. Evaluating learning in this domain might involve the creation of something artistic, the writing of an essay, or the compilation of a portfolio of student creations. The *psychomotor domain* refers to physical skills and dexterity, and evaluation typically requires the demonstration of a particular skill by a student at a clearly prescribed standard of performance using a rubric. Lastly, the *cognitive domain* refers to the thought processes, whose development can be assessed in a number of ways that are addressed in Chapters 10 and 11. Of the three domains, the cognitive is likely the greatest concern to the majority of adjunct professors.

In 1956, Benjamin Bloom published his renowned *taxonomy of educational objectives for the cognitive domain,* a concept critical to the knowledge base of any effective teacher. The taxonomy (see Figure 4.1 for a visual representation) delineates six levels of cognitive complexity, ranging from the *knowledge* level (lowest), through *comprehension,* to *application,* then *analysis,* followed by *synthesis*, and ending with the *evaluation* level. Figure 4.1 displays the taxonomy, identifies opening verbs commonly associated with learning objectives at each level, and provides guidelines for integrating the taxonomy into your course management. Introductory-level college courses will typically focus on learning objectives at the lower levels of *Bloom's Taxonomy*, whereas capstone courses target objectives at the higher levels. The second or third courses in a sequenced curriculum would likely focus in the middle of the range. From another perspective, the first few weeks of a course typically begin at the level where introductory students are likely to be intellectually engaged with the material, or at the closing level of the previous course in the curriculum sequence.

FIGURE 4.1   Bloom's Taxonomy of Cognitive Objectives

Usage Guidelines:
1. Assess, then start where the learner is.
2. Set achievable learning objectives.
3. Move learning upward systematically.
4. Evaluate students at a level no higher than that at which instruction is delivered.

Evaluation

assess	predict
defend	recommend
evaluate	support

Synthesis

compose	formulate
create	plan
design	propose

Analysis

analyze	compare
appraise	contrast
categorize	differentiate

Application

apply	sketch
demonstrate	solve
illustrate	use

Comprehension

arrange	explain
classify	interpret
discuss	sort

Knowledge

define	list
describe	name
identify	recall

Source: Lyons, R., M. McIntosh, and M. Kysilka (2003). *Teaching College in an Age of Accountability.* Boston: Allyn and Bacon.

After determining where the course fits into the program curriculum, the specific goals of the course must be clearly identified, along with an understanding of how the course will dovetail with other courses.

For existing courses, a variety of resources are available for help in planning, including your instructional leader and those who have previously taught the course at your institution. From your instructional leader, collect an official course outline if one has been developed and several syllabi of others who have taught your assigned course and carefully compare course design and strategies.

For courses being created for scratch, begin again with your instructional leader but consider also the input of leaders of other disciplines at the institution whose curricula might include the course, discipline leaders at other institutions who have developed a similar course, employers or clients of students who complete the course, and perhaps others. Early in the process, begin to research possible textbooks, not for the book alone, but for the increasing array of textbook-companion resources (e.g., web pages for each book, CDs that can be bundled with the textbook for student purchase that provides short videos for watching at home, and so on). Unfortunately, instructional leaders often do not make adjunct professors aware of these resources, and part-timers do not know they can pursue them on their own, when it is all free for the asking.

Once the overall goal of the course is formulated and a *course description* is reviewed or, in the case of a new course, developed, specific learning objectives will need to be identified. You will probably find it useful to think in terms of what educators call *behavioral objectives* (i.e., what you expect students to be able to demonstrate at the conclusion of the course). Stating objectives in this fashion encourages use of action verbs such as *identify, contrast, explain,* and *analyze,* rather than *understand* or *know,* thus creating a sharper focus for both instructor and learner. The goals and objectives of the course will provide the overall course structure and drive such other decisions as the selection of effective learning activities, choice of textbook, methods of assessing student learning, and so on.

Continue your planning with a thorough analysis of the personal resources you bring to the course. The SWOT analysis that you were encouraged to develop in Chapter 2 would be the ideal place to start. Thoroughly reflect on the following questions as they relate to the course you have been assigned; then write down the specific points that each elicits:

1. What are your specific *strengths* for delivering this particular course? Focus on those professional experiences likely to be valued by those who will later enter the field, not simply longevity in the field.
2. What are your *weaknesses*—gaps in knowledge, personal comfort level, and so on? Every instructor has some, so you will want to recognize them up front to develop a course plan that minimizes their impact.

3. What *opportunities* are presented to you from teaching this course? Does it provide a potential "signature" that others in the department lack? Is it a way for you to get a particular message to a group of students who might not otherwise be made aware of it? Is it a forum to discuss issues that impact your success in another arena of your life?
4. What *threats* accrue from your teaching the course? If it will significantly reduce the time you have available for other essential activities in your life, you should thoughtfully plan course assignments and the number and nature of examinations, all of which require extensive time to evaluate, accordingly.

As you plan your course in detail, your common-sense strategy should be to maximize your strengths and opportunities while minimizing your weaknesses and threats. For example, if organizational and writing skills are among your strengths and dynamic speaking one of your weaknesses, you would be wise to structure your course with a significant amount of student-participation activities rather than extended blocks of lecture/demonstration. If you view teaching the course as an opportunity to interest students in careers within the industry that employs you full time or in which you invested much of your career, you might want to incorporate a brief face-to-face appointment with each student early in your course so that you might more effectively maximize your stated opportunity.

Another tool that you developed, the *Personal Practical Theory* (PPT), would be very useful at this stage of your course planning as well. As you recall, your PPT enables you to identify and more thoroughly analyze your personal beliefs about learners, the role of the instructor, the subject matter, the classroom climate, and the process of learning. The PPT then serves as a guide to developing a course that reflects your personal beliefs. From an operational perspective, the PPT will:

- Guide the continuity of subsequent class meetings throughout the course
- Help you organize individual class meetings and maximize focus during class
- Aid your developing assignments that are better received and foster more grounded learning in students
- Guide your establishing an effective process for evaluating students

In short, the PPT helps you create a course that embraces your values and personal style and enables you to make more effective decisions as the course evolves over the term. The time and energy invested in developing the SWOT analysis and PPT will not only make your next course much more rewarding, but also provide you greater insight into the larger scope of college teaching.

IDENTIFYING POSSIBLE INSTRUCTIONAL RESOURCES

Throughout your course planning, be sure to carefully review key sections of the college catalog, adjunct faculty handbook, and other institutional documents that might affect your teaching. While you will no doubt need to return to these documents for clarification of policies and procedures as your course progresses, it is critical to launch each course with a clear understanding of current official guidelines toward attendance, grades, withdrawal from courses, and so on, so that your approach dovetails appropriately.

When your teaching assignment becomes firm, acquire the assigned course textbook and its ancillary materials (e.g., instructor's manual, test bank, and so on) from your instructional leader or directly from the publisher. At the same time, request copies of course examinations used by previous successful instructors of the course, even if those are dated and/or based on a previous textbook. Besides saving time from developing your examinations "from scratch," these will enable you to better gauge and align the level of your evaluation practices. Remember that instructor-developed materials require time and energy to prepare, so thank their providers appropriately. In return, offer teaching resources you later acquire or develop that your colleagues are likely to value. Through this process, you may well launch a mentoring relationship that will be mutually rewarding throughout your teaching career.

From conversations with your discipline leader and/or mentor, you will develop a more clear understanding of how your assigned course fits into the flow of the entire curriculum and a more accurate perception of the nature of students you can expect. Clarify also the degree of latitude you are permitted in delivering the course:

- Must you "cover" every chapter in the book?
- Which concepts are considered the most critical and challenging for students to master?
- Which assignments are "standard operating procedure" for this particular course?

As you review the syllabi of previous course sections, focus especially on:

- The textbook chapters addressed and any deviation in sequence with which they were addressed
- The nature, length, and complexity of course assignments
- The number, format, and length of examinations
- The overall scheduling of the course

If possible, talk with the providers of the syllabi to ensure your understanding of their strategies. As you note ideas for your syllabus, be conservative in deviating too widely from the syllabi you have reviewed, in terms of assignments, reading requirements, number of examinations, and so on. An appropriate maxim to embrace is "seek to fit into the department culture before standing out." The exception would be to include modifications that might be specifically suggested by your discipline leader.

Next, review the textbook as thoroughly as possible. Although your initial perception may well be that the book is not as effective as others with which you are familiar, try very hard to find a great deal about the book that you can embrace. If students are required to purchase the book, avoid the temptation not to rely on the book and thus risk students' perceiving their money has been wasted. Many adjunct professors have made relations with other faculty members and their teaching time very difficult by criticizing the adopted textbook to students. Although veteran faculty members openly question the ability of a new colleague to effectively evaluate the appropriateness of a specific book for this particular setting, students might interpret such remarks as reasons why they need not keep up with assigned readings. If you become convinced during the course that the text is in fact not a good fit with your curriculum, quietly solicit and review those used by other schools. If you find one that you prefer and your relationship with the instructional leader is sound, request a *desk copy* from the publisher for their review. Before developing your syllabus, you should have read the first four or five chapters completely and the summaries of the remaining chapters. This textbook review should permit you to have identified any chapters that might be of little value and which, with the discipline leader's concurrence, you might be able to omit from your syllabus. The course might also call for supplemental readings, which you would review and evaluate in a similar vein.

DEVELOPING YOUR SYLLABUS

As you draft your course syllabus, keep in mind that it should provide the increasingly overextended students who will populate your class with a complete and detailed course overview and agenda. Remember also that you are not preparing simply to deliver a single course but a vital component of the entire degree program. As such, one of our goals should be to challenge students to assume greater responsibility for their own learning. A well-developed syllabus contributes to achieving that goal. It should be a thoroughly conceived, effective, and appropriate communications tool for the specific type of student your course is designed to serve (Grunert, 1997).

Instructors often provide overly lengthy syllabi for their courses that require extensive time to review, but the one- or two-page syllabus that leaves common questions unanswered is a far more serious concern. To ensure that your syllabus is a good "fit" for your particular teaching assignment, continue to seek additional syllabi for courses similar to yours, especially from those with glowing reputations. If your assigned course is a new one, continue to seek syllabi from institutions that have longer histories with the course. Developing a syllabus with insufficient regard for what other professors have done lends itself to creating a plan that is out of touch with the department strategy and contributing to the redundancy within courses.

Because your major goal is to facilitate your students' mastery of the course content, your syllabus should eliminate barriers to learning by anticipating nearly any reasonable question that a student might have about the course. Be aware, however, that in recent years, the syllabus has become more than the course plan. In our evermore consumer-oriented and litigious society, the syllabus has evolved into a binding contract between the instructor and the student, with all the implications we typically associate with that term. In your draft syllabus, provide answers to the questions you might ask as a student, such as "what's in the course for me?" If you intend to impose penalties for attendance you consider unsatisfactory, assignments that are submitted after their stated deadline, or similar situations, your policy should be consistent with college and department guidelines and must be spelled out clearly in the syllabus. Because it is not uncommon for today's students to question authority, the astute professor will always safeguard him- or herself against unreasonable challenges with a well-developed, detailed syllabus.

Given the factors described above, I have included in Appendix 5.2 a model syllabus for your consideration. It is not designed to supplant any guidelines that your discipline leader might have provided or to address all aspects of every teaching assignment. Instead, it seeks to help you develop a "grounded" syllabus, prompt you to consider critical points that may not have been obvious, satisfy the perspective of "consumer-oriented students" and save time and energy that you might invest in other aspects of planning your course. The rationale behind each section included in the "model syllabus" is as follows:

Class: This section enables students to confirm basic information about the course, including complete course identification number, meeting place and time, and so on, with that provided them during the registration process. Students who are registered for another class can easily excuse themselves without having to disrupt the classroom environment after focus has become more intense.

Description: Providing students with a brief summary of the overall goal of the course, such as how it fits into the overall curriculum and what role/status they will occupy on its completion, will enable them to reconcile their preconceived and sometimes incorrect expectations of the course with your paradigm. Make sure the description is consistent with that which appears in the official college catalog.

Textbook: Sometimes colleges or departments allow professors to adopt textbooks for their particular sections of the course, while others embrace a universal adoption for all sections of the same course. Textbooks might be adopted for only one term, a single academic year, or an indefinite time frame. The philosophy varies widely. Therefore, it is very possible that students might have bought, borrowed, or traded for an inappropriate book. (In recent years, many professors have developed *course packs,* a collection of instructor-developed materials and articles from journals that are perhaps more current than the material included in the typical textbook.) This section on the syllabus clears up any text-related questions, and theoretically provides a "check" for the bookstore if an exchange or refund is appropriate.

This section might be extended to include *supplementary readings,* or, if those are extensive, an additional section might be added. If readings are to be reserved by the instructor in the library, critical information about its policies and procedures should be included. When additional readings are assigned, provide students with a brief rationale (e.g., currency of information) for their inclusion.

Related courses: This section provides the names and call numbers of specific courses that students should have completed before yours and might be called *prerequisites* if those courses are specifically mandated in the college catalog. Seeking to communicate the rigor of their course, some instructors identify additional, unofficial prerequisite courses and in the process, limit enrollment in their course dramatically. Increasingly cost-conscious instructional leaders are not likely to approve tactics that reduce enrollment below reasonable projections. Contemporary educators view this section as a tool for helping students make their own well-informed decision on whether their enrollment is likely to lead to success.

Instructor: This section is designed to establish the professor's credibility, academically and professionally, to instruct the course. It should be stated rather briefly and then embellished during the first and subsequent class meetings.

Office: Adjunct professors typically are not provided individual offices, but it is accepted practice to make yourself available to students on a regular basis in a secure place within close proximity to the classroom. A quiet, semiprivate area within the student union or in a vacant classroom where students would likely feel comfortable sharing problems related to their progress in the course is a common choice. In this section of the syllabus or in another logical place, provide a telephone number and e-mail address where students could reach you between class meetings. Identify time parameters that balance accessibility for students with convenience for you.

Students with disabilities: As explained in Chapter 3, it has become increasingly critical to provide students with physical or learning disabilities with information about accessing support services. Most institutions have developed detailed policies and handbooks from which you could craft an appropriate statement for your syllabus.

Teaching methods: Students with an increasingly consumer mentality want and deserve a clear idea of the instructional methods you intend to employ, especially if those methods are likely to be perceived as somewhat unusual. Listing your methods also serves as good protection should a student later criticize your methods to a discipline leader.

Concepts and skills: This section may well be entitled *learning objectives* or "course goals." Its primary purpose is to give students a clear idea of the specific concepts they will acquire in the course and start to focus their mental energies from the outset. A secondary purpose is to reinforce the perception in students' minds that you are organized and focused. Your list should probably include at least one objective for each of the textbook chapters you will cover in your class. These objectives are typically listed in the course outline provided by your discipline leader or in the textbook or its ancillary materials.

Attendance policy: Students will likely question this section for clarification, so your classroom attendance policy should be developed only after thorough research. You first need to know the college and department policies, if any, and the common practices of the majority of full-time and veteran adjunct faculty members within your department. You also should consider the lifestyles of your students, which might be quite hectic, and your own values. The important thing is to formulate language that is as specific as possible without overly limiting your flexibility. It is impossible for your discipline leader to defend a punitive action against a student's excessive absences that is not spelled out succinctly on the course syllabus.

Grading criteria: One of the most critical components of your syllabus is its grading criteria. Therefore, its formulation should consider a number of factors. As stated earlier, students will compare your course to others in their degree programs, so your grading criteria should be consistent with those of other professors in the department. To give only two examinations when other professors are giving four or entirely essay examinations when others are giving primarily multiple choice may well be perceived as highly risky to students fearful of failure. To require a significantly greater number of lengthier or more complex assignments would give many students a reason to drop your section and add an easier professor's section, or to avoid enrolling in your subsequent courses. Once you have established your reputation, you might give another look at such factors and raise the bar if appropriate. This section should also spell out your policies on course withdrawal, and the awarding of "incomplete" grades, providing support at the end of the course should you take an action that a student regards as unfairly punitive.

Grading scale: When formulating this section, first determine any institutional or departmental policy that might exist on the numerical scale. Some mandate 90 percent to 100 percent as an "A" and so on, whereas others view the development of the scale as a prerogative of academic freedom. A number of colleges and universities are now differentiating between plusses and minuses in their calculations of students' grade point averages. Some schools also have formal and informal policies on the distribution of final grades, such as no more than X percent of students should achieve a grade of "A" and so on. Again, determine all of the critical formal rules and common practice of full-time and veteran adjunct faculty members before formulating your grading scale.

Methods of achieving success: This section simply outlines the time commitments and strategies for a student to obtain satisfactory results in the class. It also identifies any potential resources that have been established to aid student success in your course.

Degrees and certificates: In the last few years, public institutions of higher education have been held increasingly accountable by their legislatures to ensure that taxpayers' money that funds their programs is invested wisely. A similar perspective has also been seen in many private institutions seeking to ensure that supporters' dollars are wisely spent. The bottom line is that there is less support than ever for students to meander through their college experience, changing majors several times, accumulating excess hours, and the like. This section is designed to influence students to complete efficiently the degree or certificate program(s) of which your course is a component.

Student organizations: This section promotes the development of students' social and leadership skills and their retention in degree programs by informing them of student organizations related to the curriculum that are available for them to join.

Tentative schedule: The final section of your syllabus should be a schedule of assignments, activities, and examinations. Stating that it is *tentative* provides you flexibility should an especially unusual circumstance occur that might cause you to want to delay an examination. But be reluctant about changing your schedule once the course is under way. Doing so creates a potential domino effect by tacitly suggesting to students that there will be further deviations, preventing you from completing the entire course.

Discretionary sections: Remembering that the syllabus is a binding contract with students and should anticipate the reasonable questions students might have about the course, you might want to consider additional sections in your syllabus. A growing number of professors are including an *academic integrity* section that cites their own and the institution's policies on cheating on examinations and plagiarism, as well as classroom civility sections designed to limit verbal conflicts and distractions. Others cite the location and operating hours of course-critical learning resources available to students, such as the college library, computer and tutoring labs, and so on. Although these sections will lengthen your syllabus, they may well provide the essential protection for yourself and help for the student that will avert unpleasant outcomes in your course.

An old management axiom says, "Plan your work, then work the plan." Apprentice carpenters are taught to "measure twice, cut once." A well-researched and formulated syllabus will make your job immensely easier and satisfying. It outlines clearly your expectations in all of the critical areas of the course, and protects you when you are challenged. As stated before, it is truly a contract that includes your offer to provide service, a tacit acceptance by students receiving it, and consideration for students' and the instructor's positions. It is entirely enforceable.

Regardless of profession, people in our society are becoming increasingly marketing conscious. Instructors who seek to thrive in the classroom must contemplate the type of image they wish to establish in the minds of their students. By using the word *image,* I am not suggesting that you attempt to present an ingenuine persona but rather am encouraging you to focus on the qualities you truly possess to make your classroom efforts more effective and thus achieve a greater sense of personal fulfillment. In that paradigm, become mindful of the effect of the appearance of your syllabus on students. Modern word-processors enable you to provide a document with excellent "eye appeal." Typos, poor-quality photocopies, and so on communicate to students that you lack professionalism, which is not an image you want to create during the first class meeting. If you teach more than one section of the same course, consider color coding your syllabus, other handout materials, and even examinations (e.g., one section on blue paper, another on white). Such a strategy not only helps you stay organized, but provides some panache to your teaching!

Your syllabus is so critical to your success that you should have your first one thoroughly reviewed, by your discipline leader, mentor, and perhaps a student, prior to having it printed for distribution to class members. If you followed the plan outlined here, you can be assured your discipline leader or mentor will be greatly impressed with your thoroughness and professionalism, helping build your confidence as you embark on your new adventure.

PLANNING YOUR COURSE STRATEGY

Many new adjunct professors seem to view themselves and the textbook as the sole focus for delivering the material of the course. A more contemporary paradigm views you as a facilitator of instruction who understands how students process information and then utilizes a range of appropriate instructional methods and strategies to provide opportunities for students to learn material in a way that is most efficient and effective for them.

Since there is a good chance that your students have been conditioned by a steady diet of rich media, it is important to design stimulating elements into your class. Guest speakers, field trips, videotapes, and web presentations are each potentially powerful vehicles for accomplishing that goal and also for enriching the overall learning experience that your course provides students. Begin early to identify potential resources—through your professional and community contacts and other faculty members—to lend credibility and richness to your course and to offer students the opportunity to develop real-world insights that textbooks and other traditionally employed materials cannot provide. It is critical to realize that the richest resources usually require significant lead time to be utilized effectively. Before committing to any specific opportunity, satisfy yourself that it effectively addresses one or more of your learning objectives and does not just liven up the class and/or fill up time. After being entertained, many of today's students have, in effect, said, "That was fun and interesting, but what did it have to do with this course?" Effective guest speakers, field trips, and videotapes will provide additional information or perspective, instead of simply rehashing what you have already delivered. At the same time, they should be perceived as complementing and reinforcing your overall approach, rather than creating a perspective so divergent that the issue fails to be resolved in students' minds.

A word of warning: like any other effective tool, guest speakers, field trips, and video presentations can be overused, creating the perception in students' eyes that the professor is more interested in filling time and entertaining than stimulating critical thinking. Is there a magic number of activities that can be effectively used in a course? Probably not; it depends on the subject matter, the experience level of the students, and the passion that the professor holds for activities. Chapter 7 provides a comprehensive set of tips for managing these resources.

Well before inviting guest speakers to your class for the first time, it would be wise to vet them with your discipline leader, to prevent a potential embarrassing conflict. Also remember that just because a potential guest speaker is an expert on some valuable topic, it does not necessarily mean he or she will be an effective presenter for your student audience. Do not risk inviting a guest speaker whom you are not sure will be successful or whom you cannot help be successful; it will not only risk problems at the time but also impair the use of subsequent guests and reflect on your judgment. Invite guest speakers who mirror the overall demographic composition of your community so that students are exposed to a rich set of perspectives and realistic role models. Once you are satisfied that those hurdles are cleared, identify the specific objectives that flow naturally out of their area of expertise (rather than items that would require additional research) that you would like the guest to address. Provide those objectives in writing or by e-mail and give ample time for the guest to assess his or her ability to effectively address the issues in a presentation. Many guest speakers have been made to appear ineffective because they were given ambiguous instructions by the instructor, so confirm by e-mail the exact date, time, location, content, and length of presentation that you would like them to deliver. At the same time, request a resumé or short biography from which you might prepare an introduction that energizes their presentation and supervisor's name and title so that you can later send an appropriate thank-you note.

The cautions about guest speakers apply in even greater intensity to field trips that you might plan for your class. Be sure to clarify the institutional policy and secure approval in writing from the appropriate administrator before announcing any field trip to students. In addition, objectively evaluate the inherent risks of the field trip. Analyze if the rewards markedly outweigh the potential risks you will bear. Consider also the very empty feeling that accrues when a teacher goes the extra mile to arrange a field trip, only to discover that it was not perceived by students as a valuable opportunity. Some of the most effective field trips can be accomplished very close to or actually on campus, such as a guided tour of an institutional facility administered by a terrific presenter or a business with a special appeal located on the perimeter of the campus.

Contemporary videotapes and website presentations also provide potentially rich learning experiences for students. Many of the same rules apply—relevancy to the curriculum, acceptability in the eyes of the discipline leader, and so on. Be careful also to inquire if another full-time or veteran adjunct with whom the students have likely had a class uses the same media presentation. A few other points should also be considered before committing to include a particular resource in your course plan. Generally, a video should not exceed a half hour in length. Feature films in a literature or social studies classes are probably reasonable exceptions but in that case should be broken into reasonable segments with debriefing sessions interspersed. Always preview a videotape before showing it to a class to ensure that the content, language, and complexity are appropriate for the students in the class.

Include any guest speakers, field trips, or major videotapes on the tentative schedule of your syllabus to promote attendance at that class meeting and reduce problems from these learning opportunities that are difficult to replicate. Integrate each strategically into the course and evaluate students' understanding through examination or other means. Avoid reinforcing the common student perception that these activities are time fillers or entertainment.

Finally, when using these enriched resources, always have a backup plan. Guest speakers become ill or get stuck in traffic. The destinations of field trips lose their charismatic hosts to other firms and experience other crises that make hosting field trips a burden at times. Equipment sometimes does not arrive or has technical difficulties that prevents the showing of media presentations. When your plans go awry, students with high expectations sometimes embarrassingly complain.

A course with a sound plan, enriched with special, well-researched learning opportunities will markedly affect your potential for success with students. Share your plan enthusiastically at your initial class meeting. Refer back to it on a regular basis throughout the course to provide students with the structure that so many need and to foster their self-direction to become lifelong learners.

SUMMARY OF KEY POINTS

- Ask for specific teaching resources from your discipline leader.
- Have dialogue with professors who have successfully taught sections of the course to which you are assigned.
- Employ your personal SWOT analysis and PPT exercise to guide your course planning and to ensure that the course will be a good fit for your abilities and style.
- Develop a sound syllabus that serves as a complete plan and contract with students.
- Plan your overall teaching strategy well in advance, drawing where possible on resources available in other arenas of your life.
- Plan guest speakers and field trips well in advance and implement plans only after thoroughly assessing all of the inherent risks involved.
- Get organized from the beginning.

THE FINAL WORD

"Having taught in higher education for 28 years and performed a number of college and community leadership roles, I believe it critical to model sound human development principles for my students, both traditionally and nontraditionally aged. Therefore, I regularly solicit and integrate their ideas into the planning of my current and subsequent course sections. Some examples include, at the first class meeting, asking their input into the sequencing of course topics; encouraging them to submit exam questions, an activity that counts toward 5 percent of their final grade; and asking those with especially rich experiences to serve as a guest speaker, in lieu of another course assignment. The major benefit of these strategies is to encourage participation and mature analysis and evaluation of the course material. A final strategy that has worked especially well has been my encouraging students to submit their perception of a valid grade for a particular major paper or essay examination. They can do this either on the paper or by e-mail shortly after submission. After I grade and return the papers, those students are then asked to compare the

grade I have assigned with the one they placed on it. If my score is lower than theirs, they are invited to see me outside of class to justify their grade. If their argument is valid and convincing, their grade is raised to a score between our two assessments. Their grade is never lowered. This practice encourages students to maturely evaluate their own work, provides a less stressful environment in which to explain their ideas, and gives me an opportunity for better insight into students' mastery of critical concepts."

—Robert Hearn, Grand Falls-Windsor, Newfoundland

■ ■ ■ ■ ■ ▬▬▬▬▬▬▬▬▬▬▬▬▬▬▬▬▬▬▬▬▬▬▬▬▬▬▬▬▬▬

MODEL COURSE SYLLABUS

PRINCIPLES OF MANAGEMENT
MAN 2021 A1
FALL 20—

Class	Tuesdays, 6:00–9:00 P.M. Springfield Campus, Blair Building, Room 111
Textbook	*Management, 9th edition,* by Burns and Schreiber, available at campus bookstore. Publisher's website for book: www.bmppublish.com/burns&schreiber.
Related Courses	Students would benefit from a prior knowledge of basic business terminology, gained through work experience or completion of an introductory course.
Instructor	Dr. Angelina Torez, Adjunct Professor of Business Management, received her B.S. in business administration, and M.A. in Marketing from Western Kentucky University, and a doctorate in business from the University of North Texas. Before entering teaching, she managed in the hospitality industry and in several sales organizations. She has been employed in management at Pax, Inc. since 1987. Her book, *Managing the Diverse Workplace,* is one of the nation's top sellers among titles focused on that workplace issue.
Office	Dr. Torez will be available to talk with students immediately following each class meeting. At other times, she can be seen in 226 during hours posted on that office door. From Madison County, she can be reached by telephone at 462-4700, or at 930-4722 from Monroe River or Jefferson Counties. Her e-mail address is *atorez@mail.amc.edu.*
Disabled Students	Students with disabilities that affect learning may be eligible for support resources through the Office of Disability Services, located in Granger Hall, room 108. Call Lori

McClendon, 786-1224, or e-mail her at
lmcclend@mail.amc.edu.

**Teaching
Methods**

A variety of instructional methods are used to provide students
with effective learning opportunities. These include role-play,
group problem solving, and self-analysis activities, in addition
to more traditional methods.

**Learning
Objectives**

Upon successful completion of this course, each student will be
able to:

1. Explain the basic management functions, skills, and
   roles.
2. Discuss management's role in enhancing efficiency and
   effectiveness.
3. Discuss the factors influencing changes in the manager's
   role.
4. Make ethical decisions that satisfy diverse organizational
   stakeholders.
5. Summarize the basic concepts of strategic planning.
6. Explain operating plans, policies, and procedures.
7. Explain the process for making effective management
   decisions.
8. Describe the function of commonly used decision-
   making tools.
9. Compare and contrast types of departmentalization.
10. Describe the dimensions and consequences of
    organizational culture.
11. Summarize the process of employee recruitment,
    selection, placement, compensation, and evaluation.
12. Contrast common leadership styles.
13. Explain the manager's role in managing conflict and
    encouraging teamwork.
14. Explain the most popular theories of worker motivation.
15. Explain effective methods of overcoming
    communications barriers.
16. Summarize the methods of controlling.
17. Explain the principles of total quality management.

**Attendance
Policy**

Although Dr. Torez provides an array of opportunities for each
student's mastery of course objectives, students should realize
the value that their experiences offer their peers. Therefore, it
is critical that you attend class regularly to be a partner in this
enhanced learning environment. Roll will be taken at each
class meeting, and your participation will be taken into
consideration in case of a borderline final grade. If class will

be missed, it is each student's responsibility to personally contact the instructor in advance regarding missed assignments. The instructor will not accept late work without valid reasons. Students are encouraged to contact the instructor any time they are not achieving their intended level of success before taking any other action. Students who need to withdraw must complete an official form and submit it consistent with college policy no later than November 9. Incomplete grades are awarded only when an emergency prevents a student from completing a minor portion of the course assignments.

Grading Criteria

Three unit examinations @ 20% (45 multiple-choice questions, one essay) = 60%
Research project (detailed standards provided at Sept. 17 class) = 20%
Final examination (comprehensive, 100 multiple-choice questions) = 20%

Grading Scale

90%–100%	A
80%–89%	B
70%–79%	C
60%–69%	D
Below 60%	F

Methods of Achieving Success

Achieving success in MAN 2021 will require a time commitment outside of class that averages three hours per week. Students benefit from completing assigned reading prior to content being addressed in class and from actively participating in classroom discussion, activities, and review.

Delta Epsilon Chi

Students enrolled in management and marketing courses benefit from participating in the college chapter of the national student organization Delta Epsilon Chi. The AMC chapter has a rich history of success in state and national competitions, as well as service to our local communities.

Certificates and Degrees

Today's workplace values many certifications and licenses as "tickets to upward mobility." This course is required within the A.S. and B.S. degrees in business administration, marketing management, accounting technology, and office support technology.

Professional Standards

An atmosphere similar to that present in most professional businesses should be displayed at all times. Thus, distractions such as personal communications devices and door slamming should be minimized, and consideration should be demonstrated to diverse opinions.

PRINCIPLES OF MANAGEMENT
MAN 2021 A1
TENTATIVE SCHEDULE

Date:	Topics/activities/assignments
August 20	Introduction, review of syllabus. Building a learning community.
August 27	Chapters 1 and 2
September 3	Chapters 3 and 4
September 10	Chapter 5; review for examination
September 17	**Examination No. 1;** return/review; research project overview
September 24	Chapters 6 and 7
October 1	Chapters 8 and 10; **project proposal due**
October 8	Chapter 11; review for examination
October 15	**Examination No. 2;** return/review; Chapter 12
October 22	Chapters 13 and 14
October 29	Chapter 15
November 5	Chapter 16; review for examination
November 12	**Examination No. 3;** return/review
November 19	Chapter 19
November 26	Chapter 20
December 3	**Projects due; presentations**
December 10	Chapter 21; review for final examination
December 17	**Final Examination: Tuesday, December 18, 8 A.M.**

■ ■ ■ ■ ■

CHAPTER 5

LAUNCHING YOUR COURSE EFFECTIVELY

"I always tell students at the first class meeting that I will know I've been successful if (1.) they learn something they can use, and (2.) they have fun."

—Larry Able, M.S., Lenexa, Kansas

FOCUS QUESTIONS

- What objectives should you expect to achieve during your first class meeting?
- Why should you and your students perceive each other as collaborators in learning?
- Why is it increasingly critical to make your expectations clear to students?
- How should you follow up your first class meeting to ensure an effective launch?

Are first impressions, truly lasting impressions? As you pursued your college degrees, you no doubt completed dozens of courses with a wide array of professors. You can likely remember at least a few terrible first-class experiences—a professor who was overtly late and obviously ill-prepared; a messy classroom with furniture in disarray; or a professor who gave a minimal introduction, distributed a lengthy syllabus with no explanation, and then dismissed the class as if its members were intruders. Today's students and other stakeholders who are clamoring for increased accountability in higher education may well have had even more horrific first-class experiences that shaped their views vividly.

Hopefully, you also have had a few exemplary first-class experiences—a professor who took her post early and introduced herself to each arriving student, a table that contained alphabetized name cards for each enrolled student, or a passionately delivered introduction to the course material that "hooked" you into a subject that you had previously decried. For many students, such well-orchestrated initial classes planted seeds that grew into a learning community, where cooperation drove steadily developing relationships between the professor and students and where students were inspired to take a more active role in learning the subject matter throughout the term than they ever believed they could (Lunde, 2000).

Replicating this kind of experience for your students is no more than you would expect if your roles were reversed. When you launch a course successfully, you will also manage successfully one of the two most significant mileposts for retaining students throughout the term (the other being the first examination). Providing you insights to do so is the objective of this chapter.

No matter how long you teach, meeting a class for the first time always evokes some degree of apprehension. Even when your thorough planning has given you a strong foundation, you may be nervous about encountering a fresh set of faces or being perceived as credible. How you and your students will perceive each other over the ensuing ten, fifteen, or more weeks will depend largely on how effectively you manage that first class meeting. One helpful strategy (Dr. Covey's fifth habit) is to try to see the occasion through the eyes of the students likely to be in your class. This chapter also contains many other suggestions intended to make the launch of your course more rewarding for students and more successful for you.

The first class meeting should serve at least two primary purposes:

1. To clarify all reasonable questions students might have relative to the course objectives, as well as your expectations for their performance in class. As students leave the first meeting, they should believe in your competency to teach the course, be able to predict the nature of your instruction and classroom management, and know what you will require of them.
2. To give you an understanding of who is taking your course and what their expectations are.

Thus, the first class meeting needs to be carefully planned and conducted in a warm, enthusiastic fashion. Many professors believe mistakenly that there is no need to conduct a full class meeting on the first day of the semester because the enrollment might not stabilize until after the first week. In reality however, few significant changes in enrollment typically occur during add-drop periods, and it is shortsighted to waste the time of most students for the benefit of a very few who might add the class later. Furthermore, conducting a solid first class meeting likely will create word-of-mouth promotion among students who drop other courses that will generate a full enrollment, which is a "win-win" for your students, your instructional leader, and you. In launching your course effectively, there are ten specific objectives you should strive to achieve:

1. To orchestrate positive first impressions
2. To introduce yourself effectively
3. To clarify the learning objectives and your expectations

4. To help students learn about each other
5. To get to know your students
6. To whet students' appetites for the course content
7. To inform students of key issues of the course and instructional program
8. To reassure students about their decision to enroll
9. To assess students' understanding of the starting position of the course
10. To ensure that everyone is "on the same page" as you begin

Each of these objectives is the focus of a section that follows.

ORCHESTRATING POSITIVE FIRST IMPRESSIONS

It is instinctive to want positive student impressions of you and your course at the first class meeting but more difficult to orchestrate them. Richard Ailes (1995), the renowned communications consultant, believes you have fewer than ten seconds to create a positive image of yourself. Since many students equate the course with you, then what you do, how you appear, how you communicate, and how you present your class syllabus will dictate how they perceive the course and ultimately *you*.

Although professors are usually no longer required to follow a preset dress code, we do know that how you dress conveys very distinct messages to your students and therefore that it is probably worth the investment to manage this factor at the first meeting. If your desire is to have a very casual classroom environment in which students perceive you as a colleague, then dressing in casual clothes may well achieve that purpose. If you want to distinguish yourself from the students and convey a professional image, then you should wear clothing appropriate for professionals in your field, ratcheting up students' aspirations. Later in the term, you may decide to change your perspective according to the nature of the activities you will engage in with your students. For example, if you have lab days, your wearing of a lab coat, protective eye gear, and latex gloves will communicate professionalism and "safety first" very powerfully. If you have field days in which students will be working in such organizations as medical facilities or specialized businesses, your adhering to that organization's dress code will "tell" students that the organization has its own culture that must be valued. Nevertheless, how you present yourself that first class meeting will convey your intent for the classroom environment to your students.

Another factor that influences students' perceptions is how you organize the learning environment. A clean board and desks in neat rows convey a sense of professionalism and formality instantly. Desks arranged in clusters, or U-shaped configurations will prepare students for an informal, interactive experience. If you are assigned to teach in a classroom with furniture fixed in place, you will have to find other ways to communicate the degree of formality or informality you wish to maintain.

When students enter your classroom, there should be no question which class is meeting in the room. The course title and your name should be neatly and prominently displayed on the board or screen in front of the room. Students who might have entered the room looking for another course can comfortably leave before the class begins. Position yourself at the door and greet entering students with a handshake and a smile. If such practice is out of your comfort level, be sure to recognize each entering student in a way that helps them feel validated.

INTRODUCING YOURSELF EFFECTIVELY TO STUDENTS

Students register for particular class sections for either or both of two primary reasons: the convenience of its time slot and the reputation of the professor. Said another way, consumer-oriented students care most about fitting the class into their already busy schedules and having their needs met by a reliable professor. While greeting the students as they enter the classroom does much to establish the environment, your self-introduction is critical either to confirming the expectations students have already formed or to creating expectations from scratch. As you read in Chapter 3, many of today's students are skeptical toward authority figures; they question the motives, knowledge, and experience levels of those in charge. Some enter your class neither highly motivated toward nor enthusiastic about learning and perhaps are intolerant of activities they do not perceive as productive. So your introduction needs to be sensitive yet highly focused on the particular course you are teaching. Convey your understanding of their limited time while also reinforcing your expectations of rigor. You will have many opportunities throughout the term to reveal your broader background, but in your initial introduction, you should strive for succinctness, humility, and a bit of enthusiasm and humor (Berk, 1998).

Your introduction should also clarify when and how students can contact you. Your syllabus will provide your office arrangements, telephone number, and e-mail address, but you also might consider sharing your home or cell phone number. Most students are mindful to try to reach you at your office, and recognize that the others are provided for true emergencies. You will also want to let the students know when you will be available to meet with them individually. Regularly reserve fifteen or twenty minutes before and after class for discussions with individual students. Although few students will take advantage of these times, your extending yourself conveys that you care about students' needs. In Chapter 9, I will discuss e-mail and personal web pages that provide asynchronous access to students.

A word of caution to readers who are assigned courses with too little lead time before the first class meeting: avoid ever saying, "This is the first time I am teaching this course," or "I was only asked to teach this class two days ago." Regardless of the rationale behind making such statements, they serve only to hamper students' willingness to trust in your ability and lower their expectations of the course. Even if you have not had sufficient time to fully develop your syllabus, you should provide an overview of the course and its learning objectives and then ask the students for feedback about their expectations. No later than the next class meeting, perhaps by e-mail before then, provide the class with a complete syllabus that includes a schedule of activities. If you do this right, students will feel that they had input into the planning of the class and perhaps will be more invested in its success (Lyons, Kysilka, & Pawlas, 1999).

CLARIFYING THE LEARNING OBJECTIVES AND YOUR EXPECTATIONS

Students should leave the first class meeting with a clear understanding of the course objectives, your expectations for their performance, and your philosophy of teaching and learning. Because today's students (and perhaps their families and/or employers) hold high expectations of what they will learn in college, you should also clarify how you perceive your role as the teacher and their role as learners. It is essential that you manage the expectations of students who view themselves as consumers by clearly explaining both the strengths and limitations of your course—that is, what you will and will not be able to accomplish because of time, space, finances, and other limitations.

Invest the time to review your carefully crafted syllabus in detail during the first class meeting, section by section. For introductory courses, you may want to create transparencies or an electronic slide presentation that enables you to isolate and focus upon each section of the syllabus. Academically mature students will usually remain focused with a mild admonition to stay with you as it is reviewed. In either scenario, be sure to solicit questions several times regarding the information on the syllabus and draw specific attention to such critical issues as attendance policy, provisions for makeup work, due dates of assignments, and grading procedures. If students do not raise questions, assure them that you will entertain questions about the syllabus by e-mail or at the next class meeting. Students who begin three or more classes within a few days of each other can probably be excused from processing all the information from all their classes at the first meeting. Do not assume that a lack of questions means that everyone clearly understands everything. Revisit the syllabus at the second class meeting and after the first examination or assignment. As I said in Chapter 4, in today's higher education environment, the syllabus is viewed as a contract between you and your students. Thus, it is imperative that both you and your students have a common understanding of its content to ensure a successful course for everyone.

HELPING STUDENTS TO LEARN ABOUT EACH OTHER

A fourth objective for launching your course effectively and an event that energizes students following the somewhat tedious review of the syllabus is an activity that helps students get acquainted with each another. Although some students might seem to not want to interact with you or their classmates, they really want and need that. Besides meeting their social needs, conducting an icebreaker provides an opportunity to assess potential study group partners and assuages their fear of contributing to classroom discussions that will make their educational experiences richer and more successful. Students who actively get to know their classmates usually become more motivated to attend class and, in an age of accountability, are far more likely to be retained within the course, the degree program, and the institution. Furthermore, when students know each other, they maintain more positive attitudes about the class and participate more actively in small-group learning activities, making your role much more rewarding.

How can you help your students to get to know each other? There are several options:

- Many professors ask students to introduce themselves to the class. This is often not optimally effective, however, when students are more focused on deciding what they will say about themselves than on listening to what others are saying.
- Ask students to form pairs or triads whose task is to introduce each other to the rest of the class. Using pairs and triads provides the students with an opportunity to launch relationships with each other and keeps their attention focused. You might add some spice to this activity by having each student nominate a peer for a fitting award (e.g., "superwoman of the month") and then providing a token prize (e.g., a fortune cookie) to the student making the most creative introduction.
- Take a refreshment break and tell the students that they need to get acquainted with at least two new people, whom they will introduce when the class reconvenes.
- Orchestrate a human scavenger hunt such as the one that appears in Appendix 5.2 that gets students up and moving around the room (a major energizer) and encourages them to meet a large number of their classmates firsthand.
- Ask students to form small groups and solve a preset problem or discuss a breaking news story related to course content. Be sure to make the activity enjoyable and to provide clear expectations of the outcome sought. After completing the task, each group can designate one reporter who will share solutions with the rest of the class and introduce the other group members.

Once you have completed one of these activities, it is critical to invest a few minutes to debrief it. The important question for students to answer is why you invested class time conducting the activity. Students should be encouraged to conclude that they are valuable resources for one another in their educational journeys and that not all knowledge will come directly from you or the textbook. They should also be encouraged to recognize several benefits from connecting with their peers (e.g., improved test scores, more effective matching of members in group activities, and so on). Said another way, by engaging students in group work during the initial class meeting, you plant the seeds for establishing a community of learners within your class, and perhaps foster a long-term appreciation for collaboration in their workplaces and other arenas of their lives.

GETTING TO KNOW YOUR STUDENTS

You can probably remember a time when a person you perceived as important surprised you by using your name for the very first time. Humans typically consider their names to be a unique characteristic, one that defines them to everyone else within their environment. To establish a bond with each of your students, it is critical that you learn and use their names as early in the term as possible.

Before pursuing this objective, do what you can to obtain an up-to-date official class roll before the first class meeting. Invest a couple of minutes to review the names a few times to help you become familiar with pronunciations and the overall gender mix. As you greet the students entering the room, you can confirm difficult pronunciations and begin to fit faces with names. As you formally begin the first class, read each name from the roll, and if you come upon one that you have not been able to confirm, ask the student to pronounce it for you. Make phonetic notes as needed so that you can correctly pronounce all names at subsequent class meetings, conveying your sense of professionalism and sensitivity to students. After calling the roll, ask for a show of hands by those whose names were not called and instruct these students to meet with you after class or during the break to clarify their situation. If you have a large class, you may decide to maximize your class time by circulating sign-in sheets so that you will have a record of who attended class.

Immediately following your icebreaker activity, distribute a Student Profile form or similar tool to each student, which you can use to learn names and gather other information throughout the term. Appendix 5.1 shows a sample form that can be used as-is or modified to fit your specific needs. Have students hand you the completed forms at the end of the class meeting to provide you an opportunity to fit name to face. If you recall their names, say them aloud as you bid good-bye. If you do not yet have the name memorized, simply read it from the student's completed student profile form. Improve your recall effectiveness even further and add a high-tech touch in the process by taking a Polaroid or digital picture of each class member and attaching it to the student profile form. Reviewing the profiles, with or without photos attached, before coming to class and keeping them readily available while you teach will greatly help you learn each student in your class. Make it your objective to learn every student's name in class no later than the time you return the first examination or written assignment.

Learning students' names comes relatively easy for many professors, but it can be a daunting task for others, especially when classes are large. Many professors assign seats for at least several weeks, a strategy that facilitates their matching of names with faces. Assigned seats also facilitate roll-taking, which is required by guidelines of many student financial aid programs, even for courses where attendance is not required. If you choose to assign seats, alert students in advance that you will be creating a seating chart and tell them why. Students with certain disabilities (e.g., poor eyesight or hearing, physical disabilities) should be encouraged to work with you to reserve appropriate seats.

Many college professors believe assigned seating is demeaning to adult learners, even though it helps in learning students' names. There are many options. Name tents, constructed by students' folding index cards lengthwise and using bold marker pens to print their names largely and clearly, can be placed in front of the student each time they come to class. Name tents enable you to respond to students by name and, through repetition, master their names quite quickly. Arriving ten or fifteen minutes early to each class meeting and engaging in conversation with each arriving student will further sharpen your recall of names and biographies.

WHETTING STUDENTS' APPETITES FOR THE COURSE CONTENT

Depending on the length of your first class meeting, you may have some time left to whet the students' appetites for the material they are about to tackle. Because students may still add your class, you do not want to address too much content, especially anything that appears on the first examination and will not be addressed a second time, during the first class session.

A number of effective professors whet their students' appetites by asking open-ended questions such as, "What do you think of when you hear [economics, sociology, and so on]?" This not only engages the students' interest but provides you a starting point for your teaching. Students might not shout back what you would hope to hear, but take their responses at face value and do something constructive with them.

An alternative idea and one that also gets students to begin working in groups on the first day is to do a no-book directed reading-thinking activity (DR-TA). The steps, which can be listed on the board or on a screen, are as follows:

1. On your own, list everything you can think of that might be in a book entitled _____. [Write the title of your textbook or the title of your course if you do not use a textbook.]
2. Get with a partner, share your ideas, and then put the ideas you both generated for Step 1 into categories.
3. Give each category a name.
4. Get with another pair and together combine your ideas. Then arrange the categories as a table of contents for this book and write it on the chart paper each group has been given.

This entire process requires about thirty minutes and is well worth every second. Students begin to focus on the course, they meet at least three other members of the class, and professors begin to develop a sense of what their students know relative to the course as they walk around listening to the groups process the task and as they observe what students write on the chart paper for display.

Seeking to open students' minds to a new perspective by asking additional, perhaps rhetorical, questions is also valuable. Sharing the front page of the morning newspaper, a video clip from a recent news broadcast, or the cover of a popular weekly newsmagazine can be very effective attention-grabbing devices for visual learners, whereas passing around examples of work projects (e.g., portfolios) appeals to tactile learners (Lunde, 2000). Experiential activities that require students to move around within the classroom engage the learning systems of kinesthetic learners. The key is to plant seeds to encourage students to examine their preexisting views without trying to win them over to your views of the subject matter all at once.

You might also want to provide a cursory review of the textbook adopted for the class, acquainting the students with how the content is organized, what study aids are included, and how those aids might enhance their mastery of the course material. If you will be using supplementary materials, such as a course pack or a website, you may want to explore those with your students, making appropriate connections to the textbook and syllabus. If you have made arrangements to have materials on reserve at the library, be sure to review procedures for their use. Perhaps you have an extended reading list; reviewing it and highlighting specifically interesting or unique articles or books would be most beneficial to your students. Remember, your goal is to encourage students to establish a foundation on which they can build knowledge and skills throughout the course and to become self-directing.

Finally, you want to be sure that the students have time to go to the bookstore and purchase the materials required for your class. This is especially important if you teach night classes, if students have limited free time, and/or if the bookstore maintains limited hours. You also want to be sure that your students, particularly if they are new to your campus, know when, where, and how to access the resources of the library, computer laboratories, and tutoring centers.

INFORMING STUDENTS OF KEY ISSUES

Like all clients that feel valued, students expect to be kept informed of key issues that might have an impact on their success. Therefore, immediately before your first class meeting, make yourself aware of information within the enrollment environment of your department's courses, such as:

- Number of vacant spaces available in your course (and in other sections of it)
- Class sections that might have been canceled because of low enrollment or other factors
- New class sections that might have been created because of unexpectedly high interest
- Drop-add dates and procedures for making schedule changes

As you approach the close of your initial class meeting, inform students of this information. It is quite possible that they, or their friends, have had changes in their schedules necessitated by a wide range of factors. Presenting the latest information not only can give you an opportunity to recruit an additional few students (if you need to), but also demonstrates your concern for their best interests. An adjunct professor's consistently increasing enrollment in his course sections during the add-drop period sends a very strong message to instructional leaders about future assignments.

REASSURING STUDENTS ABOUT THEIR DECISION

Whenever students start a new class, they typically experience a condition psychologists refer to as *cognitive dissonance*—that is, a state of doubt that sets in after a major decision is made. Tuition, fees for textbooks and other materials, opportunity costs, and other factors become the focus of their evaluation. Marketing professionals refer to cognitive dissonance as *buyer's remorse,* and they invest ample resources in reassuring customers that their decisions were wise. Thus, they foster repeat business or what higher education calls *retention.*

Before ending your first class meeting, briefly review with students the reasons why your course is a good investment of their time, energy, and opportunity costs. Emphasize the important and relevant content they will learn, highlight the influence of their peers, and share your enthusiasm for a dynamic classroom experience. Ensure that when they leave your classroom they will want to return for more. For many professors, the first class meeting is the single most critical one to the retention of students throughout the term.

ASSESSING STUDENTS' UNDERSTANDING OF THE STARTING POSITION

As students conclude their first week in your class, it is wise to assess their perceptions in an anonymous, nonthreatening manner. Doing so at this critical juncture helps you identify potential stumbling blocks before they possibly grow into large barriers later in the term that lead to student withdrawals, or otherwise reduce the success that students could achieve.

At the end of the meeting, invest just two minutes to distribute index cards on which students may reply anonymously to several open-ended questions such as:

- Who was the most interesting person you met today/tonight?
- What things are you most looking forward to in this class?
- What concerns you about your ability to be successful in this class?
- What questions do you have that are not yet answered?
- What has surprised you most about this class so far?

Ask students to place the completed cards at a convenient spot close to the door as they exit. Wish them well. Further details on processing this potentially valuable activity are addressed in Chapter 13.

FOLLOWING UP THE FIRST WEEK OF CLASS

Together, the face-to-face greetings, completed student profile forms, and ending assessments provide a rich set of data with which to begin your new class. Closely review the student profiles and make notes in whatever form is convenient to help you better fit your course strategy to your students' needs. (Continue to use the forms to log results of conferences with students, reflections on messages received from them, and so on throughout the term.) Again, seek to fit the face with the form so that you can call as many students as possible by name when they enter your class the following meeting. Review the completed assessment cards as well and note any patterns in responses that seem especially significant. Reflect on the first week as a whole and identify any actions that you might want to consider taking.

In addition, send a carefully crafted e-mail message to all members of the class (use "blind cc" so addresses are not revealed to all). Share with them some positive reinforcement of their performance in the first class meeting. Clarify responses you provided during the class, and any issues that might have arisen through your review of the student profiles, the assessment cards, and/or your reflections. Tell them how much you are looking forward to the course and why, and then remind them of the reading assignment and activities for the following class meeting. Invite students to reply with questions or comments. You will likely be very surprised by the quality of feedback that you obtain from the quiet opinion leaders within your class. Use that feedback to open your second class meeting and continue the positive momentum.

Those who develop the richest relationships with students and are attaining outstanding retention results are increasingly benchmarking a strategy of the late author and professor, Leo Buscaglia. Early in each of his courses at the University of Southern California, Dr. Buscaglia (1990) required each student to visit him in his office for what he called a *voluntary-mandatory* office visit of ten to fifteen minutes duration. His primary goal was to establish individual rapport before the time when any kind of "bad stuff" (e.g., failing examination grades, excessive class absences) might occur. His strategy served to prevent many students from experiencing that bad stuff, and his student retention was exemplary.

To implement this strategy, circulate a sign-up sheet divided into fifteen-minute increments at the second class meeting of each course. Ask all students to reserve a convenient time and to bring with them any questions or concerns they might have regarding the course. The information that students divulge during these office visits is not only illuminating but also critical to being prepared to address each student's specific learning needs. Once a personalized bond with each student is created, open sharing becomes commonplace. Why not try this proven strategy in your classes this term (Lyons, McIntosh, & Kysilka, 2003)?

SUMMARY OF KEY POINTS

- Plan for a substantive first meeting that addresses students' needs and gives you useful information and insights.
- Create a positive visual image of yourself and the classroom for arriving students.
- Extend a personalized welcome to as many students as possible.
- Learn and begin using students' names right away.
- Earn the right to teach the class by introducing yourself convincingly, yet humbly.
- Clarify your course objectives and performance expectations by reviewing the syllabus effectively and embellishing it with useful detail.
- Orchestrate an enjoyable way for students to meet each other.
- Whet students' appetite for the course by sharing material they will perceive as interesting and pertinent.
- Provide students an overview of the textbook and other critical course resources.
- Reassure students that the course will be a wise investment of their time and resources.

- Gather feedback that will enable you to identify potential problems early.
- Provide e-mail feedback prior to the second class meeting.

THE FINAL WORD

"Promoting student ownership in the classroom has always been important to me, because I feel it increases students' commitment to successful class outcomes and helps ensure self-policing behavior among classmates. This semester, I began our second class meeting with a small group activity designed to establish the class ground rules by student suggestions and opinions. This method, which has worked most effectively, began by asking students to work in groups of three to four members to create three rules related to classroom behaviors. These can include behaviors they expect from their classmates or from themselves, as well as how they wish to be treated during class, rules for participation in discussions, and attitudinal preferences toward each other and the instructor. After five minutes, each group reports out and their answers are recorded on the board or an overhead transparency. Once all are displayed, I ask if there are any rules that anyone can't follow every time the class meets and delete the ones that can't be agreed upon. Although I exercise it cautiously, I reserve the right to challenge, ask for rewording, or even delete any that are out of bounds. Once finalized, I ask what appear to be two responsible members of the class to record the list and forward it to me by e-mail. I then create the final ground rule list, and at the next class meeting, I provide a copy for each student and orally review the list to foster commitment. I have found that the modest time investment that this activity requires pays big dividends in the long run."

—Dawn Hall, Bowling Green, Kentucky

STUDENT PROFILE FORM

Date _____

The information you volunteer below will enable me to meet your individual needs more fully. All information will be kept in strict confidence.

Name _____ Course _____

Complete mailing address _____

E-mail _____Tel (day)_____(night)_____

Employer/title _____ Avg hrs week ___

Goal in taking course_____

Ultimate educational goal_____

Background _____

Hobbies/interests _____

Personal accomplishments _____

_____

Special situations _____

_____

Most memorable learning experience _____

Learning challenges _____

_____

How do you learn best?_____

Signature (indicates receipt of syllabus) _____

Questions/concerns related to class? (Use back if necessary.)

ICEBREAKER ACTIVITY

The objective of this exercise is for you to become acquainted with at least twenty other students in this class. Find one person who fits each of the following criteria (or a creatively modified version) and neatly enter his or her name in the blank beside the clue.

1. Is a fan of (local sports team) _____
2. Has seen (name of musical group) in concert _____
3. Regularly surfs the Internet _____
4. Has traveled outside the country in the past year _____
5. Has shaken hands with a governor or senator _____
6. Recently saw the movie (title) _____
7. Has two or more siblings _____
8. Is an avid reader of Stephen King novels _____
9. Has flown on an airplane within the last month _____
10. Has viewed a lunar eclipse _____
11. Can identify what D. W. Griffith did for a living _____
12. Has been skiing within the past year _____
13. Once read *The Diary of Anne Frank* _____
14. Has driven over the Golden Gate Bridge _____
15. Has never had a broken bone _____
16. Is a regular viewer of (name of television show) _____
17. Can tell you in which country the current Pope was born _____
18. Can tell you the latest winner of the Stanley Cup _____
19. Owns a dog named Jake _____
20. Voted in the last presidential election _____

CHAPTER 6

MANAGING THE CONTEXT
OF YOUR COURSE

*"When I began teaching as an adjunct professor some 17 years ago, I thought that
what I said and did was the most important part of the educational process. It didn't
take long however for me to discover that it was how I orchestrated, facilitated, and
incorporated everyone else's knowledge and wisdom that was the most essential
factor in deep learning. My practical experience as a therapist was important, but
my students' perception of those experiences fueled the inquiry."*

—Lawrence Anthony, Ed.D., Cincinnati, Ohio

FOCUS QUESTIONS

- How do you get effectively organized and remain so throughout your course?
- How should you organize a class session to ensure efficiency and effectiveness?
- How can you manage communications and challenging situations with students?
- What are the critical professional practices for you to display consistently?

"Honey," frustratingly cried the returning student to her spouse who had been
babysitting the children, "two of my three classes have over a hundred students.
We're afraid to raise our hands, even when we're totally lost. One professor
jumped all over a student tonight for asking an 'ill-conceived' question. Students
who get to class late sit in the aisles or stand in the back of the classroom.
There's always chatter going on around me—people trying to figure out where
the professor is in the textbook—so I can't hear half of what is being said up
front. And after class, the professors walk right out of the room—totally
unapproachable."

At the beginning of each new academic year, thousands of students on
campuses throughout North America no doubt share such frustration with
partners ill-prepared to respond. Such students often react by dropping classes,
complaining to deans, or writing letters to trustees and legislators. In the process,
stakeholders have been angered and respond by questioning rising tuition costs

and institutional procedures and fueling the accountability movement. Many factors are beyond the control of adjunct professors, but the interchange between the individual student and professor—the root of many problems in higher education—is very manageable. This chapter focuses on strategies for effectively managing the context of your courses.

After planning your course thoroughly and launching it successfully, your next challenge is to maintain the momentum you have established. As a student, you probably studied under some well-organized professors and a few "absent-minded" types who seemingly had to scramble to locate a copy of a handout or syllabus from among a pile of unsorted papers. Even if such experiences were decades ago, you can very likely describe the frustration you felt when your reasonable requests were not satisfied. The expectations of today's students are every bit as high, if not higher, than yours were then (Fallows & Ahmet, 1999).

Even without a campus office to call your own, getting fully organized for the remainder of the course will be relatively easy, if you attend to it immediately. Waiting until the first student assignments are submitted or your first examination is administered will make getting organized far more challenging and time consuming. Heed the often-repeated admonition of effective managers from varied fields: "Plan your work, then work your plan, and most problems will be minimized."

ORGANIZING YOUR COURSE MATERIALS

Organizing your course materials is critical to achieving your own peace of mind, as well as fostering optimal student learning. Three models that you might want to consider include:

1. Insert all critical course documents into a single course binder, and use tabbed dividers or a blank sheet to divide sections. This system would include several copies of the course syllabus, the official class roll, and the alphabetized student profiles completed at the first class meeting. As they are developed, lesson plans for each class session, pertinent notes, and extra copies of materials you hand out to students would be inserted. Since students inevitably will misplace materials or ask for those distributed when they were absent, this system could readily support their needs. In addition, having these materials immediately available provides a sense of security for you and your students.

   Another section of your course binder could be designated for copies of your examinations, quizzes, answer keys, and study guides, to which you may refer during class when reviewing. Include also all project assignment handouts with their respective scoring rubrics, which you will want handy when your students ask specific questions.

2. A mobile organizational strategy that many adjunct faculty members employ is to file all course materials into a single briefcase, plastic file cabinet, storage crate, or expandable cardboard file, which with a small wheeled carrier can be transported easily, from an automobile or mass transit provider to the classroom or home office with great convenience. The storage unit, which can even be color-coded by course if you teach more than one, might contain file folders or large manila envelopes that hold examination, handouts, extra copies of the syllabus, and so on. This method also enables you to store a copy of the textbook, assignments collected from students, and videos or other instructional materials to be used during class. Those using this strategy are more confident, knowing that all of their course materials are located in one convenient, reliable place.

3. A growing number of adjunct professors are building web pages, often with the support of textbook publishers, on which they post their course syllabus, directions for assignments, course handouts, and other materials for each of their classes. Students can view the materials in the privacy of their living quarters and print hard copies as needed. This strategy, which will be further highlighted in Chapter 9, not only provides students with around-the-clock access to critical documents but also reduces the need for adjunct professors to transport bulky materials to each class meeting.

The key to each of the strategies described above is planning a system that fits your needs and then relying on it to provide its benefits. When course materials are managed effectively, students will perceive you as professional and caring. The systematic use of this strategy will also free your mind to manage other aspects of your teaching more effectively, including the interpersonal aspects of teaching.

In Chapter 4, I emphasized the development of a sound syllabus and in Chapter 5, the impact of the initial class meeting on student retention. As you advance deeper into the term, open several class meetings by revisiting your syllabus with students to reinforce focus and direction in your decision making. Avoid making abrupt changes, especially those perceived by students as inconsistent with the foundation you have already built, which trigger confusion and frustration. Although you will recognize changes you would like to make in subsequent delivery of the materials, nature of the assignments, content of the examination, and so on throughout the term, note those changes without making dramatic deviations from the current course syllabus.

LESSON PLANNING

The planning of each class meeting is another important organizational function, which as I stated earlier should include two distinct phases: evaluation of the last session and strategizing for the upcoming session. Although establishing an agenda may keep your class flowing from activity to activity, what you plan to accomplish in those time segments must be clear in your mind and must facilitate the achievement of your course objectives. The degree of detail in your lesson plans is directly related to your teaching style, experience with the material being taught, and comfort level in the classroom. Strategic lesson planning focuses on four elements: establishing objectives, planning learning experiences, identifying required materials, and evaluating student progress. Each is discussed below.

1. **Establishing objectives:** In Chapter 4, an overview of Bloom's Taxonomy, the most widely recognized system for guiding the development of cognitive learning outcomes, was provided. You might recall that Figure 4.1 identified common verbs used to describe student behaviors consistent with that level. During your planning, you developed the broad areas of student performance. Before each class meeting, you should also identify more specific expectations of student performance to be attained by the end of the lesson. Writing your objectives with respect to Bloom's levels will help you identify effective classroom activities and an evaluation process that measures student success.

2. **Planning learning experiences:** Focusing as best you can on students' existing knowledge levels, learning styles, overall maturity, and related factors, your next task is to identify activities and teaching methods to match the objectives you clarified above. Chapters 7, 8, and 9 will prepare you to make better decisions related to learning experiences, but it is critical to answer some foundational questions, including: What content do you need to present, and what is its appropriate level of complexity for this course? Does that content lend itself to using an overhead projector, an electronic slide presentation, or some other form of visual device to focus students' attention? How do you intend to keep the students engaged in the lecture? Would it be desirable to have students immediately apply their knowledge in a group activity? If so, how will you structure that activity? What is the ideal size of groups for this activity and how will you select members? What directions do you need to provide so that students can be successful in their group work? How will they share their group findings? What key points do you need to make in debriefing the activity? Do you plan to engage students in discussion? If so, what are the key questions to ask? Given your group of students, what cognitive level of learning should they reach?

Bloom's Taxonomy can guide the formulation of answers to these questions, just as it can clarify objectives. Begin to plan your later evaluation of student learning at the level at which instruction is delivered. When you target the higher-order cognitive functions, plan to evaluate at that level, but be mindful of the concerns of students' employers, professional groups, and legislators who complain that college graduates have trouble with higher-order thinking. Invest the energy to ensure that students' higher-order thinking skills are developed to the fullest extent.

3. **Identifying required materials:** When planning your in-class learning experiences, make a list of the specific materials you will need. Are you planning to show a video? Do you have the video close by, or must you retrieve it from someplace else? Do you need to reserve it ahead of time? Is equipment always available in your classroom, or do you need to order it? If you are planning group work, do you have all the materials you need to share with the students? Make a list of resources you need for each lesson in advance. I have found it worthwhile always to have a toolkit of materials: whiteboard markers, self-stick notes, name tags, a three-hole punch, index cards, scissors, and so on. You may or may not need all in any given class period, but it promotes a feeling of security to have them already packed, just in case.

4. **Evaluating student progress:** How are you going to know if the students accomplish the objectives of the lesson? Your evaluation strategies should not only be appropriate for the objectives of the lesson but dovetail with the overall evaluation process for the course. If your evaluation strategy indicates that students did not achieve the objectives of the lesson, you can review the material or try a new approach the next time the class meets. It is far better to re-teach missed concepts than to continue to plow ahead without the comprehension of the students. An important adage for many adjunct professors to remember is "Less is more." Rather than "cover" the material, we should be more concerned with students "learning" the material.

After each class, note what worked and what did not. Such reflection will allow you to make adjustments in your plans for the next class meeting and will give you a head start when you rethink your class for another term. Reflecting on your practices can also help you focus on problems with clarity, potential examination questions, and alternative sources of materials. Although I do not advocate that you "teach the test," I do believe that what you teach and what you assess must be correlated. Too often students complain that a test did not measure what they studied. If this is a legitimate complaint, it can be traced back to the professor's not planning the instruction and assessment concurrently.

Inevitably, students will ask you, "Is this on the test?" Although that question can be annoying, you should be able to answer it honestly. Answers such as, "This specific problem won't be on the test, but I will expect you to be able to demonstrate the process used to solve the problem," or "I will not ask you to write out definitions of these terms but rather to use the terms appropriately in your explanation of related phenomena" convey to the students what is important (concepts and process) and unimportant (specific facts).

DEVELOPING AN AGENDA

To ensure that each class meeting is managed efficiently and effectively, it is critical to have an agenda that divides your scheduled time into segments. Such planning will assist you in pacing the class productivity. Some professors like to write the time allotments on the chalkboard to provide structure for those needing it and to encourage the students to stay on task as well. A typical agenda may look like the following:

1. Reflections on last class meeting (10 minutes)
2. Review of homework assignment (10 to 15 minutes)
3. Overview of new material (10 minutes)
4. Lecture on new content (20 minutes)
5. Break (10 minutes)
6. Group activity over new content (25 minutes)
7. Group debriefing (15 to 20 minutes)
8. Explanation of assignments (10 minutes)

Note that the above agenda reinforces mastery of material addressed in the previous session and does not address new content until twenty or twenty-five minutes into the class meeting. Students are not required to be "on" the minute they step into the classroom, allowing some time to transition from their previous class, workday, and other mental focus areas. In addition, students whose schedules or last-minute conflicts might have delayed their arrival would not be severely penalized by this schedule. Attention to the most critical content is concentrated in the core period of the session, when students are most likely to experience optimal mental engagement.

Strategic agenda preparation requires that you spend some time with your course plan to identify activities that foster the achievement of course objectives for a particular group of students. It will also enable you to experience the sense of self-satisfaction all teachers need. The confidence that an agenda engenders also enables you to focus on fostering a personalized relationship with your students.

MANAGING YOUR CLASS TIME

Establishing an agenda and a good lesson plan for each meeting should enable you to keep your class on target. However, unpredictable events sometimes affect even the best planning. To minimize their impact and to provide you with the optimum amount of time to address your objectives, you would be wise to adhere to the following guidelines:

- *Begin each class precisely on time.* When students know that their tardiness will not affect your class management, they will typically extend themselves to arrive on time. On occasions (e.g., when there is severe weather), you might decide to begin slowly by reviewing previously taught material or even by talking individually with students regarding their progress, but start on time nonetheless.

- *Adhere to your agenda.* Students often complain that professors go off on tangents and tell irrelevant stories. Adhering to your agenda and lesson plans, perhaps by writing the plan on the board or sharing it a day in advance by e-mail, should keep you on target. Remember, however, that you have developed your agenda and lesson plans on assumptions about your students' ability to learn. If they are exhibiting comprehension difficulties, you should adjust your agenda and lesson plan and regroup, rethink, and perhaps re-teach on the spot.

- *Schedule breaks strategically.* In long class sessions, students require breaks for mental and physiological reasons, so assess the specific aspects of your course section strategically before scheduling them. In a class lasting longer than one hour, release students for a ten-minute break midway through the session after planting a seed that requires reflection or incubation. For classes of three or more hours, when students' needs are likely more intense, you have the option of scheduling two breaks of ten minutes each after an hour's session, or a single one of fifteen or twenty minutes' duration. If you maintain the discretion to use either option within a given class meeting, you will likely attain greater student mental engagement than if students know you always take a break at a particular time. The starting time of the class and its proximity to typical mealtimes, the walking distance to facilities, the extent of special needs of students, and so on should also be factored into such decisions. (It might be wise to solicit your students' input on this decision at your first class meeting, thereby fostering the perception that it is their class.) Announce and write on the board the exact time students should return from a break, and restart your class on time afterward. Otherwise, students are likely to get caught up in conversations or activities that delay your agenda, affect instructional effectiveness, frustrate highly focused students, and foster ill will. You might also want to double-check attendance after the break. Immature students increasingly use the break as an excuse to skip out early, so address the situation proactively at the first class meeting by explaining its effect on your management of the class and requesting that anyone who must leave early tell you so at the start of the break.

- *During discussions, shut off nonproductive talk.* Whether with the whole class or in small groups, discussions must be targeted to your learning objectives. When a student makes a tangential comment, you can confirm the interesting nature of the point and then redirect discussion to the central issue. When students are working in small groups, circulate among them actively, especially at the beginning, to ensure that everyone fully understands the goals of the activity and remains on task to accomplish them. Chapter 8 presents more details on using small classroom groups effectively.

- *Whenever possible, relate course content to everyday events.* Integrate breaking news from the international, national, and local scenes, as well as from pop culture and sports into your content if you can. Add relevant cartoons or quotations to your presentations. Find props to enhance your students' engagement. Pay attention to your voice projection, volume, enunciations, and variety (e.g., when properly employed, dramatic elongated pauses can engender student reflection). Use gestures to emphasize important ideas and concepts and move throughout the room to nudge the disengaged into the dialogue. Communication theory tells us that nonverbal cues are stronger than verbal cues, so be sure that your nonverbal gestures reinforce and do not discount what you say. Most importantly, plan to make your class relevant to the specific group of students enrolled and have some fun. Even if you are "humor-challenged," you can probably apply your points by telling a story to which your students are likely to relate. The idea is to provide students an extra reason to attend when their lives hold so many diversions that they might be tempted to skip class.
- *Utilize the class time in its entirety.* Avoid being swayed by some students' requests to go home early, which are usually made by a few highly vocal but relatively unmotivated students. Your most motivated students silently reject the suggestions from their counterparts to cut classes short. Which students would you want to reward for their behavior, the motivated or the unmotivated?
- *End class on time.* If you became sidetracked from your agenda, you cannot expect students to remain after the scheduled ending time to address missed topics. The next session will need to be used to catch up. Many of your students have family, work, or other school obligations to meet after class, and making them late discounts your standing in their eyes. Being overly free-flowing does not foster a positive learning environment in your classroom.
- *Before dismissing the class, remind students of what they can expect during the next session.* If you have a special event planned, such as a guest speaker or a highly controversial video, convey that information enthusiastically to the students so that they will look forward to returning. Their energy will feed the occasion.

Ineffective adjunct professors often embrace a paradigm that views the class period as time to fill so that students stay busy. Strategic professors realize that with clearly established learning objectives, well-chosen resources, and strong teaching and learning methods, time management is a relatively easy issue.

MANAGING YOUR CLASSROOM ENVIRONMENT

Managing your class time strategically will prevent or help you overcome most of your challenges. There are, however, several additional practices that will help ensure that the environment is conducive to maximum learning, perceived as fair by students, and supportive of your own peace of mind. Depending on the characteristics of your students and your own comfort level, you might be able to allow students to contribute to one or more of these practices.

First, develop a workable system for taking roll. Student financial aid programs generally require participants to attend class regularly, so roll-taking is mandatory even when attendance is not factored into final grades. You might want to circulate a roll sheet, reminding students that they are responsible for neatly entering their names, even if they arrive late. As mentioned earlier, seating charts can help you check attendance at the start of each class meeting. Whatever method you choose, follow it systematically and explain it orally and on your syllabus so that each student fully understands your policy.

Next, anticipate and plan for the arrival of late-arriving students. Locking the door behind you as you enter the classroom is no longer considered a defendable option at most institutions. A viable possibility, however, is to designate specific seats close to the door for late arrivers and admonish those who do so to enter quietly and follow the attendance record-keeping protocol you have established. This strategy minimizes distractions and allows you and your students to remain focused on your learning objectives.

Finally, colleges and universities are increasingly engaging their students in "service learning," in hopes of their developing a more grounded understanding of their obligations to their communities. As their exemplar, you should model such behavior in the most basic of ways, by demonstrating responsible housekeeping practices in your classroom. No professor or student should have to follow another group into an unkempt classroom. You should accept the responsibility to leave the classroom in at least as good a condition as you found it. Boards should be erased clean, furniture properly arranged, and trash placed in a proper receptacle. Besides modeling responsible behavior for students, you will also maintain the respect of the housekeeping staff. If you are tempted to not appreciate the custodian's role, imagine having to ask a custodian to unlock your classroom if it was left in a mess the previous session! The custodian whose area of responsibility has been consistently well-treated by your students is likely to come to your aid generously.

IMPROVING INTERPERSONAL COMMUNICATIONS

As emphasized throughout this book, a major key to success for adjunct professors is the ability to recruit a few additional students for class sections and retain the overwhelming majority of those who enroll. As in most arenas of human interaction, effective communications is the key to success. Below are some useful guidelines to employ:

- Listen to your students (free of preconceptions) at least as often as you speak. Students want to communicate; give them the opportunity to do so.
- Perception is important. Choose your words and tone carefully to demonstrate respect of social and cultural differences among your students.
- Both praise and criticism of individual student's work are best given privately. Excessive praise in front of the class can be as uncomfortable to the student as excessive criticism. However, private written praise or constructive feedback on assignments and in e-mail messages can be extremely constructive.
- Do not argue with your students. Students often like to verbally joust with you or their fellow students and can push your limits. Arguing in front of the class rarely works; although you may win the verbal battle, ultimately you will lose the battle for control. If there is disagreement, encourage the student to stay after class to continue the dialogue. Both in class and privately, control your emotions.

An especially effective tool for managing your communications with students (and others) is transactional analysis (Stewart & Joines, 1987). Developed by psychotherapist Eric Berne (1964), this theory recognizes that each of us has developed three ego states that determine the communications patterns we regularly employ. The first ego state is that of "child." It is a totally emotional state characterized by self-absorption and dependency on others for need satisfaction and is often observed in either pouting or being rebellious. Language is very *I* centered: "I want," "give me," "I expect," "I need."

The second ego state is that of "parent." This is also an emotional state, one characterized by either judgmental or nurturing attitude and language, such as: "You made me very proud," "You make me angry," "You cannot seem to do anything right," "You demand a lot of attention," "You will not graduate if you do not start applying yourself." Note that the parental ego state uses *you* language.

The third ego state is that of "adult." This is an objective, analytical ego state that emphasizes higher-order and critical-thinking language: "Let's analyze what we have said here and determine where we are," "We have been very creative in our thinking; let's examine our thoughts," "We have been doing a lot of evaluating here; can we look again at our criteria and see if we are applying them equally and fairly?" Language in this state is often *we* language and indicates the equality of the people involved in the transaction.

Within a particular transaction one ego state dominates an individual. However, all three might come into play during a single class session. The effective professor will seek to elevate interaction to adult ego states and keep the class dialogue objective and collaborative. Enjoying a resurgence of popularity among those in the helping professions, transactional analysis is a practical tool that can help you cope in your classroom with the variety of challenges students will pose.

Transactional Analysis Exercise

In each scenario below, identify the ego state from which each of the three statements that follows is generated (HINT: there is one parent, one adult, and one child in each). Then select the most effective statement for the situation.

1. At the end of the first meeting of a new class, a student asks, "This class really has a lot of work required. Do many students flunk?" The professor responds:
   a. "Only the lazy ones who don't get with it right away."
   b. "I do everything I possibly can to make sure everyone passes."
   c. "The course material is challenging, but I provide many resources for helping everyone learn it. Nearly all students are successful in this course."
2. During the second class meeting, the professor states a well-developed position on a controversial topic. A student heatedly attacks the professor's position. The professor responds:
   a. "It's clear you've been brainwashed by one side of this issue."
   b. "Can I see a show of hands of those of you who support that position?"
   c. "You've stated a viewpoint that many people believe to be true. One of the most important reasons we attend college is to be exposed to divergent points of view; this exposure helps us make more grounded decisions throughout our lives."
3. Thirty minutes into the third class meeting, a student's cell phone rings, and he gets up to go into the hall to answer it. The professor says:
   a. "Oh noooooooo!"
   b. "The syllabus warns you not to let that happen! See me after class!"
   c. Nothing at the time, but before dismissing class says, "Now that we're up and running, I want to remind everyone that our syllabus asks you to keep personal communications devices in the mute position. If you're ever in a potential emergency situation expecting a call, please let me know before the class begins."

4. During the review of the results of the first examination, a student emotionally states that a certain question was tricky. The professor says:
   a. "Tricky? If you really knew the material, you wouldn't say that!"
   b. "Really? I used the test bank. You'd think all the questions would be good."
   c. "Hmm. What about that question do you believe is unfair?"
5. At the end of a class during which the professor returned the first scored papers, a struggling student approaches to question her less-than-perfect grade. The professor says:
   a. "You look disappointed. Would you like to talk about the paper?"
   b. "Cheer up, it's only one grade."
   c. "You made above the class average, a very acceptable grade on the first paper."

Exercise Answers and Discussion

Communications experts say that when messages are mixed, only 7 percent of the meaning is attributable to the words themselves, whereas 38 percent is attributable to the tone of voice, and 55 percent to the body language used. Thus, in the response exercise, because you have only words on which to base your answers, your choices might vary from those given below.

My perception is that in scenario 1, response *a* comes from a judgmental parent, *b* from an unresponsive child, and *c* from the adult ego state. Using *c* prevents the parent from being hooked by the question and fosters an objective communications dynamic as the course gets launched. Note the parent and child ego states react emotionally, whereas the adult ego state responds objectively.

In scenario 2, response *a* comes from a judgmental parent, *b* from the irresponsible child, and *c* from the adult ego state. As in the first scenario, *c* is clearly the most effective response.

In scenario 3, response *a* comes from the child, *b* from the judgmental parent, and *c* from the adult ego state. Again, the adult response is the most effective, reminding students of the agreed-on policy while also recognizing that there might be legitimate reasons to have a personal communications device. If the professor controls his or her tone of voice carefully, the dignity of the student is protected.

In scenario 4, response *a* comes from the judgmental parent, *b* from the irresponsible child, and *c* from the adult ego state. Again, the adult response is clearly the most effective.

In scenario 5, response *a* seems to come from a nurturing parent, *b* from a child or perhaps a judgmental parent (seeing only the words prevents us from knowing for sure, but it is definitely from an emotional ego state), *c* comes from the adult ego state. In this case however, the adult response is probably not the most effective for a struggling student. The nurturing parent response *a* demonstrates a sensitivity that the student would likely perceive as helpful.

Individual students maintain powerful, vivid memories of their transactions with professors, throughout the term and well into their futures. Students not involved in such evocative transactions but who observe them learn vicariously about the emotional intelligence of the professor, in the process becoming more attached to or detached from the classroom environment.

Although my discussion of transactional analysis is limited, you can see that it has great potential to affect the effectiveness of your course management. It is but one of many tools presented here with which you might experiment and test their ability to improve outcomes with students, and thus make your teaching more consistent and rewarding.

Remain open to trying new approaches, even if they feel uncomfortable at first. Such openness is critical to accessing students' vulnerabilities, where some of their deepest learning occurs.

SPECIAL STRATEGIES FOR MANAGING LARGE CLASSES

Over the past few years, finances have constrained academic decision making significantly. The strategy of employing large introductory classes to subsidize small upper-division and graduate-level classes is now a fact of life at many institutions. At the same time, the accountability movement will no longer permit some of the common shortcomings of large classes, such as students' disengagement and easy tests that measure only surface knowledge. These tactics lead to low evaluations from students and other stakeholders and a perception of reduced learning. Adjunct professors rarely are assigned large classes, but accepting one might be an opportunity that you want to consider. Besides dealing with security, confidentiality, and other logistical issues, those who teach large classes must markedly scrutinize their management of the learning process to ensure student success (Golding, 2001).

Although true in a class of any size, the planning and organizing functions are especially critical in the effective management of large classes. Issues that should be addressed before the first class meeting to maximize student focus and minimize unproductive time, include:

- Visiting the classroom well in advance so that you can leverage its size and equipment to orchestrate compelling "events" that could not be duplicated in a small classroom ·
- Staggering dates of examination and submission dates for papers with those of your other courses to avoid bottlenecks in paper flow and delays in returning scored projects
- Developing systems for expediting roll-taking, distribution of handouts, collection of student assignments, and other logistical tasks (Davis, 2001)

- Dedicating a seating area near a classroom door for early leavers and late arrivers and promoting noise minimization
- Selecting a cadre of student aides, from previously proven students or new ones you get to know early in the term, and providing a system of incentives that will foster their high achievement of quality service to students

In your decision-making process, consult with veteran professors to see what has worked well and poorly for them. Your strategies on the points that directly affect students must be clearly communicated in your syllabus, reinforced orally at the opening class meeting and in other meetings, and modeled throughout the remainder of the term. Be cautious about ignoring negative feedback on your systems or changing them because a few students complain. Instead conduct an informal evaluation by all students in the class part way into the course to ensure that the policies and procedures are workable in the majority of students' eyes. (See Chapter 13 for more information on informal evaluations.)

Often, professors believe that the only workable instructional method in a large class is lecture. After all, the rooms where we teach large classes are called *lecture* halls. I would like to propose, however, that lecture is only one of the methods that can be used effectively in a large class. Research conducted by Graham Gibbs (1998) indicates that the effectiveness of large introductory classes is increased when the focus is on learning rather than on teaching, assessment is strategically employed to foster focus on learning objectives, students do for themselves and for each other some of what the professor once did for them, and peer support and pressure are fostered. Therefore, rather than employ the common authoritative approach, whose judgmental-parent ego state is likely to trigger students' surreptitious rebellion and irresponsibility, you might want to consider an alternative instructional strategy. Another critical key to success in large classes is making them at times "psychologically small," by dividing large classes into small groups for some of the learning experiences, starting from the very first day. Students thus have a smaller number of classmates to get to know and start to feel psychologically safe more quickly. When larger groups are needed, the professor can combine two or more smaller groups, gradually expanding the number of students who interact comfortably.

Part of making a class seem psychologically small is to learn as many students' names as early in the term as possible. This strategy was discussed in Chapter 5, but learning names in a large class and thus encouraging participation by students who are more likely to feel anonymous is more challenging. Students can make a note of every time they participate by asking a question, making a cogent comment, and so on and then be directed to turn in the notes with their names at the end of class each day with enough description to allow the professor to identify the comment or question. The professor can then write back to each student with encouragement, answers, or whatever else is appropriate. A professor can also choose to give participation points to those students who take advantage of this learning opportunity.

A variation on this idea of participation notes also enables a professor to take attendance. All students are given an index card on the first day. They write their names on the top and, from then on, pick up their cards as they enter class. The professor can see which cards are left in the box and thus record absences. Either during the class or as a closure for the day, students are to write on their cards a question, comment, summary, or point they would like to see reviewed in an upcoming class. After class, the professor can quickly read through these cards and get a sense of what was understood, what might still be muddy, and where an appropriate starting place for the next class period would be. They can also write back to the students to heighten the sense of connection that is so important to learning.

Teams of four to six students can be employed to provide diversity of experience and motivation and are small enough to manage. In a class of several hundred, you might designate the teams with names of states or other geographical regions, or the names of well-known political figures (e.g., Pierre Trudeau or John F. Kennedy). Allowing students to pick their own team members, following an icebreaker exercise (see Chapter 5), would reduce logistical challenges. You might also allow individuals to opt out, in which case they would do the entire team project themselves or with fewer partners. In giving broad assignments, make it clear that team members must divide the work equitably. Team members could then evaluate the contribution of their teammates by assigning shares of a total point allocation and communicating this allocation to you by private e-mail. For example, if you use five-member teams, each member would be expected to divide 400 points among the other team members (i.e., the rater excludes him- or herself). The scores from one member for the other members might be 120, 110, 90, 80. All of the team members' scores will be averaged, creating the individual team member's score on the project. (To guard against punishment by peers, a minimum threshold of 50 points might be imposed.) You should probably meet early in the term with each team to clarify understanding of the syllabus, assignments, and so on, or you might have the teams select captains with whom you will meet. You can also create e-mail lists for each team and the class as a whole to dispense information throughout the term and facilitate feedback as projects move along. Such a setup can establish a didactic environment not only between you and your students but also among the students themselves.

You need not limit the use of teams to outside assignments. Learning within the classroom is greatly enhanced when students are expected to play a more active role than they typically play in a large lecture-driven class. For example, after delivering a certain amount of material from the front of the room, have students discuss that material in pairs or "buzz groups." Display several questions to be answered within the small group and then shared with another group across the aisle. In such a process, students advance in Bloom's Taxonomy toward a greater understanding of critical course concepts.

Employing teams and group discussions not only facilitates management of the large course but also creates opportunities for support and competition that will likely make the course more enjoyable for students while improving the quality of their learning. Working in teams also gives students an opportunity to develop their interpersonal skills and fosters learning beyond the classroom. Finally, this strategy helps you manage your time effectively by allowing you to focus on issues that emerge throughout the term as teams meet, rather than dealing with an array of questions all at once. Once you have experienced the results of this approach and have worked through the loss of ego gratification that comes from being the "sage on the stage," you will likely ask yourself why it took you so long to understand that education is more about student learning than it is about teaching.

MANAGING THE FIRST EXAMINATION OR MAJOR ASSIGNMENT

No event demonstrates your success as a professor more than your first examination or major assignment. As I noted in Chapter 4, this is typically the most critical milepost in retaining students through the conclusion of the course. Therefore, it is imperative that the assessment of the first examination or major assignment is well designed, and perceived as fair by the students—issues that will be addressed comprehensively in Chapter 10. Drafted well in advance of its administration, the first examination or assignment should not be made artificially easy; in fact, it should reinforce high standards. However professors should provide students with clear expectations so that their preparation time is focused and the scores reward those who produce most effectively.

As you teach, prompt students to concepts that you will include on the examination. Provide a comprehensive review, both in writing and orally, and perhaps a short sample exercise that includes items similar in approach and wording to those that will appear on the examination. Also tell them the format(s) that the examination will use—multiple-choice, short-answer, essay, and so on—the number of each item, and how much time they will have to complete the examination. If you intend to use essay questions, provide sample questions and a rubric for how you will evaluate the answers. Remember, examinations should not serve the purpose of catching the ill-prepared student but should instead help you and your students evaluate their understanding of the content they have been studying.

Following critical first retention milepost, some students will inherently sense how they performed, whereas others will require a scored document. Typically some will underperform and be the most likely to drop the course.

Anticipating this result, strategic professors must develop a strategy to deal with the situation. "Curving" the test results, in which students are awarded unearned points so that the total class results more closely approximate a bell curve, is not defensible in an age of accountability. An analysis of the test results perhaps facilitated by a Scantron system or other technological tactic, in which the test items that were most commonly missed are evaluated a second time for their clarity, validity, and other salient features, is one possibility. That tactic might identify several questions that should be deleted, with scores then recalculated. Another possibility is to offer students the opportunity to drop their scores on the first examination, while ratcheting up their commitment to improve on subsequent examinations. After all, some students add the course late, are delayed in purchasing the text, or have other valid reasons for not being as prepared as they might be. A syllabus that lists five total assignments, each weighted at 20 percent of the final course grade, can be modified through a "Plan B" in which the four remaining items are weighted at 25 percent of the final grade. Students who select Plan B simply write that phrase on the next scored assignment. It should be made very clear that there will be no "Plan C, D, or X." Retaining one or two students who would have otherwise dropped the class makes the tactic worthwhile (Lyons, Kysilka, & Pawlas, 1999), while retaining integrity.

If your scored assignment is a major paper or project, consider breaking the assignment into several more manageable chunks, and provide feedback to your students on each. For example, on a major paper, you might have students develop a theme statement and an outline of the argument to submit for review and scoring. The second chunk might focus on the resources they intend to use to develop their argument, a third chunk on their first draft, and the final piece on the completed paper. This strategy also reduces the likelihood of students' plagiarizing. Every major written assignment or project should also be coupled with a rubric (see Chapter 11) that is shared with the student at the time the assignment is made. By giving students the scoring criteria up front, students can focus their time and energy more precisely in completing the assignment. If students perceive that you are fair in the assignments and feedback you give, they will be more likely to persist in your course.

SURVIVING WHEN YOU ARE NOT PREPARED

At one time or another, multitasking adjunct professors will face a class for which they are not prepared because of emergency illnesses, family problems, other employment, or other reasons. Most students understand the first time this occurs. However, they will not tolerate a consistent lack of preparation and are not shy about expressing their dissatisfaction either on student evaluations or directly to instructional leaders. The following strategies can help you manage being unprepared to meet your class:

- Seek help from a colleague who has an area of expertise that can fit into your curriculum. Understanding professionals are sometimes willing to become a last-minute guest speaker, and may even enjoy conversing with your students on a topic they are really excited about.
- Have students engage in brainstorming activities focused on a critical concept presented in a previous class. Through the brainstorming, they can examine ideas from a variety of perspectives and perhaps gain a more grounded understanding.
- Break students into small groups of three to four and have them develop questions they think would be appropriate on their next examination. If you use this tactic, you must then follow through to incorporate their suggestions into the examination you administer. Such an activity not only serves as a review for your students, but also provides you with information about what they perceive to be the most critical concepts, which is often a valuable insight.
- Locate a video at your institution's media center or a video rental store that can embellish your most recent instructional unit. The video may provide an opposite viewpoint, reinforce important concepts, raise specific questions, or provide students context and depth.
- Have students work in groups, perhaps excusing them to go to the library or computer lab, to work on an upcoming assignment. Busy adult students especially appreciate having some class time and convenient access to otherwise difficult-to-obtain resources. Hold students accountable by having them report at the next class meeting.
- As a last resort, admit to students that you are not as prepared as you intended to be and ask them how they could best use the class time. This option requires that you have established a large amount of trust and understanding, so it is probably best used later in the term. Whenever you give students a voice in decisions, you are obligated to reflect that voice even when it pushes your comfort level. In letting students plan activities, you should establish parameters by saying, for example, "Why don't we do some brainstorming? Anything but canceling this class is a valid option." Then select the one that would be of greatest value.

Being spontaneous and relaxed will help you through such awkward moments. If a legitimate emergency arises at the last minute that causes you to miss class, be sure to notify the administrator who is designated to notify your class, and send students an e-mail that clarifies the situation as soon as possible. When you return to class, apologize to your students and adjust your syllabus accordingly.

ADHERING TO ETHICAL CODES

Like all professionals, adjunct professors must adhere to a code of ethics that serves as a guide to fair and equal treatment of all students in their classes.

Behaving in ethical ways requires you to familiarize yourself with your institution's policies regarding students' rights and responsibilities and to view situations through the eyes of their stakeholders. Read both the student handbook that outlines students' rights and the faculty handbook that indicates your rights, responsibilities, and rules of conduct. In the absence of written rules provided by your institution, the following guidelines related to commonly occurring challenges could serve you well:

- Discuss student progress or problems *only* with the student. In the rare cases where the student is a legal minor, you may be asked to speak to a parent or guardian, but this should be done in the presence of the student. Most students are legal adults; the Federal Educational Rights and Privacy Act (FERPA), enacted in 1974 and amended in 2000, protects them against inappropriate disclosure of critical information.
- If students share troubling information with you, such as details about illegal activities or mental/emotional distress, encourage them to access support resources available to them on campus, such as free counseling services. If students are hesitant about contacting these services, you might ask if they would prefer that you make an appointment for them. In that way, you can help them avoid the awkwardness of having to call a stranger for help. If a student refuses to get help and you believe that student can become dangerous to him- or herself or to others, seek the advice of your administrator. Together, research institutional policies and procedures and other resources to find a way to help the student, or at least to protect other students and yourself.
- Do not accept payment from students for tutoring, consulting, or similar duties that are a logical extension of your role. Similarly, if you use books you publish or other materials you own in your classes, royalties that you earn from those materials should be donated to your institution's foundation. Books and materials sold to students of other institutions can of course contribute to your income.
- Be careful about socializing too much or too energetically with your students. Many professors like to celebrate the end of a term with their students, particularly if the class was an exceptionally good one. Bringing snacks to class is usually acceptable, but check your institution's policy beforehand. Celebrating at a restaurant or pub, however, may be risky. If you meet at an establishment where alcohol is served and your underage students are caught drinking, you could be held liable. Even when all of your students are legal age, in today's litigious society you may find yourself involved in a lawsuit if a student attending is injured or injures someone else. Decline any invitations by your students to parties away from the campus. Another note of caution: under no circumstances should you celebrate with only one or two students. Not only could your reputation be tarnished, perhaps irreparably, but you also risk putting students in an extremely awkward situation with their families, peers, and

campus or community authorities. This precept includes dating students, even if they are single and close to your age. Dating students puts both parties into uncomfortable territory and can jeopardize your future employment.

Professional Practices Exercise

Because professional challenges arise suddenly, let us present some potential situations, give you an opportunity to respond, and then debrief with some useful insights regarding each scenario:

1. At the conclusion of your Tuesday evening class, you leave the classroom, only to be approached by a person waiting outside the door. She introduces herself nervously, saying, "I'm Mary Smith, the mother of April Miller, who is a student in the class you just completed. You probably noticed that she didn't attend tonight." You invite her into the classroom and ask her to have a seat. She continues, "April didn't come home last night, and we're worried sick. For the past couple of weeks, she has been behaving erratically. Has she been having problems in your class?"

2. In your largest class, Chris is clearly one of the brightest students. Seemingly without having to exert himself, Chris was able to achieve scores on the first two examinations in the low 90s. Earlier today, as Chris submitted the first term paper, you overheard a conversation between him and one of his friends that led you to believe that his paper might be questionable. Giving it a quick review in your office, you notice that although it is well written, the paper does not fit several of the specific criteria you identified at the time the assignment was made.

3. Samantha struggled the entire term in your class. She came by your office nearly every week to get tutoring on difficult issues. By the end of the term, she had made very good progress, scoring an A on the last unit examination. On the last day of the term, barely 10 minutes after completing her final examination, Samantha appeared outside the classroom door with a gift-wrapped package in her hands. Extending the gift toward you, she expressed how thankful she was for the help that you had provided her in the course and asked that you accept the gift as a symbol of her appreciation.

4. Your Wednesday evening class has been an absolute joy to teach. Mostly working adults, the students have arrived promptly, have been well prepared for each class meeting, worked cohesively in small-group situations, and performed well on all of your assessment activities. Tonight, as you distribute the final examination, one of the informal leaders announces, "We're meeting down at The Thirsty Scholar to celebrate after the test is over. Won't you join us?"

Debriefing

1. Unfortunately, Ms. Smith's situation is becoming increasingly common. When her daughter was younger, she may well have had the child's behavioral issues addressed proactively by the teachers and administrators of schools that April attended. Now, however, April is seemingly at least eighteen years old and is no longer considered a minor. FERPA protects even young adults from unwarranted disclosure of their educational progress. While using your emotional intelligence to demonstrate genuine concern for Ms. Smith, it is critical not to divulge information that would put yourself, or potentially April, at risk. Politely provide her the name and telephone number of the student affairs administrator.

2. The challenge that this situation presents has been complicated greatly by the advent of the Internet, the rise in the number of classes with large enrollments, the changing perceptions of what cheating means, and other factors. The potential problems here are many and varied, but it is critical to address the situation soberly, without accusing Chris of cheating. The possibilities include, but are not limited to, Chris's having downloaded a paper from a web vendor of such products, his resubmitting a paper written for a previous class, and his using material provided by his peers. Your most responsible strategy might be to ask the department chair to be present when you meet with Chris after your next class for a clarification. Broach the topic clearly by stating what you actually saw and heard. Then say, "Chris, I have questions about the goals and direction of the paper you recently submitted. Would you help me understand how you approached it?" As you listen closely to his response, you might—rather than asking additional, pointed questions too quickly—rephrase and reflect his explanation so that you become clear on all salient issues. Submitting downloaded papers is clearly plagiarism and likely subject to your institution's disciplinary policies. It may well be that Chris did not understand the implications of his resubmitting a paper with few or no changes. Other scenarios must also be anticipated and strategies for dealing with each clarified by the department chair.

3. The acceptance of any gift from a student enrolled in your class jeopardizes your role and more specifically risks your being viewed as compromised in the determination of final grades. Thank Samantha for her thoughtfulness but tell her that your help was provided with no expectation of reward. Encourage her to extend the gift to a family member or friend for whom such an expression of gratitude is appropriate.

4. Never drink alcoholic beverages with students while they are enrolled in your classes. Besides the absence of professionalism that the acceptance of this invitation would display, there are at least three major risks to you. First, if you attend, your students' pub outing may well appear to an

administrator, a judge hearing a drunken-driving/injury case, or some other official to be a sanctioned class event, a perception that some students might confirm on interrogation. Second, if even one of your students is underage, your pub appearance could make you liable for contributing to the delinquency of a minor. Finally, if even one of the students has a history of substance abuse, you risk contributing to a relapse and initiating a series of potentially tragic events. You can either ask the class to move the celebration to a venue that does not serve alcohol or politely decline the invitation while telling students your reasons.

DEALING WITH DISRUPTIVE STUDENTS

In all areas of society, higher education included, many people feel that incivility has escalated in both degree and frequency. Remember that students arrive in classrooms with increasing amounts of "baggage"; you cannot expect your classroom to be immune from disruptive incidents. Although no guarantee or prevention, the suggestions made in this book about getting to know students and understanding their learning styles will go a long way toward preventing the frequency and degree of disruptive behavior.

Nonetheless some situations arise that inevitably trigger unacceptable reactions in some students. Such reactions are likely to include loud or excessive talking, profane or defamatory language, or physical invasion of others' space. In an increasingly accountability-minded and litigious society, you cannot fail to respond when students cross the line with you or with their peers. Not responding effectively to unacceptable behavior from students creates a hostile environment for innocent students, discounts the impact of instruction, and detracts from your standing with students and colleagues. I suggest that the following practices become a part of your repertoire.

- Include an appropriate statement on your syllabus.
- Become familiar with campus support resources and refer students who can benefit.
- Confront disruptive students proactively: individually and quietly outside of class.
- Employ your adult ego state and resist becoming angry, sarcastic, or accusatory.
- Go the extra mile to preserve the dignity of all concerned.
- Do not share private issues with other students or anyone who does not have a legitimate reason to know.
- Document actions and words immediately and inform those who have responsibility for student affairs.

Interacting with students in class can be one of the most rewarding aspects of your career. To become highly successful in that endeavor, answer the following questions for yourself:

1. What would you expect from the class if you were a student?
2. What activities would you enjoy most if you were a student in your class?
3. What other activities should you plan to meet the needs of the diverse students in your class?
4. How can you make large classes seem small?
5. What were the communication strategies of your best professors?
6. What are the fundamentals of ethical practice?

By answering these questions, you will have guidelines for success in your classes. If after you launch your course, you reexamine your efforts by thinking as a student, you should be able to make your classes both enjoyable and challenging. Remember, students really do like to be fairly challenged. Also keep in mind that a good teacher is a good listener who can alter conditions as necessary to ensure good learning by the students.

SUMMARY OF KEY POINTS

- Develop a means to organize your materials that works effectively for you.
- Plan your agenda and have lesson plans for each class meeting.
- Provide feedback to your students, privately and in open classroom settings.
- Start and stop your classes on time.
- Plan breaks accordingly and restart your class on time.
- Plan for such logistical factors as roll taking, late arrivals, and housekeeping.
- Develop alternatives to the lecture format for large classes.
- Strive to engage your students at adult levels of conversation.
- Prepare the first examination or major assignment carefully to ensure fairness and relevance, and equip students for success.
- Have a contingency plan when you are unprepared or have to cancel a class.
- Adhere to a code of ethics and professional practices.
- Address disruptive students proactively.
- Remember to have fun!

THE FINAL WORD

"I have attendance policies for all classes I teach. Several years ago, a very promising student told me early on in the term that he was a pre-med major.

When he returned from missing several class meetings, I approached him to ascertain if there was a problem. He responded that his old car had proven itself unreliable. I gently reminded him that his patients would expect him to be both dependable and punctual and suggested that he should therefore develop alternative forms of transportation. While he replied that if he were a doctor, he could better afford a dependable car, he nonetheless attended each subsequent class meeting. Face-to-face 'tough love' is sometimes critical in your teaching."

—Rebecca Keith, Jerome, Indiana

CHAPTER 7

INSTRUCTOR-DIRECTED LEARNING METHODS

"The most painful statement I hear about faculty members is that they're boring! To insulate myself from such statements about my teaching, I now regularly use two effective attention-getting strategies: relevant personal stories and unexpected visual objects. When told as the masters have through the centuries with enthusiasm and vocal variety, stories have great power to rivet the attention of students. When pulled unexpectedly from beneath a podium, a flak jacket, an ice cream churn, or a birdcage has great potential to encourage student participation."

—Jodi Decker, Phoenix, Arizona

FOCUS QUESTIONS

- How do methods that you direct help students learn effectively?
- How do you create an environment in your classroom that is conducive to learning?
- How can you enhance the effectiveness of lectures with today's students?
- What measures should you take to maximize learning outcomes from video presentations and guest speakers?

Do you often feel pressured by your instructional leaders to ensure that all of the material in the adopted textbook and course outline are "covered"? How critical is it to you to maintain decorum within your classroom at all times? How important is it for you to reinforce high standards of the institution for which you teach? Most adjunct professors do feel these pressures, especially early in their teaching experience. The rather human strategy for managing each of these outcomes is to pursue control at every turn. Teaching methods that demonstrate control can be helpful in achieving the objectives above and providing students from undisciplined backgrounds with the structure they require to make sense of the body of knowledge that you teach. In a larger sense however, such methods should be seen as only a portion of the teaching tools that an effective professor will use to foster learning.

A CONTINUUM OF METHODS

One of the primary goals of this book is to help you develop a teaching style that is not only effective with your students and accountable to other stakeholders but also personally satisfying and rewarding. Most adjunct professors, especially early in their teaching experience, teach as they learn best and as they were taught by their better teachers. Unfortunately, these models and techniques may not be effective with many of the students you read about in Chapter 3. Helping today's students achieve learning success requires you to understand deeply your philosophical base, which was clarified through the exercises in Chapter 2. It also obliges you to become familiar with the principles upon which sound teaching methods are built, as well as to understand how students perceive and process the information flow that you create within your classroom.

This chapter and the next address the seemingly opposite ends of a continuum. At one end are instructor-directed learning methods; at the other are student-driven learning methods. The strength of instructor-directed teaching methods lies in their potential to provide students with structure, scope, and sequence, and so it is with these methods that we begin. Keep in mind as you read both chapters that ultimately, deciding which methods to use will depend on your determination of the most effective way to achieve a particular learning objective (Cranton, 1989).

As you finalize plans for your teaching, it would be helpful to reflect on your own student experiences. You may have had deeply traditional professors who, in a misguided effort to stress their high standards, boasted how few students ever earned A's in their class, or even worse, how many dropped out. Such a boast suggests a paradigm in which the professor is the sole intellectual resource in the classroom and therefore bears the entire burden of imparting knowledge to students, as with the students who were characterized by Professor Kingsfield in the movie *The Paper Chase* as having "minds of mush" (Bridges, 1973). Teaching, in this paradigm, entails having students avail themselves of the professor's view of the course material, integrating that perspective into the formulation of "enlightened" insights, and then regurgitating their "learning" in carefully crafted essays—or else!

Our purpose is not to denigrate any particular position on teaching. However, those who are most knowledgeable about teaching and learning have concluded that employing the traditional paradigm as a primary strategy is untenable in the contemporary environment. This conclusion is based on (1) a change in the generational conditioning of those who are now college professors, (2) an increased focus on accountability for what happens in the classroom, and most importantly, (3) new research findings about how human beings learn.

TODAY'S TEACHING AND LEARNING PARADIGM

Chapter 3 detailed an array of factors that have had an effect on how today's students process information. It serves little purpose here to debate whether that impact is good or bad—it is reality. Currently, many television ads run only ten to fifteen seconds (experiments are being conducted with three-second advertisements), and some rather complex stories are being made to fit 50 or so minutes (plus time for commercials) within an hour-long television drama. Compare this with ads of a generation ago that lasted 60 seconds, and epic movies that ran for 3 hours or more. Factor in the processing speed of today's computers and other forms of technology that provide instant feedback to users, and you can see why "lecture-as-monologue" should no longer be the sole or even primary vehicle of instruction in higher education. Today's students do not learn very effectively from such a format (and yesterday's students also would likely have learned a lot more from varied formats) (Hativa, 2000).

An even more important argument for an updated paradigm, however, is that recent brain research has fundamentally changed what we know about how students learn: the student-as-receptacle model does not match any of the up-to-date research (Ratey, 2001; Restak, 2001). The healthy human brain has a virtually inexhaustible capacity to learn—to detect patterns, to remember, to self-correct from experience, and to create. Achieving the learning outcomes that you have established for your courses requires an ongoing understanding of and attendance to students' learning systems and styles.

Assuming that you believe you are accountable for the student learning that occurs as a result of your teaching, should orchestrating maximum student learning not be your paramount role? You want how and what you teach to fit within the ultimate goal of maximizing learning in all of your students. If so, then when you strategically choose to use instructor-directed teaching and learning methods, you are deciding that in order to reach that goal, you will be the director, creator, supervisor, and manager of the learning experiences. You must know the focus and the level of mental engagement, both on your part and that of your students (Royse, 2001).

Teaching and learning situations can be analyzed in three different dimensions: (1) who is directing the teaching/learning experience, (2) who is engaged in the teaching/learning experience, and (3) how deep is the level of engagement. As with any model, these dimensions are not absolute, but they will serve as a guide for thinking about the ideas we will be presenting throughout this chapter and the next. Strategic professors learn to think of themselves as masters of their craft. Not unlike a master cabinetmaker or surgeon, professors must develop a wide variety of tools for completing the total job most efficiently and effectively. Generally, craftspeople who reach the level of master employ the largest variety and most effective tools currently available. In higher education, the instructor-directed tools of a master professor include lectures, video presentations, and guest speakers. The following sections highlight each of these tools, along with ideas for using them most strategically.

STRATEGIC USE OF LECTURE

In spite of mounting evidence of decreased effectiveness, lecturing remains the most common method used when teaching adults (Bligh, 2000). We do not suggest that all lectures are bad, but like any other kind of ineffective teaching, poor lectures need to be eliminated. Our purpose in this section is to help those who choose to use lectures as part of their strategic teaching to be able to do so effectively. Traditionalists and revisionists vary on the value of lecturing, but the following are widely accepted as reasons one might choose to use lectures (Brookfield, 2000):

- To establish the broad outlines of a body of material
- To provide guidelines for independent study
- To model intellectual attitudes you hope to encourage in students
- To foster learners' interest in a topic or perspective that is relatively new to them
- To set the moral culture of discussions

As you can see from Figure 7.1, lectures can fall anywhere along a continuum anchored at one end by completely one-way lectures (monologues) to highly interactive lectures. Given the limited attention spans of many of today's students, relying primarily on lectures that fall at the far left of the continuum is likely to be an ineffective strategy. Therefore, when you choose to lecture, be sure to (1) limit the length of your lecture segments to no more than fifteen minutes, (2) inject a variety of visual and auditory stimuli, and (3) engage students frequently and actively in processing the lecture information.

FIGURE 7.1 Lectures are designed and delivered anywhere along this continuum. Where do yours fall?

Lecture Continuum
←――――――――――――――――――――――――――――――――→
Monologue, scripted   Highly interactive Completely one-way   Students may seek clarification anytime

An effective strategy today is to lecture in fifteen-minute segments, interspersed with what Middendorf and Kalish (1996) call *change-ups*. The purpose of a change-up is to *reset students' attention clocks*. Before giving examples of change-ups, be aware that:

- Change-ups can be brief interludes that shift to a different learning domain, such as from cognitive to psychomotor. The idea is to direct students' attention elsewhere and then to redirect it back to your lecture without losing anyone in the process.
- Change-ups can be shifts to a different instructional method. You might lecture for fifteen minutes, show a fifteen-minute video clip, and then conduct a structured, small-group debriefing that relates the video to the previous lecture.
- Change-ups must be integrated with your learning objectives. Telling an unrelated funny story or taking a break does not contribute to achieving learning goals and thus are not change-ups.
- Change-ups should become natural and instinctive, but their use must be deliberately planned and scheduled in your lecture notes.

Change-ups can be used with individuals or groups and can vary from having students reinforce ideas presented in the lecture to having them make connections between a new concept and a previously learned one. The following are some popular change-ups:

- *Whip-around pass:* With this change-up, you pose a question to the entire class, and then call on a specific student to respond. After his or her short response, you "whip-around" to other students dispersed throughout the classroom for other rapid responses—no time for long-winded answers with supplemental comments. The pass part of the strategy allows students without an answer, or whose answer has already been stated, to "pass." There are times, especially with a small class, when so many fresh answers are coming that you might choose to whip-around the class more than once. If a class is very large, you may whip-around one segment of the class for the first question, another section for the second question, and so on. The goal is to keep it active and fun. One professor who uses this strategy threatens students that she will bring in a whip to crack, as a reminder for them to be quick.
- *Quick questions:* Distribute blank index cards at the start of class. When you sense the need for a change-up, ask students to read through their notes quickly and write on the card one question that they have regarding the lecture. Collect the cards, read some aloud, and answer the questions. You can also have students exchange the cards, read them over, and then return them to the question writer with an answer.

- *Question, all write:* Ask a question regarding some of the content just addressed in the lecture. All students are to write an answer; using self-stick notes or colored index cards adds to the novelty. After everyone has responded, ask a few students to read what they have written, or ask all students to compare their answers with someone else's.
- *Note review:* A change-up that requires no additional materials and thus can be conducted extemporaneously is the note review. When the class needs some new energy, stop and ask students to get with a partner and compare notes. They are to find differences in what they wrote down—omissions, differences of opinion or perception, or differences in style. The comparison provides students a check on the completeness of their notes and a reinforcement of the content, and resets their attention clocks so that the lecture can proceed with renewed effectiveness.

Although change-ups are fun, they more importantly foster student engagement and deeper learning. Investing a few minutes in a change-up can help you ensure that the material in your lecture will make it into your students' memories. When your teaching seems rushed, the thought may cross your mind to hurry up and "get through" the material and dispense with the change-ups. If so remind yourself of the ultimate goal (student learning), which requires periodic refocusing time. Getting through the material does not mean that the students learned it. As a strategic professor, keep your eye on the learning target, always considering and reconsidering the best way to reach it.

AUGMENTING YOUR LECTURE WITH VISUALS

Today's students have grown up with high-tech, high-color, high-intensity, high-speed visuals. Even the formerly staid national evening news reflects the change in viewers' habits and preferences. The venerable Walter Cronkite and others have given way to news commentators who are on the screen for no more than a minute at a time, surrounded by supporting visuals.

Achieving effectiveness with today's learners requires supplementing your lectures with compelling photographs and graphics. So much is available for most topics that it is easy to locate appropriate stimuli to complement a lecture. Many faculty members are using Microsoft PowerPoint or similar presentation software to supplement and/or guide their lectures. For strategic teachers, presentation software neither replaces the lecture nor serves as a backdrop only; it enhances learning by providing visual cues for students' mental organization. Think twice about using features of the software that create sizzle but add little to genuine learning. If you are a novice user, consult with one of the growing number of campus specialists who have responsibility for effectively integrating use of such technology into teaching.

Most faculty members who previously used slides have converted those to some type of presentation software. There are two primary benefits: (1) electronic slides are easier to sequence than traditional slides and (2) the classroom lights can be left on so that students can continue to take notes. Neither benefit should be discounted. Remember, however, that just because the lights are on, students are not necessarily engaged. Their attention clocks still require periodic resetting.

Video and sound clips can also help keep students engaged in the lecture. Better than your words, they can help illustrate a point, demonstrate a concept, clarify a confusing notion, provide background information, or deliver a figurative punch. A clip may be as short as ten seconds or as long as twenty minutes, but used strategically, it can powerfully reinforce the lecture in students' minds.

Props, from everyday household items to historical artifacts and artwork, are underutilized in most college classrooms. Some would view props as unsophisticated in a high-tech age, but their value lies in their surprise factor. They are valuable in helping students connect with particular concepts in a more personalized way. Props support the use of powerful metaphors and analogies. For example, when helping students understand the concept of inertia, an old-fashioned, hand-lever water pump can be employed so that students really internalize the meaning.

Traditional transparencies (either professionally produced or hand-drawn) displayed on overhead projectors enable you to prepare presentations on short notice and add color and panache to your lecture. Unlike a chalk or marker board, they also allow you to face the class as you use them. Some textbook publishers continue to provide professional-looking transparencies to professors using their company's textbooks, although this practice is giving way to PowerPoint and other presentation software that is less expensive for them to produce.

From a psychological perspective, flip charts (large pads of paper set up on an easel) provide a bit warmer tone than transparencies and seem to foster better student participation. They are most effective in courses with small enrollments that focus on interpersonal issues and skills. From a logistical perspective, flip charts can be prepared in advance or can be spontaneously constructed during the class. Either way, you can keep the chart intact and easily refer back to previous pages or tear off sheets that can be tacked or taped around the classroom, reinforcing students' ability to sequence the material. Because they do not require electricity and are portable, flip charts are especially convenient and reliable for adjunct professors.

The chalk or marker board is best used in situations in which spontaneity and student input are critical to the success of your lecture. Avoid writing long passages that require you to keep your back turned to students for extended periods. You would be wise to start at the very top of the board and to print in letters viewable to those furthest from the front of the room. Keeping extra chalk, markers, and erasers in your briefcase is prudent. An easy-to-remember acronym for effectively using the board is SUE: *s*ay it before writing; check for *u*nderstanding; and *e*rase energetically before introducing new material. (It is also thoughtful to erase the board before leaving the room so that it is ready for the following class.)

Professionally produced maps, charts, globes, or other visual aids have great potential to enhance your lectures as well. These are often available for check out from the instructional department and campus library. Plan in advance how to arrange seating so that students can easily see these materials, thus maximizing the effectiveness of these learning aids.

OTHER CONSIDERATIONS FOR THE STRATEGIC LECTURE

Besides using change-ups to help students process the information in your lecture, you might foster their fuller participation through additional tactics. For example, when soliciting their agreement or understanding of an idea by enthusiastically nodding or shaking their heads or by displaying a "thumbs up/thumbs down" response. When having them work problems, you can ask them to hold up their answers as a way to infuse energy into learning and demonstrate their understanding. Some professors and students are comfortable with using more outrageous techniques than those mentioned above (e.g., giving students noise makers that they can use when they stop understanding), but you will have to determine your own comfort level with those. The idea is to keep students fully engaged and to keep you informed of their engagement.

An astute professor learns to monitor students' body language during the lecture. It is astonishing to watch a classroom where, judging by the body language, the only person engaged in the lecture is the professor! It is even more amazing that the professor either has not noticed or does not care that students are not paying attention to the lecture. It is perfectly acceptable to stop periodically and say from in front of the classroom, "Hmmm, apparently I'm interested in this, but I haven't sparked any interest in you," or "Wow, I guess I got carried away all by myself. I want to pull you back into this. What do I need to do?", or the like. You can be honest with your students, and generally they will help you connect more effectively with their minds.

An extension of reading students' body language is interpreting their facial expressions. Although the "whatever" visage of some young students is difficult to read, most students send discernable signals. Students whose eyes are lit up, who are smiling when you are, who are looking pensive when you ask them to reflect, who are wrinkling their brows over a difficult problem or situation you have posed, who have rolled their eyes or closed them, or who even have shut down their faces altogether are all signaling you. Read the signals and respond appropriately.

Demonstrate actively to students what you mean by participation during lectures. Challenge through your actions those who seem to think that by merely showing up they have fulfilled their responsibility for class. Because you are holding yourself accountable for your students' learning, always expect much more than just showing up. Consider providing a handout early in the term that explains what you mean by participation. Reasonable expectations include:

- Coming to class prepared (having completed whatever was assigned)
- Sitting so that learning will be optimized; considerations include sitting where you can see the professor and the class members, avoiding distractions (certain people, sounds, sights), and maintaining an alert physical stance (leaning forward and making eye contact with each speaker)
- Offering comments that are pertinent to the material
- Asking questions when you have them
- Supporting others in the class who are asking questions or making contributions
- Disagreeing constructively when appropriate
- Attending class regularly (that means all the time, barring physical illness or the like)

Creative professors have found it valuable to demonstrate actively what they mean by participation. For example, Hal Blythe, in *It Works for Me* (1998), writes that when his questioning is met with a deafening silence, he uses a form of role-playing. Leaving the lectern and taking an empty seat in the classroom, he raises his hand, and says, "Dr. Blythe, I've got an answer," then gives it. He then returns to the lectern and thanks his alter ego for the valuable insight. He then finds another empty seat and asks the lectern another question. Blythe reports great success engendering a dialogue that real students enthusiastically join. Benefits of this technique include the following:

- It stimulates everyone in the class.
- Once you invade students' space, they no longer feel secure in their silence.
- Once "one of their own" responds, the rest of the class is often willing to join in the fun.
- Your alter ego allows you to pose questions students never do.
- Your alter ego speaks in their language, which helps quiet students become part of the discussion.
- Your movement is kinetic. A body in motion tends to create other movement.
- The technique provides variety. Your student alter ego can either ask or answer questions. Blythe says that he has even sent his alter ego to the

board and that, on one occasion, in sort of an exchange program, a real student wanted to move to the podium.

■ It creates a more open, dynamic class atmosphere, in which the professor is perceived as having ingenuity and a sense of humor.

This section has introduced you to a variety of techniques to make your lectures effective. You can add even more variety to your lectures by interspersing them with some of the other instructor-directed teaching/learning methods highlighted in the following sections.

STRATEGIC USE OF VIDEO PRESENTATIONS

Video and computer-generated presentations can contribute markedly to the richness of your course, but you must select them carefully to ensure an appropriate fit with the curriculum and to prevent students from perceiving them as time-fillers or gimmicks. In some courses, such presentations might not be appropriate at all. They tend to be most effective in introducing units of instruction (by providing appropriate contextual information) and in concluding instructional units (by providing applications of concepts studied).

To effectively use a video presentation in your classroom:

■ Check with colleagues to ensure that the video is not commonly used in another course within the curriculum.

■ Limit the length to twenty minutes or less. If it is critical to show a longer work, divide the showing into segments with debriefing sessions interspersed. As with lengthy lectures, students can become disengaged or focused on extraneous issues during a long video. Remember to conduct change-ups or other quick checks of understanding periodically.

■ Preview the video prior to using it in class to ensure that its content is appropriate to the instructional unit and your particular group of students and to confirm its technical quality and currency.

■ If using traditional viewing equipment (rather than a computer-driven system), order it well in advance; many campuses have a limited supply. Keep handy the names and telephone numbers of the technology contact person so that you can reach them quickly if there is a problem.

■ Check the equipment before class to make sure that it is working properly and that you understand its controls.

■ Provide students an oral "advance organizer" or handout guide that lists specific things you would like them to look for as they watch the video (see Appendix 7.1).

■ After showing the video, debrief and synthesize its content with the other activities of the instructional unit.

Unless you are teaching a video production course or have another very good reason, limit your use of videos or any other single method of instruction throughout the term. Especially early in your teaching, you do not want to develop a reputation among students and colleagues for taking shortcuts and failing to provide sufficient rigor to your course.

Although web-based demonstrations and other technology-delivered visuals each have slight tactical differences compared with videotapes, their usage guidelines are generally similar. Because these are typically more current and include integrated graphics, they can be powerful teaching and learning resources. As technology evolves, their glitches are becoming more rare, but always have a contingency plan when using the Internet or other technology as part of a lecture. Connections go down, websites are shut down for a variety of reasons, and so on. When they work, web demonstrations can be fabulous with today's tech-savvy students; but when glitches occur, standing there without a viable option is frustrating and lonely.

STRATEGIC USE OF GUEST SPEAKERS

Hosting a qualified guest speaker can be an excellent way to increase student learning and add richness to your instruction. As with video presentations, however, be careful not to overuse this tactic so that students might discount your standing as the professor. When using a guest speaker, be sure to observe the following guidelines:

- Qualify (or "vet") any guest speakers through reliable sources.
- When inviting the guest speaker, clearly identify the learning objectives for your students. A common objective is to have the speaker demonstrate how course concepts are applied in the "real world" or to address an important issue on which your knowledge and/or the textbook is relatively weak or not as current as students should have.
- Obtain a resumé or biographical sketch in advance so that you can prepare an appropriate and enthusiastic introduction that energizes the speaker and prepares the class for the learning opportunity. Also ask the speaker for names, titles, and addresses of those who should receive copies of thank-you letters.
- Clarify explicitly with the speaker, well in advance, the time parameters of the presentation, the interests of your students, their career goals, and so on.
- At the close of the class meeting before the presentation, encourage students to ask questions at the end of the guest's presentation and clearly indicate areas that are out of bounds. The last thing you want is for the speaker to become embarrassed.

- Several days in advance of the presentation, confirm by telephone or e-mail the guest speaker's appearance and the details you have previously agreed on.
- Develop a contingency plan in case the guest speaker cancels at the last minute; conflicts develop unexpectedly, traffic accidents and illnesses occur, and so on.
- During the presentation, play an active nonverbal role, maintaining consistent eye contact with the speaker that encourages students to do the same.
- If the speaker starts to exceed the time limits significantly, simply stand and move to the side of the classroom.
- At the conclusion of the presentation, thank the speaker aloud and reinforce key points made during the presentation while providing specific linkage to critical concepts.
- Announce a short break, during which time you should thank the guest outside the classroom.
- After the guest departs, discuss the presentation with students with the objective of positively reinforcing instructional objectives. If it arises during this discussion, deal constructively with any student criticism of the speaker.
- Promptly mail the guest speaker a professional letter of thanks with a photocopy to his or her designees, if appropriate.

After class, discuss with student opinion-leaders their perceptions of the guest speaker's effectiveness. You may decide to ask the speaker to return for subsequent terms, but be cautious about asking for too much and always demonstrate appropriate gratitude. Many guest speakers feel an obligation to serve their local communities by making themselves available in this way, but most have their limits (Lyons, McIntosh, & Kysilka, 2003).

Adjunct professors instinctively want to be treated as the professionals that their education, career achievements, and other life experiences should predict that they would be. As our colleague Peggy Roche stated in opening Chapter 2, we must often earn that level of respect in others' eyes. Consistent modeling is perhaps our most effective strategy for accomplishing that objective. There is something very special about watching true professionals work, be they physicians, carpenters, or college professors. In many ways, teaching is a craft like so many others that requires the mastery of a core set of values and vision of a desired outcome. It also requires the regular display of a growing kit of instructional tools. Each tool has a specific purpose, and when used in situations for which it was not designed, it loses its effectiveness. A carpenter who uses a wrench as he would a hammer will not only lose efficiency but also risks damaging the wrench in the process, causing it to lose its effectiveness in the tasks for which it was designed. Instead of relying only on straight lecture—the control device of many adjunct professors—continue to build mastery of tools that fit best for increasingly precise tasks. In the process, you will develop a far more effective and rewarding teaching style. Keep thorough notes throughout your course, in which you evaluate the strengths and weaknesses of teaching tools you employed in each component of your course. Like a good carpenter, continually look for new tools that will increase your effectiveness. Exchange knowledge of techniques with peers not only to increase your own success but also to foster the type of community that improves teaching for all (Davis, 2001).

Invest also in refining the communications skills that differentiate the truly effective professor from the average. Vocal energy and variety are qualities you can develop when your focus is sensitized. Carefully observe and, where appropriate, begin to adopt the effective techniques you see. This chapter has provided only the most essential information on the major instructor-directed strategies available for delivering your course. This set of skills is critical, but others hold the potential for increasing the effectiveness of student learning and enriching the personal rewards of teaching as well. The following chapter will challenge you to trust your instincts that some sense of control can be sacrificed in order to achieve deeper student learning.

SUMMARY OF KEY POINTS

- Adjunct professors must develop an array of instructor-directed teaching methods.
- Instructor-directed teaching/learning methods are comfortably familiar to many professors and students, and can provide structure, organization, and sequence.
- Lectures occur along a wide continuum, from the one-way monologue to what appears to be a free-flowing interchange between students and the professor.
- Learners must have their attention clocks reset through the use of change-ups or other quick-check techniques designed to help them focus. This is true for all learners, regardless of age or sophistication.
- Visual stimuli, including but not limited to presentation software, props, transparencies, flip charts, and web-based demonstrations, are essential in strategic lecture.
- Video presentations must be selected carefully, limited in length, and synthesized with other course material.
- Incorporating guest speakers into a course requires careful planning and follow-up to increase student learning.
- Trust that deeper student learning can be facilitated when you begin to let go of some of the control strategies you have adopted out of necessity.

THE FINAL WORD

"A math instructor, I have many adult students whose confidence in their math skills is very low. Having been out of school for a number of years and not usually engaged actively in study, they need the structure that my lectures and demonstrations provide. However, once they start to get a concept, they need to complete and practice their learning of the concept through hands-on activities, which again must be highly-structured, so that I can provide precise, useful feedback. One of my favorite activities uses group learning, or, can I say more precisely, full-body experiences. To introduce graphing, I take the students outside on campus (that alone was mysterious for many—how can a math class go outside for an experiment?) and use a rope and student movement as a metaphor for the mathematical process. The first time I tried this, I was not sure how my adult students would accept the exercise. Willing to try nearly anything once if it helps students master a key concept, I was rewarded with their enthusiastic involvement in this nontraditional activity and have subsequently used it in each section of the course while refining its dynamics to variances in class size, student maturity, and so on. With the rope held taut between two students representing the number line, students are directed to shift from their original physical points to represent the dynamics of the mathematical process. The part I like best in this activity is watching the students' thinking processes emerge. The walk back inside the classroom building provides time for incubation, and we immediately debrief the activity and use the board to display the critical mathematical concepts involved. Unlike asking them to relate to dry textbook material, the students can easily remember their involvement outside and how processes unfolded and are better able to transfer grounded thoughts to paper. I have been teaching for 25 years, and in comparing the way I started with the way I teach now, student learning is so much more exciting for them and me. The combination of instructor-directed and student-driven methods is a perfect fit for me."

—Beverly Gates, Sidney, Michigan

SAMPLE VIEWING GUIDE FOR VIDEOTAPE

Please complete the following viewing guide as you are watching the movie *Twelve Angry Men* so that afterward our debriefing can be more thorough:

1. In a few words, what are your initial impressions of Juror #8 (Henry Fonda)?
2. What is "guilt beyond a reasonable doubt"?
3. Who was the second juror to vote "not guilty"? What about him do you believe drove his decision?
4. What are your thoughts about Juror #10? Do you believe he would be accepted as a jury member today? Why or why not?
5. What are your thoughts about Juror #11 (the East European watchmaker)?
6. What do you believe the writer and director wanted us to believe when we viewed their movie? Why?
7. What was the single most critical moment in the movie? Why?
8. How does this movie remind you of another issue in our society today? How? Why?
9. Does this movie help you understand some issue of human nature or leadership better than you previously did? If so, what? How? Why?

CHAPTER 8

STUDENT-DRIVEN LEARNING METHODS

"My role is not so much to instruct students but to provide an environment that exudes not only determination and motivation to learn but also one which is nurturing and supportive; a place where students who have gotten off track can get back on."

—Laura James-Ezzidio, London, England, and Fort Pierce, Florida

FOCUS QUESTIONS

- Why do students benefit from directing their own learning activities?
- What are the proven student-driven learning strategies?
- How can classroom discussions be made effective for today's students?
- How can you incorporate contemporary strategies into your teaching?

Reflect back to a time when a magical curiosity drove you to pursue a deeper understanding of a particular idea. Perhaps it involved a science experiment you devised yourself, an historical figure with a shrouded past on whom you developed a presentation, or a seed planted by a guest speaker in one of your classes—whatever it was, you were dramatically challenged to push the limits of your known world. The pursuit of knowledge for the sheer pleasure of understanding is a powerful force. The best professors demonstrate an awareness of this phenomenon in their teaching, and moving at a pace that fits their students, seek to move each learner toward greater self-directed learning.

Extending the attention on teaching and learning strategies begun in Chapter 7, this chapter focuses on the methods largely controlled and directed by students themselves. We should note, first, that we understand why many professors would question the wisdom of employing such methods. After all, today's students appear to need a great deal of structure to guide their learning—in and outside the classroom. Extensive research (Dunn & Griggs, 2000; Light, 2001) has identified some common learning challenges, many of which we discussed in Chapter 3. Traditionalists might ask, "If students are so capable of directing their own learning, why are colleges and universities even needed?" The answer lies in the ultimate goal of higher education in today's world as empowering students to access and process rapidly changing knowledge themselves—in effect, to become their own lifelong teachers. Keep this paradigm in mind as we describe the potential benefits of incorporating an increasing ratio of student-driven strategies into the courses you facilitate.

As we said in Chapter 7, ultimately, of course, the methods you select will depend on your determination of the most effective and efficient way to achieve particular learning objectives. Although you will initially make the strategic decision of which instructional method to use, it is your students who will decide how much of the responsibility they feel confident in accepting.

THE CONTEMPORARY VIEW

At several earlier points we stated that the strategic teacher must start where the learner is, and suggested that many learners may not be where you hope they would be. At the same time, other students will be well beyond where you might expect them to be. Television, the Internet, and other forms of rapid-turnaround information-delivery systems have expanded the quantity, and enriched the realism and currency of information to which students have been exposed. In the 1940s, Americans read newspapers or listened to radio accounts of World War II battles, sometimes days after they had concluded. Today, citizens watch live battles on television, complete with instant analysis by former military officer/commentators knowledgeable about the strategies of the warring parties. In their schools, homes, and work, personal computers have empowered today's college students to pursue information of their own choosing and at their own pace. Today's web searches are far more efficient and effective than the library visits of earlier generations.

Several decades ago, a professor who assumed that students would arrive in the classroom without much knowledge of the subject at hand could feel secure in shaping and controlling the information flow that influenced the students by categorizing information into discreet compartments. In contrast, today's instructors typically face students whose greatest need is to *sort out* and *make sense* of the vast torrent of information that rushes around them—a paradigm commonly referred to as *contextual* or *constructivist* learning. This approach flows from the research of renowned educational psychologist David Ausubel, who identified that the single most critical factor influencing learning is what the learner already knows (1978). He cautioned all educators to ascertain students' existing knowledge base before developing their course delivery strategies. The dynamic shift in the flow of information, along with discoveries about how people learn, has fueled a movement that emphasizes helping learners make connections between their pre-existing knowledge bases and new information or perspectives.

ACTIVE LEARNING

Student-driven learning methods are based on the concept of *active learning*. To clarify that term, let us once again employ a continuum. If at one end we put active learning, what might we call the opposite extreme—passive learning? Or is that a state that does not exist? Do lectures, video presentations, and guest speakers engender passive learning? After fifteen or so minutes (for most learners), does the mind typically become occupied with other thoughts? The research would indicate that it does.

Active learning can be defined as an approach selected by a professor in which the teaching and learning environment is designed for the learner to be actively engaged in the acquisition and processing of knowledge and information. In an active learning environment, students are doing much of the work, at their own pace, to achieve their individual learning objectives.

Richard Hake (1998), a professor of physics at Indiana University, prefers a synonymous term, *interactive engagement*. He says that such learning involves methods "designed in part to promote conceptual understanding through interactive engagement of students in heads-on (always) and hands-on (usually) activities that yield immediate feedback through discussion with peers and/or instructors" (p. 65).

Although theorists and practitioners give nuanced definitions of this approach, those definitions commonly include students' drawing on prior knowledge to make mental connections at ever-higher levels of learning. Whatever sources you consult on the topic, and whatever differences you find among them, keep your individual conceptualization of active learning in mind as you progress through this chapter.

Adjunct professors—often even more than full-time faculty members—are increasingly accepting accountability for the student learning that occurs as a result of their teaching. We know instinctively that *student learning is paramount.* Every decision we make about *how* we teach and *what* we teach is made with the ultimate goal of fostering student learning. Therefore, when you strategically choose to use student-driven methods, you are deciding that, to reach that ultimate goal: (1) students will be directing the learning at a point on the continuum that fits their abilities; (2) the primary focus will be on a unique collection of students; and (3) students will be doing the majority of the work in the classroom and classroom-related activities. Your major work comes outside of class when you are designing and preparing the learning experiences and assessing and providing feedback.

Proponents of *active learning,* Angelo and Cross (1993) stated, "Learning can and often does take place without the benefit of teaching, and sometimes even in spite of it, but there is no such thing as effective teaching in the absence of learning" (p. 3). As a professor in the age of accountability, you must make the extraordinary effort it often takes to ensure that students are actually learning what you are teaching.

Unfortunately, sometimes it is easier to convince professors of this than it is to convince students. But convince them we must, because students must increasingly be taught to embrace this axiom, and thereby accept at least as much responsibility for their learning as we have. For some, it will be a challenge. In a compelling article in *The Chronicle of Higher Education* (June 4, 1999), Mark Benvennto offers the following, in response to what a student had written on an evaluation (i.e., "Get up to the f---ing board—that's what we pay you for!"):

> Although many students may not want to hear it, for most of them, interactive learning is the same thing as taking your medicine. You may not like it, but it is good for you. You will learn more by being engaged in a class rather than just listening to a lecture. You will learn more by teaching your classmates, and asking them and the professor questions, than by just listening and answering others' questions. You will learn more working in a group than working alone. You will learn more if you use your mind than if you come to class simply to be entertained. (p. B9)

We need to upgrade students' perceptions of their responsibilities as learners. When we are strategic teachers and they are strategic learners, the teaching/learning experience is incomparable in its efficacy.

STRATEGIC TEACHING USING STUDENT-DRIVEN METHODS

Teaching exclusively as you have been taught or how you prefer to learn may be comfortable, but it is often not very effective with the diverse range of today's students nor is it preferable, given what is now known about the brain and learning. Wherever you are in your teaching career, you can enhance your success by developing a teaching style that regularly employs some student-directed learning methods. This will require ongoing experimentation, analysis of results, and reflection on your efforts. It will be especially helpful to begin a dialogue with one or more colleagues grounded in active learning methods (Silberman, 1996).

To begin, consider ways to promote learning both inside the classroom when the students are right there with you, and outside the classroom. The primary student-directed learning methods for use inside the classroom include discussion, learning in small groups, role-playing, case studies, and student presentations. Methods for outside the classroom include experiential learning, fieldwork, and focused study time. Each of these broad areas will be explored in the following sections.

STRATEGIC USE OF CLASSROOM DISCUSSION

Students learn best when their minds are actively engaged. Research indicates that mental engagement during discussions is superior to that which occurs during one-way lectures (Sousa, 2001). Some degree of lecture or demonstration *may* be required to present new material, but a controlled whole-group discussion can help that information take root in students' minds. Discussion is appropriate for enabling students to:

- Apply information delivered through instructor-directed means to situations they perceive as relevant
- Analyze the perspectives of other students within the class—a significant goal for younger students especially
- Synthesize material delivered from diverse sources—the textbook, the lecture, the visual presentations
- Evaluate the validity of their previously held beliefs
- Evaluate the evidence and logic provided by others against their own developing knowledge base
- Gain motivation for pursuit of additional learning

Like teaching and learning methods explained earlier, discussion approaches can be differentiated along a continuum, as displayed in Figure 8.1. The key to success is to identify where your students are in their learning and employ a strategy that fits best in trying to advance them up Bloom's Taxonomy. Be aware also that discussions are an especially valuable tool in helping students develop their affective skills (e.g., difference in attitudes between individuals of diverse backgrounds—a major factor in higher education affirmative action debates).

FIGURE 8.1 Discussions can be conducted at any point along this continuum. Where should yours fit?

Discussion Continuum
← ─────────────────────────────────────── →
Highly structured   **Student-driven**
Focused on low range of   **Focused on high range of**
Bloom's Taxonomy   **Bloom's Taxonomy**

To make controlled whole-class discussions most effective for achieving the learning objectives of an introductory course, Davidson and Ambrose (1994) make the following recommendations for balancing content and process functions:

1. Begin by posing largely closed-end questions that identify the baseline for existing student knowledge.
2. Listen proactively by hearing not just the words but also the tone and the underlying message.
3. Use your peripheral vision to make sure that all class members are as engaged as you want them to be. You can then use your eyes, your body language, and other questioning techniques to pull in and address what your peripheral vision has told you.
4. Empathize with speakers and encourage the class to do the same. Make sure that ideas are not simply dismissed out of hand.
5. Maintain your sense of timing, knowing when to ask a question, when to summarize, when to make a connection to an earlier comment, and when to be quiet.
6. Help clarify ideas that are poorly explained by either restating them or using visuals to give them structure.
7. Separate yourself from the discussion part of the time. Although you are the director of the discussion, in this case, you need to let the students take the lead sometimes and not try to restate every comment or respond to every idea.
8. Vary the pace and tone of the discussion. Keep the tempo brisk when needed or slow it down when appropriate. Encourage and allow levity if that is required and stay focused on a more serious tone when that is needed. Support or confront, when necessary.
9. Make connections with both individuals and groups. Although this is challenging when you first try it or before you know the students well, it fosters active engagement for all.
10. Share relevant personal information, remembering that self-disclosure can be powerful when it is done appropriately but perceived as self-serving when it is not.
11. Be flexible in allowing the discussion to take off even if it does so in a direction you originally had not intended. If necessary, change the format to affect learning outcomes positively.

You can see that making sure a whole-class discussion is productive involves a great deal of energy and focus. Inexperienced faculty often think that holding a discussion will let them off the hook for a while and might be something to do if the lecture has left them drained or if they have not had time to plan adequately. This is far from the truth. A productive discussion takes both advanced planning and careful, keen orchestration throughout.

Students retain information most effectively when discussions are frequent, nonthreatening, lively, and mentally challenging. Leading discussions with all of these qualities is a significant challenge in contemporary classrooms, populated as they are by diverse students with varied experiences. Large classes are probably the major obstacle to orchestrating effective discussions. Fear of embarrassment, lack of knowledge, low self-esteem, and the desire not to stick out from the crowd are among the many reasons students are reluctant to participate actively in large-group discussions. You can probably relate to those reasons from your own experience, so be sensitive to your students' feelings. To achieve an atmosphere in which classroom discussions achieve their fullest potential, employ the following common sense practices.

Strategies for Early in the Term

- Break the class into groups of no more than five students (sometimes called *buzz groups*) to discuss a critical question.
- Decide what the objective is for the small group.
- Establish ground rules for discussion groups, such as "value all opinions" and "each member must participate."
- Before discussion begins, have students introduce themselves to each other and select a spokesperson for reporting their collective conclusions.
- Monitor the discussion within groups to ensure that students understand and follow the ground rules.
- Prompt participation from all students by posing nonthreatening, open-ended questions.
- Have each group report their findings in an orderly way, encouraging amplification of key points.
- Summarize the overall activity, by citing appropriate points you heard within groups and asking for illumination from individuals making those points.

Strategies for Later in the Term

- Expand the size of discussion groups incrementally to increase diversity of inputs.
- After establishing an appropriate class culture of tolerance and openness, begin posing relatively broad, yet not overly abstract, questions to the entire class. Then encourage applications of course concepts through subsequent questions.
- After posing a question, pause to allow students ample time to process it and form a thoughtful answer. Doing so will help build students' confidence and heighten their engagement.
- Call on respondents who have raised their hands or indicated a willingness to participate through some less obvious nonverbal signal.

- When calling on subsequent respondents, create a more dynamic atmosphere by scanning the room and choosing people who are physically distant from each other.
- Avoid calling on those whose body language indicates they are not mentally engaged; it will only stifle the discussion and their future involvement.
- When you encourage input from nonparticipants, do so out of earshot of other students.
- Provide feedback on the positive components of responses, especially from those who had previously been reluctant to participate.
- Avoid calling a response incorrect; instead, ask whether anyone sees another way to answer. Be sure, however, to clarify correct objective information before moving the discussion along.
- Be extremely careful about providing the correct answer to a factual question before students are ready to hear it. Doing so will condition students to wait for you to find them answers in subsequent discussions.
- When a discussion bogs down, summarize appropriate points before posing an additional question.
- Close discussions positively by asking if someone would like to have the final word or by stating how the conclusions apply to the course objectives (Lyons, Kysilka, & Pawlas, 1999).

Even the best discussion leaders experience challenges in achieving a free-flowing, highly engaged dialogue. Four of the most common problems are (1) lack of broad participation, (2) dominance by a small number of students, (3) diversions into areas inappropriate for your course, and (4) highly personal or emotional reactions by students. These problems are likely to occur, especially during the early stages of your teaching, but anticipating them can help you reduce their frequency and severity. Some tips for dealing with each of these challenges are as follows:

1. Even after you have achieved a positive environment for classroom discussion, you sometimes will sense passivity from the majority of the class. This is especially common as the course winds down and students are overwhelmed with assignments due at the end of the term. Avoid the tendency to slip into your *judgmental parent* ego state and to punish students for their nonparticipation. Instead, build common ground by saying something like, "You look a little drained" and giving students a chance to vent some emotion. If the discussion still lags, you might shift the order of your lesson plan slightly and provide more instructor-directed activities. Later in the class meeting you might elicit discussion most effectively by employing the small-group strategy, which you used early in the term, and a debriefing that is more humorous and engaging than normal. Also, providing increased positive feedback to individual students,

as well as comments to the whole class, such as "I'm really proud the way this class has . . . ," will likely pay big dividends.

2. Discussions that are dominated by only a few students lead noncontributing students to become disengaged, take the focus off your learning objectives, and risk establishing a pattern in the class. In the interest of building a positive classroom atmosphere, many adjunct professors are reluctant to silence those who overparticipate but then spend the remainder of the term feeling a loss of control. To avoid this, speak in private with those who tend to dominate, first thanking them for their involvement in class discussion but then going on to ask their help in encouraging the less involved by allowing you to seek their participation.

3. Occasionally, permitting a degree of wandering can make the discussion more lively and engaging. At the same time, you must be willing to step in early to refocus on your goals. Do so by first acknowledging the collective experiences of the speakers and then asking a transitional question that returns the discussion to its proper focus. If such measures prove ineffective, be proactive and remember the *Pareto rule*, which in this case should alert you that 80 percent of your challenges will come from 20 percent of your students. For the student who repeatedly makes unrelated comments, you might say something akin to, "That's an excellent point, and one that we will explore further when we get to the next chapter." The key is to intensify the students' focus on the learning goals. As with most problems, the best solution is prevention. Clarify the parameters of the discussion at the outset and reinforce them through use of the board, overhead projector, electronic slide presentation, or other visual aid. If the discussion starts to wander, a simple reminder of the parameters is usually effective and nonthreatening.

4. Affected perhaps by the overall lack of civility within today's society, students sometimes contribute highly emotional or personal reactions during classroom discussions. Some of these reactions lead to arguments that divide the class along gender, racial, political, or religious lines. Furthermore, students may directly challenge your authority. The keys in such situations are anticipating potential outbursts, knowing your personal comfort level with such situations, and knowing your students' limits. If discussions become heated, stay appropriately involved with your most calm and rational tone of voice, asking questions designed to return the focus to objective points made in the textbook, lecture, or discussion. Using a visual aid to list points or summarize facts can deescalate the emotion, minimize repetition, and engender objectivity.

Like so many other activities in teaching, orchestrating effective classroom discussions is a balancing act that stretches students' comfort zones and content understanding while recognizing reasonable professional boundaries. Stated once again, discussions are most effective when carefully planned with your learning objectives clearly in mind. In an increasingly complex world, our objectives include fostering students' critical thinking skills on issues within our courses. In short, we want students to understand vital issues from perspectives other than the one they held when they started the course. Through controlled discussions early in the term, one of our major tactics should be to clarify our understanding of individual students' perspectives, assess their levels of openness and assertiveness, and gauge which students are developing influence with their peers (noting these on the individual student profile form would facilitate your management of subsequent discussions).

Once a working knowledge base of these factors is developed, test your emerging assumptions gently. Employing the tactics listed on page 138, move on to orchestrate "point/counter point" dynamics. Hear out those who choose to speak on one side of an issue, then make eye contact with individual students who you anticipate will have an opposing view, thus encouraging that perspective to be articulated. Keep the discussion moving by summarizing and questioning, so that all students remain engaged, or you will find the effectiveness of this potentially rich tool waning after fifteen minutes or so. As the number of class sessions grows, students mature in the material and in their discussion skills, and the issues gain complexity, you will likely want to inject some reflective pauses into the discussion. As you begin a discussion, prompt reflection by simply saying something akin to: "In a few minutes, we are going to discuss the following question . . . (then write it on the board). Please take a minute to reflect on your views on this issue, and in a minute I will start us off." Even deeper into the term, you might select several individual students to enunciate a position that you believe would be contrary to their existing beliefs on the issue. Leveraging this strategy employed by debaters over the centuries enables students to analyze and even appreciate a point-of-view that they would otherwise reject out-of-hand.

As your course evolves, you will likely see benefit in empowering students to play a greater leadership role in the structure and direction of classroom discussions. The following are some techniques to use when you are having the students direct whole-class or large-group discussions themselves:

- Designate an item as the "speaking stick" or some such moniker. The person holding the item is the only person who may speak. Different rules may govern when and how this person passes the item to the next speaker, but the key factor is that total control of the speaking and turn-taking is literally in the hands of the students.
- Even without a speaking stick, students can be in charge of calling on the next speaker. They should, of course, be encouraged to include as many different speakers as possible and to make sure that all parts of the room and both genders are represented fairly. (Men tend to be called on much more frequently than women, even by other women.)

- Use speaking chips. Purchase several sets of poker chips to distribute at the beginning of a discussion period. Either you or the students decide what each color represents and how many of each color the students should receive. For example, blue might represent questions, red could represent disagreements, and white could represent clarifications. Participants must give up a chip when they want to speak. They must be clear on which color they are using and then channel their comments to stay within that category. Limiting the number of chips keeps the discussion focused and prevents any single person from dominating.
- Conduct a fishbowl discussion. A reasonable number of students sit in a circle in the middle of the larger class. They are asked to discuss a question, topic, or issue. The other students observe the discussion but may not speak until it is their turn in the middle. Whole groups may take turns in the fishbowl, or students can form tag teams whose members trade off as the situation requires. There is a lot of movement and engagement in this process.

The following can make student-led small-group discussions more productive:

- Present questions or problems for the group to discuss simultaneously. You may have generated these, or the students may have. Give them adequate time to formulate answers. Then have them either "report out" one group at a time or confer with another group to share what they determined.
- Present different questions for each group. This works particularly well if the questions are ones that the students brought to class—questions for which they want answers. Then, after adequate time, each group can give their answers to the whole class.
- Provide groups of six to ten students with a controversial statement related to course content. Each group then prepares both "pro" and "con" positions. After adequate time, the group is randomly divided and must conduct a debate for the class. Thus, the members do not know ahead of time which side they will have to take. You can expect high energy on this.

Once concluded, invest time debriefing and reinforcing the learning that has occurred during a discussion period. Too often, students are conditioned to take notes only when the teacher is talking, so they fail to record critical information during discussions. Emphasize the amount of learning that has occurred, the valuable points made by students, and the new ideas you have garnered as a result of the discussion. You might also say something to the effect of, "I made some excellent notes today for ideas that I want to address in our next examination. I hope that you made extensive notes as well." If they did not take notes this time, they will next time!

STRATEGIC USE OF SMALL-GROUP LEARNING STRATEGIES

A popular instructional development of recent years has been the use of small groups within classrooms to provide students an engaging, nonthreatening learning experience. The strategy leverages the tenets of the *constructivist approach*, whose adherents believe that students construct new knowledge within the parameters of their existing knowledge, rather than come to the course with a "blank slate." Although purists differentiate *cooperative learning* (teacher controls activities, monitors work closely) and *collaborative learning* (students direct their own learning while the teacher serves as a resource) along a continuum, many practitioners treat the terms as largely synonymous (Panitz, 2001). There is value in considering the connotations of each term individually, but we will focus initially on their common elements:

1. *Positive interdependence of goals, roles, resources, and rewards*: Students must believe that they are linked with others such that one cannot succeed unless the other members of the group also succeed.
2. *Face-to-face promotive interaction*: Students must help, assist, encourage, and support one another's efforts to learn.
3. *Individual accountability*: Each student's performance is assessed, and the results are given back to the group and the individual.
4. *Social skills*: Taking the lead, making decisions, building trust, communicating, and managing conflict are all practiced in small groups.
5. *Group processing*: Members monitor how well goals are being achieved and how well effective working relationships are being maintained.

It is these five elements that differentiate cooperative/collaborative learning groups from traditional discussion groups and a well-structured cooperative/collaborative learning lesson from a poorly structured one (Johnson, Johnson, & Smith, 1991).

Strategic use of small learning groups contributes to an egalitarian environment in the classroom and shifts the role of the instructor to that of a *facilitator of learning*. To facilitate means to draw on the existing collective knowledge base of a given assemblage of students and to then integrate additional sources when appropriate. A cooperative/collaborative classroom is a more participatory and flexible learning environment than is an instructor-centered classroom. Since cooperative/collaborative learning mirrors the movement within the American workplace toward use of self-directed work teams, many professors who prepare students for occupations employ it widely.

Like any tool, cooperative/collaborative learning has both strengths and weaknesses. Its advantages include the following:

- Engaging the learning systems of each student actively, through positive interdependence
- Empowering students to pursue learning that each perceives as relevant, thus creating individual accountability
- Building the interpersonal skills necessary for success in the larger society
- Developing solutions that integrate multiple perspectives
- Allowing the instructor to effectively manage the learning environment by monitoring group work and interceding where most appropriate

The major disadvantage of cooperative and collaborative learning is that some students (typically a small minority) may take advantage of the ostensible freedom of this approach to piggyback on the efforts of other group members. To prevent this, the instructor must do the following:

- Teach students how to be effective members of cooperative groups
- Decide on group sizes and numbers, placement of students within groups, room arrangement, and planning materials
- Specify objectives for the learning experience
- Monitor student behavior, including assistance with the task, processing of discoveries, and bringing closure to the exercise
- Structure "win/win" outcomes, individual accountability, and intergroup cooperation
- Intervene, when necessary, to ensure that students are practicing civility and contributing as appropriate
- Evaluate the quantity and quality of students' learning

Before employing a more collaborative approach that provides students greater input into these tasks and responsibilities, the professor should assess the comfort level of students with a looser approach. Collaborative approaches typically extend learning to outside the classroom, where students are conducting research and holding meetings (albeit some in cyberspace) to accomplish project goals.

The time you invest in additional planning for cooperative/collaborative learning activities is usually rewarded by the freedom you gain to monitor implementation and the opportunity you gain to provide individualized coaching for students whose needs are greatest. Your initial efforts at employing these strategies might leave you wondering if you have performed your duties, but you will likely soon realize the advantages of being able to circulate around the classroom to become more familiar with the needs of individual students.

The size of the groups should vary according to the task, but groups of four to seven students typically work most effectively. The smaller the group, the less information and experience there is on which to develop solutions. The larger the group, the smaller the opportunity is for individual students, especially shy ones, to contribute. Larger groups also lend themselves to being dominated by one or two students, yet they can also be more diverse. Discussions are livelier, and solutions are more broadly based, when members are diverse in age, gender, race, and other factors. To ensure diversity, it is typically more effective to assign students to groups, rather than allowing students to select themselves.

When the group work will be done in class, random assignment usually works well. Simply divide the total number of students present in the class by the number you want in each group to determine the number of groups you will create. Then, beginning at a convenient place within the class, have students count off up to the number of groups you need. Then have all the "number 1's" gather in a designated area to conduct their discussion. Proceed with the "number 2's" gathering in another area, and so on. You can also form random groups by having students draw numbers, items of a particular type, or a colored token from a container that will serve to identify their group.

Random assignments typically do not work well for groups that will be meeting outside of class because of students' disparate schedules, areas of residence, and other factors. One of the biggest complaints that students have about cooperative/collaborative groups is the difficulty finding time to meet. Such activity typically also does not foster the spirit of collaboration that is intended to maximize students' learning and also sometimes leads students to divide the work too narrowly and piece it back together at the end, resulting in insufficient mastery of the total learning objective. Therefore, strategic professors take students' schedules into account as they assign groups. Proactively creating groups that *can* meet will significantly increase the likelihood that they *do* meet and will lower what David Yamane (1996) calls "transaction costs"—that is, the prices students pay for having to work collectively.

The effectiveness of small-group learning depends largely on the quality of the learning experience you design or have students design with your review and approval. Having students group together to answer the review questions at the end of the textbook chapter may be only slightly more effective than assigning the same material as individual homework. Using a custom-designed case problem with interesting characters and situations is more likely to provide a dynamic learning opportunity that cannot be duplicated at home or in the library (Colberg, et al., 1996). Employing a competitive classroom activity such as the Circle of Knowledge in Appendix 8.1 can lead to a far greater mastery of course material than you otherwise would be able to achieve. Learning experiences that require students to explore their personal values and discuss them with those of diverse beliefs create a truly synergistic environment. As always, think about why you are having students take apart in a particular learning experience. Never use group work for its own sake. Rather use it because it will lead to outcomes superior to those of another instructional method.

Regardless of their size, composition, and place of meeting, groups must have their work monitored to ensure progress. When you are using groups within the regularly scheduled class meeting, move quickly throughout the entire classroom during the initial phases to gauge all groups' understanding of the assignment and outcome to be produced. Then, observe from a distance and circulate more deliberately to help any groups that get stuck. Rather than simply providing information, ask questions that will stimulate students to uncover clues for solving their own problems. You will see some students emerge as teachers of their peers within each group. This benefits all students: teaching others helps students synthesize their own master of concepts, and learning from peers helps students understand information and concepts they might not have understood from a lecture or textbook (Millis & Cottell, 1998).

When students are involved in small-group learning outside the regularly scheduled class meetings, you must be diligent to ensure that everyone understands the tasks, roles, objectives, time frame, and so on. Some professors make time to meet with individual groups working on long-term projects. Others establish specific times for the group leaders to consult on challenges. Still others use e-mail to allow student teams to convey overall progress, problems, issues, and the like.

Following any group learning experience, it is essential to facilitate a debriefing that enables students to develop a sense of accomplishment and place their discoveries in a proper context. Ask questions, both rhetorical and pointed, to bring the activity to a satisfactory level of closure. A debriefing might include additional out-of-class research to develop a more comprehensive solution, which the group can present at the opening of the next class meeting.

Another small-group strategy coming into widespread use is problem-based learning (PBL). John Cavanaugh sorts out the place of PBL among the various learning strategies as follows:

> "Imagine a family tree: Active Learning would be at the top. Cooperative/ Collaborative would be a subset of that, and I see PBL as a subset of Coop/ Collab based on cases. All forms of group work do not center on cases; problem-based groups do." (Rhem, 1998)

Whereas typical cooperative/collaborative groups are set up to reinforce learning of material that an instructor has already presented, PBL introduces students to new material through a problem addressed in small groups. The goal in doing so is to stimulate higher-order thinking. PBL is used extensively in health sciences education because it gives the students opportunities to continually apply pre-existing knowledge and build on it, rather than just trying to learn new material that has no link to what they already know. Professors in other disciplines also have begun writing PBL cases for their students because the power of this learning format is enormous (Spence, 2001).

In your first efforts to employ one of the various modes of small-group learning, you might feel unnecessary once the groups get going. You may even feel guilty about either not being in charge of the classroom or not covering more material. A few students, imprinted by the consumer mind set, might imply that you have somehow shirked your responsibilities by not directing the class. After observing the quality of the discussion, monitoring students' overall reaction, and speaking with experienced facilitators, you will likely overcome your negative feelings and find yourself looking for additional opportunities to employ small-group learning strategies.

One last recommendation concerning small-group work is to evaluate group cooperation and collaboration along with the final product. Students consider graded activities to be especially important. Therefore, if we do not assess their cooperation and collaboration along with other aspects of their work, they will not attend to increasing their team-building and emotional intelligence skills. You must determine what percentage of the overall grade will be for teamwork, and provide it in writing at the time the assignment is made. A handout for the project could say the following:

> There is a reason why I am having you complete this task as a group. I believe that in many cases two or more heads are better than one. So that you know I am serious about what I am saying, 40 percent of your grade will be based on the effectiveness of your collaborative effort. I will make that judgment by considering the following:
>
> ■ *Observations of your group interactions when you are in the classroom.*
>
> ■ *Explanation of the role(s) that each group member played in the final product.* Each member of the group will write an explanation of what everyone in the group did (including self).
>
> ■ *Weekly scores given by each member of the group to the rest of the members.* Those scores will be divided as follows: Assuming that you have four members in your group, each member of the group will have 100 points to divide up among all the members of the group. Each person *must* give him- or herself 25 of the points and then award the other 75 points based on a rubric-driven evaluation of how well each of the other members of the group contributed to the project. Sharing the aggregated scores on a weekly basis provides invaluable feedback to individual members of the group, which provides increasingly specific focus and motivation.
>
> ■ *The overall sense that the rest of the class and I have about whether or not you are working "seamlessly" as a team when you do your final presentation.* We have all, unfortunately, witnessed group presentations that were done by a minority of members who had divided up the workload and never communicated about what was being done or what was being learned. What I want to see is a group presentation that showcases each member's ability to take over any one of the other roles, because you are so familiar with all parts of the material and those parts fit together.

More and more students arriving in college and university classrooms are used to working with other students, but they may not know how to be members of a true team. Employers and community leaders are looking for people who can be contributing members of work teams. There is much we can do to give our students this experience (Matthews, 1996).

STRATEGIC USE OF ROLE-PLAYING

As a learning method, role-playing seeks to help students discover personal meaning in a given subject, or resolve personal dilemmas with the aid of their peer group. Whenever students take risks, as they do in improvisation, they typically achieve a valid educational payoff. In a more intensive and personal way than other teaching-learning methodologies, role-playing:

- Allows students to develop an understanding of others' perspectives
- Encourages students to work with others in analyzing situations and developing workable solutions
- Provides students an opportunity to apply concepts they have learned in a rich, realistic environment
- Gives students the chance to gain insights into interpersonal challenges they are likely to face in their careers and private lives
- Enables students to effectively contrast problem-solving methods or take on diverse perspectives
- Offers a constructive channel through which to express feelings and process feedback
- Presents students with a forum for building self-esteem and confidence
- Helps students realize that college courses can be fun (Lyons, McIntosh, & Kysilka, 2003)

Whether the scenarios selected are deadly serious or lighthearted, or whether they focus on the *affective* (i.e., *emotions and character*), *psychomotor,* or *cognitive* learning domains (or a combination of these), role-playing can have a dramatic impact on student learning. It can make an important contribution to students' long-term retention of fundamental concepts. The varieties of scenarios and learning goals are endless, but in each case the instructor must do the following:

- Identify and introduce to the class a sufficiently explicit problem and the surrounding issues
- Explain the rules that will guide the role-playing exercise
- Match and orient students to the roles within the activity
- Involve even extremely shy students, perhaps as chief observers or evaluators
- Set the stage for students, which includes establishing observation tasks
- Monitor the activity to ensure it achieves an appropriate direction

- Debrief the participants afterward to ensure accomplishment of desired learning outcomes

Role-playing is an especially effective teaching/learning tool within the social sciences and occupational disciplines. What more effective way to learn about the judicial system could be found than by conducting a mock trial? Or what more valid means of understanding entrepreneurship could be used than developing a business plan, and presenting it to a (peer) group of potential financial backers? How might students better develop conversational foreign-language skills than by role-playing an everyday situation staged in an appropriate location?

When they know they will be closely scrutinized by their peers, many otherwise passive students will prepare extensively to deliver an authentic representation of a given role. With prompting, they will ask themselves all sorts of what-if questions, continuously improving the quality of their learning up through and including the presentation. Such learning activities clearly have the potential for enriched learning unmatched by other instructional methods.

STRATEGIC USE OF STUDENT PRESENTATIONS

Most students master and retain learning quite effectively when they present their work to others. Many people can remember details of a school presentation they made long ago. Regardless of the discipline area, your students will likely benefit from making presentations also—as long as you follow sound practices.

We instinctively know that a major fear of most adults is public speaking, so your students, whatever their age, are likely to need a great deal of reassurance. One key form of reassurance that many professors overlook is providing students with an adequate overview of the assignment. As a result, students commonly make unfocused, disjointed presentations, which contribute to feelings of inadequacy the next time around. Therefore, students should be provided, in writing and well in advance, the objectives of the presentation, as well as a detailed scoring *rubric*. In a large course or when building teamwork is an especially desirable goal, you might consider having students make presentations as members of a forum or panel discussion. Or individual students might present to a subset of the entire class. Presenting to a small group is less frightening than presenting to a large group, particularly if the chosen subset of the class has been working together on various projects throughout the term.

If yours is an introductory course and/or students voice considerable anxiety, provide individual coaching or model effective presentation skills, showing students how to gain viewers' attention, use visual aids, achieve a powerful conclusion, and so on. You can also have a student with a proven track record in another professor's class demonstrate effective presentation skills. Videos on how to develop an excellent presentation are another possibility. A final but far less desirable option is to deliver a model presentation yourself, emphasizing in advance the key techniques students should look for. Some students would likely have difficulty separating such a presentation from regular lecture or demonstration, whereas others might view such a presentation as *the* model and work so hard to duplicate it that they appear unnatural.

Viewers and speakers can derive full value from presentations only when feedback is plentiful, objective, and consistent. We recommend allowing viewers to contribute to the evaluation of their peers. One commonly used method is to give viewers index cards on which they are asked to do a "three by three"—that is, they are to write down three strong points and three suggested improvements for each presentation. These are turned in at the end of the presentation and then attached to the evaluation form completed by the instructor.

The student who makes the presentation should not be the only one who is engaged and learning. Therefore, you should measure the learning that occurs among the audience. This helps indicate to the student presenters the effectiveness of their efforts. It is sometimes worthwhile to base at least a portion of the presenter's grade on how much the other students learned. Remember, what gets measured gets done, and most students value those measurements (i.e., grades) highly.

Deliver modest praise for student presentations in public and give genuinely constructive criticism in private. This way of delivering feedback is critical to achieving a supportive learning community among your students. Keep in mind that such an environment increases students' retention of the material they have already presented, as well as what they have heard their fellow students present. It also contributes to the enhancement of students' efficacy.

Finally, remember that nearly any good idea can be overdone. Unless yours is a public speaking course, resist the increasingly common tendency, especially in graduate courses, to have students learn the majority of the course content through their own and peers' presentations. Consumer-oriented students are likely to perceive that such an arrangement denies them access to the expertise of a professor for whom they invested considerable time and financial resources.

STRATEGIC USE OF EXPERIENTIAL LEARNING

For decades, occupational programs have placed students in internships and externships—jobs in actual work settings—to link classroom or laboratory learning to the requirements of the real world. Many can attest to the learning value of those experiences and the accompanying opportunities they provided to make valuable career-building contacts. Experiential learning is highly motivating to many students and offers them a rich opportunity to develop the higher-level skills of Bloom's Taxonomy. It has the potential to change students' perceptions of their communities and their roles within them, and it assuredly helps participants make informed career and lifestyle decisions. Experiential learning includes not only internships and externships but also fieldwork and service learning. In all of these experiences, students direct their own learning outside the classroom while the professor assumes the role of resource and mentor (Kelly, 1997).

In the late 1960s, when student idealism led to the demand for increased relevancy in higher education, various types of experiential learning projects became a significant part of the curriculum in many discipline areas. Now called *service learning*, that practice has returned in full force to many campuses, holding promise for the inspired Millennial Generation members to contribute to the betterment of society. Service learning exposes students to the needs of the larger community, engages them in addressing those needs through proven service methods, and connects what they learn in the classroom to real-world situations. At its best, service learning is a powerful teaching method that allows students to reflect why experienced situations exist and what their democratic responsibilities are in addressing them. A study by the Higher Education Research Institute comparing service learning participants with nonparticipants showed that participation in community service positively influenced every one of the thirty-five measured student outcomes, which fell into the broad categories of academic development, civic values, and life skills (Astin, et al., 2000).

A major challenge with experiential learning is ensuring the legitimate role of each experience in achieving predetermined learning objectives. Students will value the independence and personal satisfaction they receive from internships or fieldwork, but we must strive to ensure what they learn is transferable to an even wider arena. Thus, the instructor must not only select sound learning activities carefully but also build reflection and analysis into the learning experience.

If you plan to include experiential learning projects in your class, a tool that you should strongly consider using is the *contract,* a written document that spells out the pertinent issues and responsibilities of the student and professor and is signed by both parties. Generating a contract generally involves a three-step procedure:

1. Develop the parameters of the experience. These include the product that you expect students to generate (e.g., reaction paper, journal, video, oral report), its evaluation criteria, and related logistical requirements. Provide a printed copy for each student along with a list of possible topics.
2. Create a proposal form that students will submit for your review before actually beginning the experience. This form will give you the opportunity to provide direction and minimize the chances that the experience will be perceived negatively by students.
3. Return the proposal along with your comments to the student. At this point, the proposal becomes a binding contract—that is, for a certain body of work, submitted according to stated time parameters and performance standards, you agree to award a particular grade.

You might want to consult with your department chair and other faculty members in your department after drafting the contract to ensure that it meets commonly accepted standards of your situation. Even after you have determined their value to students, fieldwork experiences need to be examined for their impact on the overall curriculum and the goals of the department and institution.

Faculty members who choose to involve students in service-learning projects need to develop ways to combine service to the community with student learning in a way that improves both the student and the community. Doing this effectively takes time, effort, and detailed knowledge of the situation into which students will be sent. A growing number of campuses are offering workshops and support for faculty who want to take advantage of this learning strategy.

STRATEGIC USE OF FOCUSED STUDY TIME

Strategic learners are deliberate and conscious. They are mindful of their strengths and weaknesses as learners, and of what they must do to be effective and efficient during the learning process. As a professor, you should facilitate your students' learning by ensuring that they know *how to learn* and are *intentional* in their learning. Becoming strategic learners will serve your students well, both while they are enrolled in college and throughout the remainder of their lives.

Often, professors say, in one way or another, "You know, nobody ever taught me how to study, and I did just fine. By the time students get to college, they ought to know how to study." We have the following responses to these sentiments:

- As professors, we are not necessarily typical of the students who are populating our classes. Although some of us were first-generation college students who did not have studying modeled for us at home, others of us had college-educated parents who schooled us, directly or indirectly, on how to be effective in college.
- Maybe no one did teach us to study, but what if someone had? How much *more* could we have learned, and how much more quickly could we have learned it?
- Students may have learned how to study before they got to college, but college is different from high school. Also, general study techniques may not be sufficient for the type of learning students need to do in a particular specialty. Should we not do everything we possibly can to ensure the learning of the students we have, even if this means including letting them in on the secrets we possess about learning our subject area?

That being said, the following list presents a few student-driven learning methods that will facilitate the focused studying that students should do outside of the classroom. Although the instructor does the prep work, the students are responsible for seeing each method through:

- Ask students to keep a study log in which they write down what they are involved in while studying and how long they spend on each task. Tell them that the only grade attached is a participation grade—you are interested in seeing what they are doing. Also suggest that if they eventually have some trouble in the course, the diary might help you advise them on different ways to study. The first time you do this, you can suggest which tasks they should be doing and estimate the time they will take. But after several semesters of collecting actual student logs, particularly of those students who were successful in the course, you can give actual examples.
- An alternative to the study log is the examination log, in which students record what they studied, how they studied, the time they studied, and what they think will be on the test. Afterward, they record how well they believe they did and why. When the tests are returned, they can reflect on why they scored as they did and why their estimate was on target or not. This is especially effective with younger, lower division students who may have little practice in studying for difficult tests and in assessing their readiness for them.
- Complete study sheets as they do the assigned reading. Your work may consist of nothing more than listing chapter objectives and leaving an adequate amount of space for students to list what they find in the reading to amplify each objective. You can collect the study sheets weekly or on test day. Once they are graded, you can compare and encourage the students to compare the study sheets of those who did well and those who did not. The differences will be plain to see.
- Have students complete a "wonder, interpret, tie-in" (WIT) sheet while they are reading. Students write down concepts, words, or facts that make them wonder; they write down their interpretation of at least one idea presented by the author; and they make statements about how what they are reading ties in with other concepts from the class. In class, students can form small groups to talk about what is on their WIT sheets.
- Require students to do what Russ Moulds (1997) calls *interactive annotations*. Students may highlight and underline their text, but they must also go further and add meaningful margin notes where they interact with the author—arguing, commenting, reflecting, asking, agreeing, referring to other portions of the text or other sources, making connections with personal experience, reacting, comparing, and so on. Students can turn in their whole textbook so that you can read through and check their annotations. It is a heavy workload, but to avoid having to carry all the grading on any one particular day, you can stagger due dates, do all the checking in class, or use some other alternative.

The time you spend helping your students learn represents an investment in their future success. You will be repaid, with interest. But larger dividends also accrue for the students as they move through college, and for society as these students move on from college to work and beyond.

SUMMARY OF KEY POINTS

- Resist the trap of teaching only as you have been taught yourself. Today's students are likely to possess a knowledge base on which you can build through student-driven learning methods.
- Work to convince students that active learning carries many benefits for them.
- For classroom discussions, use small groups until students attain a satisfactory comfort level.
- Use collaborative and cooperative learning techniques to enable students to effectively process and apply material from your presentations.
- Employ role-playing to enable students to understand diverse perspectives.
- Develop experiential learning initiatives to increase student engagement and higher order learning.
- Integrate student presentations into your course to increase students' retention of material and to build their self-esteem.
- Plan to teach students how to become strategic learners. Doing so fosters their learning efficacy, which benefits them in your course and in their future learning.

THE FINAL WORD

"It's absolutely essential that today's students develop their writing skills, even though they often come to us quite deficient in this area. To minimize the "gotcha factor" and get them invested in a focused job of revising and editing, I provide an incentive to motivate serious effort. While I always give the initial submission of each paper a fair grade based upon a standardized rubric, I offer students the opportunity to enhance that grade by submitting a revised version within one week. Some students, of course, do not avail themselves of this opportunity either because they are satisfied with their initial grade or because they do not have the time. But most do. The resulting revisions are often astounding in their improvement."

—Jay Crockett, Blacksburg, Virginia

CIRCLE OF KNOWLEDGE

The Circle of Knowledge (Dunn & Dunn, 1999) is a highly motivating group strategy for reinforcing learning of factual material, before moving to upper levels of Bloom's Taxonomy. The steps are as follows:

1. Divide students into teams of three or four and distribute the teams throughout the classroom.
2. Pose a brainstorming question to all students in the class, providing a specific time frame between two and three minutes (e.g., two minutes, thirty-five seconds) for completion of the task.
3. Taking turns and moving clockwise, each team member is to whisper to teammates an answer that meets the criteria of the question (e.g., the name of a muscle in the body).
4. One member is designated as the recorder, using paper and pencil to record each response.
5. The recorder participates as a member and provides responses in his or her turn.
6. No member may skip a turn or give more than one answer in a turn.
7. If a member becomes stumped, teammates are allowed to draw or act out an acceptable response but not to say it out loud or write it down.
8. Progress cannot continue unless each member satisfies his or her obligation to whisper an answer not already on the growing list.
9. At the end of the predetermined time, the facilitator calls a halt and makes all recorders put down their pencils.
10. Using a board or overhead projector, the facilitator writes each team's number at the top of a column.
11. The first team's recorder calls out an answer. Facilitator writes this answer in that team's column.
12. On each, the recorder should then scratch out that answer from his or her team's list to avoid a possible penalty as the activity progresses.
13. After the last team calls out its answer for the master list, a new round begins. The team that went last in round one goes first in round two and so on.
14. A team may call out only those answers that appear on its list.
15. When a team runs out of answers on its list, it calls out "pass" but should stay active in the game.

16. All team members should watch the master list as it builds. If an answer is given that essentially matches another answer already on the board or is an incorrect fit with the criteria, anyone may call out "challenge."

17. If the facilitator determines that the challenge is valid, the challenging team receives a bonus point (written at the top of the team column), and the team providing the duplicate or incorrect answer is denied credit for the answer.

18. If the facilitator determines that the challenge is incorrect, the challenging team is penalized one point (written at the top of the team column).

19. The rounds conclude when all teams have passed. Each group may then discuss missing correct answers, and the first team to call out a missing correct answer is given one additional point.

20. When the game is concluded, the facilitator tallies the points for each team—correct answers, plus challenge points, minus penalty points—in full view of the teams. The winning team is the one with the most points.

■ ■ ■ ■ ■

CHAPTER 9

INFUSING TECHNOLOGY
INTO YOUR TEACHING

"An instructor's ability to infuse technology into the course has become a way that students measure credibility. Communicating with students via e-mail is a great way to build accessibility and create one-on-one time, while accepting drafts and assignments builds a sense of invested interest in students. Students' perception of a fear or discomfort on our part with technology tells them we may not be in touch with larger current trends or best practices."

—Todd Hattori, Salt Lake City, Utah

FOCUS QUESTIONS

■ How can everyday technology be employed to improve your teaching efficiency and effectiveness?

■ How can instructional-specific technology be infused easily into your teaching?

■ How can technology be used to engage students more actively in their learning?

Readers of this book range from those who have developed their own websites and written programs to those who do not own a computer. This chapter employs little technical language and seeks to provide readers with insights on how to use both general purpose technology and hardware and software specific to the academic environment. Most colleges and universities today are encouraging all of their faculty members, both full and part time, to become early adopters of new developments in instructional technology and are offering more training in that arena than any other. Because it is nearly all free, you would be wise to take advantage, not only for the skill building provided but also for the exposure it provides to instructional leaders and the networking opportunities that potentially provide many rewards (Woodell & Garofoli, 2003; Katz, et al., 1999).

Unquestionably technology holds huge potential for improving the *efficiency* of your instruction, enabling you to prepare instruction in less time and deliver it with less in-class effort when there are a myriad of factors

159

influencing your delivery. As I suggest specific tactics for achieving greater efficiency, however, keep in mind technology's potential to improve the *effectiveness* of your instruction as well. Many have noted an increasingly significant paradox between society's increased use of technology and its concurrent expectations of increased emotional intelligence from those from whom they receive service, a dynamic called the *high-tech, high-touch paradox.* In my experience, students have shown themselves to be especially mindful of this paradox. How and when we use technology and with what expertise and quality we use it are thus very crucial in our instructional success and to our reputations with students and instructional leaders alike (Grabe & Grabe, 2001).

To highlight the potential of technology's use in the classroom, let us again employ a continuum to focus our discussion. Imagine at one end professor-initiated, teaching-centered tools, and at the other, student-managed tools that fit their individual learning styles. Leveraging the full range of technology can help you develop more effective learning relationships with students, manage the instructional process, enhance your professionalism, foster deeper learning, improve your assessment of students' performance, and manage your grading system.

FOSTERING RICHER LEARNING RELATIONSHIPS WITH STUDENTS THROUGH TECHNOLOGY

The effective use of common technologies can provide more opportunities than obstacles for fostering richer learning relationships with students and thus overcoming the high-tech, high-touch paradox. Strategies with especially strong potential are the ongoing use of targeted e-mail messages to students, use of courseware programs, distribution lists, and listservs.

Targeted e-Mail

In Chapter 5, I suggested the strategic use of e-mail to increase student retention, beginning with a reassuring message immediately after the first class meeting. That message should carry a friendly tone to support your classroom-expressed desire to foster a community of learners within your course—a community that encourages the sharing of its resources and insights. That first e-mail message may also summarize some of the informal feedback you received from students as they departed the class meeting and could perhaps clarify issues regarding the syllabus. You could also use that e-mail to remind students of key issues that may have gotten buried in the rush of the first week of class.

There is, of course, no absolute number of e-mail messages to send to your class, but I recommend approximately one per week, sent at a regular time. You might even choose to call it a weekly e-newsletter to increase student awareness and expectations. This weekly message can be used to:

- Reinforce key ideas from the previous week's class.
- Build anticipation for the upcoming week's topics.
- Remind students of special arrangements they need to be making.
- Provide learning tips or study helps, especially online resources.
- Offer answers to a question from one or a few students that might have application for all of the students enrolled.
- Clarify difficult passages in the text by offering a variant explanation or sources for other views.
- Commend the class genuinely on something that went particularly well in class.
- Share anecdotes passed on by class members who have attained some success with a study method, means of accessing data, or some other pertinent experiences.
- Provide feedback on overall results of examinations, assignments, and in-class activities.
- Stay connected!

This last reason is widely reported by students as being of special importance. Whether you are teaching small or large classes, it is difficult to connect face to face with all the students in the class every week. E-mail can let students know that you are thinking about their learning and provides encouragement for them to think about their learning. Many administrators are so sold on the retention and other benefits of e-mail that students and adjunct professors are assigned free accounts, making using e-mail especially efficient.

In your weekly e-newsletter to your students, give them a special reason to get in the habit of reading them and target the key retention mileposts for special emphasis. Just before the first examination or submission of the first major assignment, send a message with some study or research tips, rhetorical questions that focus attention, or evaluation rubrics. Before the midterm meeting, your e-mail might summarize the progress students have made in the course and clarify a timeline for the rest of the term. As the term draws to a close, some tips for time management and multitasking might be in order.

The following list of tips for employing e-mail in your course includes those of David G. Brown (2001), Greg Kearsley (2000), and Kerry Hannon (2001):

- Create e-mail groups for each course section.
- Enter the course number on the subject line for easy recognition and sorting.
- In class, give students directions for how to create an e-mail group so that they can do so with their study group or another small project group.
- At your first class meeting, when you gather students' e-mail addresses on the student profiles, state that you expect each student to check e-mail messages at least once a day.

- In your second class meeting, ask for a show of hands of those who received your first e-newsletter and ask how they felt about it. Others will catch on to the value of reading it.
- Use e-mail for general and good news only. Deliver bad news face-to-face, in private.
- Tell students that you expect all e-mail communications to be civil; avoid sarcasm, flaming, and the use of ALL CAPS. They should also be sensitive to the different ways in which their fellow students might perceive the content of an e-mail message and who should be copied on messages.
- Use e-mail for managing the flow of your course to distribute materials and updates.
- In small classes, send specific, personal notes to those who might need extra encouragement.
- At the end of class sessions, encourage students to e-mail you about unclear issues.
- At the end of difficult sessions, send a group message that summarizes and clarifies details.
- Consider allowing students to submit drafts of work by e-mail. You can comment on these drafts using any of a number of software functions.
- Encourage students to e-mail each other.
- Consider requiring each student to e-mail you once per week.
- Check your e-mail messages every day and a second time the evening before major assignments are due or an examination is to be given.
- When responding to an e-mail, include the entire message you received, relevant parts of it, or a simple summary of what you are responding to.
- When responding to an e-mail, note whether it is necessary to respond to an entire group to whom the e-mail was addressed or only to the sender, saving others from excessive mailbox clutter.
- If you refer to a specific website in your e-mail message, include a link to it.

One extra caution. Install and regularly update reliable virus protection software and ask your students to do the same. New viruses and worms are often reported, and although some are merely annoyances, others are capable of shutting down the networks of large institutions. No longer can faculty or students claim ignorance when they have exposed someone else to a virus. There are several common and widely respected virus protection software packages available. You can set them to check DAILY (and, yes, I am shouting) for upgrades. Students should do the same.

Courseware Applications for e-Mail, Distribution Lists, and Listservs

Many e-mail programs have sorting provisions. If you have this option, be sure to establish a unique location for student inquiries and comments. That way, you do not have to sort through all of your e-mail messages to address the concerns of your students. If your college or university has licenses for WebCT or Blackboard, you can use the internal e-mail application to confine your students to the specific websites for your courses where you are using these applications. These applications allow students to post to open forums or privately to you. They also allow you to set up group discussions and follow threaded conversations. Both WebCT and Blackboard are primarily asynchronous, meaning students can access them at any time and are not confined to a specific time slot to communicate with their classmates. However, both applications also allow you to set up "live" (synchronous) chat rooms, in which participants are all logged on at the same time.

If your course has a large enrollment, you might consider setting up a listserv for each class. A listserv differs from a distribution list in that a distribution list is for one-way communication from you to your students and a listserv allows anyone who is registered on the listserv to initiate a communication. The listserv is great for making announcements, asking students to react to some relevant news event, or asking for help on a class assignment. Explore the e-mail options you have at your institution and see what you can arrange so you have a focused means of using technology to communicate with the students in your classes.

ORGANIZING THE INSTRUCTIONAL PROCESS

As a strategic professor, you begin each term by providing students a syllabus that is understood to be a contract with you and addresses the array of functions highlighted in Chapter 4. During your initial class meeting, you likely follow up the syllabus distribution with an explanation of all its critical details and nuances. At succeeding class meetings, you likely get requests for a copy of the syllabus or handouts from students who either missed a class meeting or misplaced the original copy distributed. Such requests not only become increasingly annoying as the term unfolds but also divert your focus from more critical issues that you need to communicate to all students. In addition, there are times between class meetings when you want to clarify wording that appears on the syllabus to ensure that the potential for the student grapevine to misinterpret your intentions is minimized.

One proactive way to organize class instruction is to leverage the technology at your disposal and create a course web page. Many colleges and universities are actively supporting adjunct professors in their efforts, for the following reasons:

- Today's students expect 24/7/365 access to a full range of course resources.

- Students like to be able to sneak a peek at the course syllabus before actually registering for the course.
- Well-designed web pages can serve as marketing tools for professors, departments, and institutions.
- Making the syllabus and its accompanying print materials available online can reduce the department's budget for paper and reproduction costs.
- In a school that charges student technology fees, students expect those fees to be used to make their lives easier; web-supported courses achieve that objective.
- Improved communications with students would seem to improve the student retention and completion rates of courses.
- Faculty web pages' potential to foster more time-sensitive communications with students will likely reduce the number of complaints administrators receive about the inaccessibility of adjunct professors.

If administration at your institution is not yet on board with adjunct faculty web pages, be aware that major publishers are increasingly providing such resources, as a textbook-companion to those who adopt their products. On a course web page, your syllabus can highlight such important dates as tests, project due dates, and so on. Posting your syllabus ensures that students will always have a copy readily available. You can also add links to clarify sections of the syllabus, provide instructions for assignments and information about how to format papers, and supply study guides for examinations and scoring rubrics for projects. Other links on your web page might lead to supplemental material such as a tutorial that will help students with specific, course-related information. All of these can be created on an as-needed basis and then readily accessed by your students.

In addition to getting help from your campus technology staff or textbook publishers, consider asking some of your students for some *reverse mentoring*. Many students are quite proficient at web design and may be able to help you identify appropriate sites with which to link your web page. Once your page is up and running, you might create an assignment that encourages your web-surfing students to find and evaluate links for the class, either as a part of their regular assignments or as extra credit. You can then review these sites, continually upgrade your page, and plan your course for the following term.

As we move further into the new millennium, there remains a "digital divide" that results in some students coming to college with extensive computer experience, and others whose families and schools had no budget for computers. You must be careful not to assume that all students are experienced and comfortable going online. Consider holding an optional after-class session for all interested students at a campus computer lab. Nearly all colleges and universities provide Internet access for students through computer laboratories, so if your students are assigned online work, it is imperative to make them aware of the locations, hours, guidelines and restrictions of these labs. If warranted, include this information on the hard copy of your syllabus, a label students can attach to a notebook, or a card that they can keep in their wallet or purse.

Faculty members who have created and used their own web pages usually believe there is no turning back. Those who experience the array of possibilities it offers for enhancing communications, convenience, and accountability to students far prefer it to low-tech options.

Besides the Internet, other computer applications allow both professors and students to be more efficient in organizing and processing information. Word processing is the most widely used application of computer technology in colleges and universities (Ravitz, Wong, & Becker, 1999). One especially valuable dimension of word processing is that it enables students to submit initial drafts, receive specific feedback quickly, and develop rewrites while the content is fresh in their minds. The growing array of word processing program features make revisions easy. By manipulating the text and incorporating graphics, students can produce professional-looking documents in which they take pride. Caution them however against substituting stunning appearance for quality text. Another caution relates to the ease with which students can cut and paste other people's work into their document. The growing concern over plagiarism in college and university classrooms will be discussed in the following section.

Spreadsheet programs allow students to manipulate and interpret numerical data. Storing, interpreting, and querying are relevant tasks in many fields: business, political science, mathematics, engineering, physics, chemistry, sociology, biology, economics, education, and finance, to name a few, so your using this software equips students better for their futures. Most spreadsheet data can also be displayed in chart and graph formats, which enable visual learners to better understand the data they have collected.

Databases are used to organize, store, and search for information and are familiar to students from the online searches they conduct. Databases organize factual information and allow the student to examine relationships within that database and are invaluable to researchers in all fields. The U.S. Census Bureau maintains a large database of census results that could prove valuable to students in many courses while providing more of that real-world experience.

Higher education is also about developing higher order thinking skills, problem-solving skills, and critical thinking skills. Technology infusion into your classes can help students develop these skills with ease and assurance. Because the Internet provides an abundance of information, students are immediately engaged in classifying, sorting, and evaluating activities. They get involved in organizing, comparing, and contrasting. Because data can be collected and imported into databases or spreadsheets, students can manipulate, sort, analyze, and draw conclusions about the data. You no longer have to do most of the work to collect and manipulate data—students can do it. Students may be able to provide much more information for you to use in your classes than you can alone, and the process itself can help them meet their learning goals.

Resist the temptation, however, to view technology as a panacea for quality improvement of instruction. Quality still depends on your ability to develop your class objectives, content, and activities. Technology is a terrific *aid* to making your ideas work in the classroom. Initially you may be intimidated, particularly if most of your students have an edge on you with respect to their fluency in technology; but most students are patient and will help you learn.

ENHANCING INSTRUCTIONAL PRESENTATIONS

Clearly one of the major advantages of technology is its ability to help professors deliver instruction in a professional manner that accommodates multiple perceptual modalities. We will explore a few of the technological advances in the following section.

Overhead Projection

In today's classrooms, some form of overhead projection is nearly as common as the chalkboard or the whiteboard. Two widely used forms of projection are the familiar overhead projector, which uses transparencies, and the newer document camera, which allows you to project from printed pages. Both tools have many advantages over the traditional board on the front wall.

The first, and perhaps most important, advantage is that you never have to turn your back to the students. Overhead projection allows you to record students' ideas on the transparency or document being projected, while maintaining eye contact for responses and questions. More students participate this way because so often when the professor's back is turned to the class, the ideas that get recorded are the ones "shouted out" by the more outgoing students.

The second advantage is that you can prepare transparencies or documents ahead of time. Using your computer to do so enables you to enhance your documents with color and use large fonts so that everyone in the room can see the print. With transparent overlays (that can be used on either the overhead projector or the document camera), you can demonstrate steps in a process, include pictures or cartoons that emphasize points in your lecture, display statistics on graphs and charts that will improve student comprehension, and much more.

A final benefit of using overhead projection, specifically the document camera, is that you can project items besides plain-text documents. Photographs, insects, pages of a book, rocks—all can be projected with ease. It is truly insightful technology because it brings the learning experience closer to all the students instead of just the brave few who sit in the front of the room.

Often the effectiveness of the document camera is diminished because teachers do not use it properly. Here are some very basic rules to help you get full use from overhead projection:

- Be sure that the print on prepared transparencies and documents is large enough for all students to see regardless of where they sit in your classroom.
- Keep the amount of print to a minimum. The transparency or document should be used to highlight points, not to give full text information.
- Writing on transparencies requires practice. You want to be certain that what you write is legible and evenly spaced for easy reading by the students farthest from the screen.
- When using the overhead, face the class. Avoid putting a transparency or document on the overhead, then turning around to read the projection to students. Keep your eyes focused on the transparency or document on the bed of the projector, pointing to items of interest.

Presentation Software

Several presentation software packages are available today, but the most popular and readily accessible is Microsoft PowerPoint, which is bundled onto most new computers. Like all other strategic decisions about your teaching, the use of presentation software should be based on what you want your students to learn and how to best orchestrate it. Presentation software allows you to highlight more content more effectively than you would otherwise be able to do, as described in the following:

- When you use presentation software to create visuals to support your lecture, its options enable you to print the text of slides as handouts and make them available on your web page. Bulleted points on your slides save students time copying information you want everyone to have and allow them instead to add supplemental information that would help them make personal sense of the information. Note, however, that unsophisticated students may think that a handout *is* the lecture, so be sure to help them know what *else* they need to be writing.
- Preparing excellent presentation slides for a class causes you to think through your course material more thoroughly, thus increasing your focus on important content and improving student engagement.
- Presenting information in more than one way appeals to students' diverse learning styles. When you use presentation software, you support your oral presentation with a visual component. Even if you only have words on your slides, the learning potential for many students is enhanced. Using more than words enables you to make an additional impact on what students retain from a class.

Other points to keep in mind when using presentation software include:

- Templates provided within the program should be selected for their ability to provide an uncluttered contrast between the print and the slide's background. The fonts should stand out so that all students can read the text regardless of where they sit in your classroom.
- Bulleted items or other data can appear to "fly" onto the screen, but be sure to keep the direction uniform throughout the presentation.
- Select sound for the background only if it genuinely complements your teaching objectives; otherwise, it is just "showing off."
- When indicating text points already discussed by fading their colors, be consistent with your technique throughout the presentation.
- Highlight only main points and keep statements concise.
- Use fonts large enough and sufficiently crisp for everyone to read.
- Limit your font variety to three types within a presentation.
- Avoid the trap of having your visual presentation carry your lesson; it should only support.
- Have a contingency plan should a glitch occur. Some presenters choose to print transparencies as backups and/or provide students with handouts of all slides.
- Because developing a good media presentation is time consuming, begin with a single lesson that is especially critical to students' understanding of the material. Then focus on a session a few weeks later where the content is especially crucial. It is unrealistic to create presentations for all class meetings within the same term.

COURSE MANAGEMENT SOFTWARE

In recent years, the market for course management systems, sometimes called *courseware*, has exploded. Providing electronic grade books, class rosters, course outlines, assignments, and quizzes, the growing array of competing products includes WebCT, Blackboard, Course Compass, and others (Olsen, 2001). If you do not have specific grade book software, you can use spreadsheet software to record and calculate grades. In a spreadsheet, provisions can be made to weight different components. If you allow students to retake quizzes or examinations several times until they get a "mastery score," you can set up your spreadsheet to count only the highest score in calculating the student's grade for the class. Spreadsheets provide great flexibility in recording and calculating grades for your classes.

As I discuss in Chapter 10, constructing effective tests can take an enormous amount of time. If you use a bank of items recorded on a CD or in hard copy that can be scanned, selecting items is easy. If not, you can develop your own test item database by using various software programs. As you write test items, input them into a database so that eventually, you accumulate a rich pool from which you can select questions for future tests. As you score tests, you can conduct an item analysis to determine which questions worked well or were not effective and adjust your database accordingly. If you continue to teach the course but change the reading materials, you will likely still have a viable set of questions for years to come. Investing the time to create a database of questions is well worth your efforts.

LEVERAGING THE LEARNING RESOURCES OF THE INTERNET

Many of today's students are entering our colleges and universities with much experience in using various technologies. Don Tapscott (1998) refers to these students as the *Net Generation*. Unlike the relatively passive radio, television, or video formats, the computer and the Internet provide active engaged time. The Internet opens a larger world to most students, eliminating geographic boundaries and time constraints. Technology advocates also claim that since the Internet knows no race, color, age, or ethnicity, users are more likely to engage in communication to learn and share more openly than they would in traditional environments.

The Net Generation uses technology more easily and frequently than older generations. They are navigators in a new world of learning. Their learning tool of choice helps them challenge current ideas and thoughts. According to Tapscott (1998), the Net Generation "is more knowledgeable than any previous generation and they care deeply about social issues. They believe strongly in individual rights [particularly] rights to information" (p. 9), and they challenge ideas and concepts with data that supports their arguments. Professors are challenged primarily to channel their curiosity, social justice ideas, and independence in positive ways.

There are literally thousands of websites that can enhance your instruction, by being linked to your class webpage, listed within your weekly e-newsletter, or simply noted on the hard copy of your syllabus. Among the most valuable are those launched by major publishers to support adopters of their textbooks. Some interactive websites can be used as either acceleration or remediation opportunities for your students, whereas others are designed to engage students in problem solving activities and/or reflective thinking strategies that are difficult to include in traditional class meetings.

The Internet holds volumes of information—some that is useful, some not. If students use the Internet for gathering data, they need to know how to evaluate the information they retrieve. College librarians can usually provide student orientations for effectively using browsers and delineating searches to retrieve the most relevant information for their purposes. Librarians can also help students learn how to evaluate the websites. There are instruments available to assess the quality of websites, such as the Credibility, Accuracy, Reason-ableness, and Support (CARS) checklist, which is summarized in Table 9.1 (Harris, 1997). Many faculty members find it helpful for students to explain how they determined a site was worthy of being included in the reference list of their research projects.

Through the Internet, students have access to libraries around the world, including the United States Library of Congress and most college and university libraries. Databases that were previously difficult to access are now readily available to students (e.g., local, state, and federal demographic and economic statistics). Using the Internet, students can view the collections of the world's finest museums and the street patterns of the world's busiest cities. The sources for information are endless and provide a timeliness that heretofore has not been available to students.

Students can access professional expertise by the Internet; television networks, professional associations, corporations, and government agencies all have websites. Frequently, they will announce that a particular celebrity, author, politician, pundit, or scholar will be available to "chat" with an "audience" at a given time. In addition, many of these recognized names maintain their own websites or at least make their e-mail addresses available to the general public. Increasingly, students in our classes are contacting authors of course textbooks

TABLE 9.1   Credibility, Accuracy, Reasonableness, and Support Checklist

Credibility	Trustworthy source, author's credentials, evidence of quality control, known or respected authority, organizational support. *Goal:* An authoritative source, a source that supplies some good evidence that allows you to trust it.
Accuracy	Up-to-date, factual, detailed, exact, comprehensive, audience and purpose reflect intentions of completeness and accuracy. *Goal:* A source that is correct today (not yesterday), a source that gives the whole truth.
Reasonableness	Fair, balanced, objective, reasoned, no conflict of interest, absence of fallacies or slanted tone. *Goal:* A source that engages the subject thoughtfully and reasonably, concerned with the truth.
Support	Listed sources, contact information, available corroboration, claims supported, documentation supplied. *Goal:* A source that provides convincing evidence for the claims made, a source you can triangulate (find at least two other sources that support it).

they are using and are impressed to be able to ask them questions about the content presented in the books. Most of the authors are very accommodating. The audio and video possibilities available through the Internet are staggering in terms of their potential to involve and excite your students. Students can hear or see real-time legislative debates, speeches, or other notable events using streaming video. Even if their home computers do not have the capability that will allow them to do so, your campus computers should. In addition, many speeches and interviews have been stored, to be accessed by anyone, anytime, using the tools of the Internet. There is no need to haul in tape recorders, record players, or other ancient means to let students listen to political speeches given twenty, forty, or sixty years ago. You (or they) need only find the websites that have stored these speeches and then point, click, and listen.

DEALING WITH TECHNOLOGY-FACILITATED PLAGIARISM

As you evaluate your students' papers and projects, you will undoubtedly come across some work that makes you question if it was plagiarized. For all the positive opportunities that have been afforded by the Internet, a major downside is the ease with which students can obtain information and pass it off as their own. There are scores of sites on the Web where students can obtain anything from well-developed essays to sophisticated research papers. Students can also use the Web to purchase papers from commercial paper mills, get translations of papers from foreign sites, participate in paper swaps, and cut and paste all manner of text. Even the traditional fraternity/sorority files or other paper-sharing mechanisms operating on most college campuses are now online.

According to Robert Harris (2001), there are several reasons why students cheat. First, many students simply do not understand plagiarism. They may have been copying material for reports since elementary school without being taught that such copying is unethical. Second, some students are sloppy about their note taking; when doing research, they neglect to distinguish their notes from paraphrased data or from direct quotes. Consequently, when they write their papers, they cannot make a distinction between their own thoughts and those of their sources. Third, stress and competition affect students' decisions. To someone balancing work, school, and parenting, the easy availability of prewritten papers or projects can be too tempting, and, since most students do not get caught, many feel the risk is worth it. Another factor that encourages cheating is self-defense. Students who see other students getting good grades through cheating believe that to survive in a competitive situation they also need to cheat. Sadly, another factor is a widespread societal one. Students routinely see politicians, athletes, businesspeople, entertainment figures, and even educators cheating in a variety of ways and not getting punished for their behavior. The perception that cheating is an acceptable practice in contemporary society is hard to combat in the academic arena. The final reason is one you can work to combat: students cheat because they believe they can get away with it. They know that some professors often only scan the assignments that are turned in. Although most professors do check student work thoroughly, desperate students are willing to take their chances with cheating and hoping they will not get caught.

There are several clues that would indicate that a student may have plagiarized, likely by using some form of computer technology:

- The quality of the work does not match that of the student's previous work.
- The language used in the paper is not typical of the student's work.
- The references and citations are not done consistently throughout the paper or are not done according to your guidelines. Many students who copy do not pay attention to bibliographic references and mix together those they have found regardless of style.
- The paper lacks references or citations altogether.
- The paper has inconsistent flow and voice or lacks logical argument. Generally this is a sign of a cut and paste job.
- The bibliographical references or the dates quoted in the paper are not current.
- There are anomalies in content. For example, a giveaway sentence would be, "The legislation is expected to pass in 2002."
- The content is very familiar to you.

These indicators of plagiarism are fairly common, but be aware that the evolution of more sophisticated software and students' technology skills require your continued vigilance.

There are several strategies you can employ to make plagiarism less likely to occur in your courses, many of which relate directly to effective planning, clarity of objectives, and specificity of requirements. They are as follows:

- Regularly ask yourself why your students would plagiarize. Perhaps they do not value the opportunity of learning, or perhaps they are working too many hours at outside jobs and allow themselves to get trapped by easy "solutions." Avoid fostering a "gotcha" paradigm (Howard, 2001).
- Include an academic integrity section on your course syllabus that clarifies your standards in easily understandable verbiage.
- Be specific with your expectations on all projects and give students a copy of your scoring rubric. The more precise your criteria are, the more difficult it will be for students to find a source from which to copy.
- Maintain samples of your students' written work. Early on in each course, give an in-class writing assignment that you can collect and place in a file for possible comparison purposes later. Or you can save a copy of an early out-of-class assignment because this is more likely to show students' final draft style than something written somewhat extemporaneously in class.

- Require students to turn in progress reports for major assignments. Set up dates on which they must identify and submit their topic, their references, an outline of their paper, a rough draft, and so on.
- Ask students to include annotated references. With the ubiquity of online bookstores and library card catalogs, keep in mind that this is not a foolproof tactic. You might want to spot-check the annotations by going online yourself.
- Require students to submit photocopies or printouts of their resources, particularly journal articles, websites, or pages from the books they cited.
- Become familiar with software and online resources that enable you to enter a questionable sentence and conduct a search for a "match" with published work.
- Have students make presentations to the class followed by a question-and-answer period.
- Require students to sign an integrity oath, which might be intregrated into your student profile form. This is done routinely at many campuses.
- Invest some class time in defining plagiarism and discussing the consequences of being caught. Review your institution's policy with students so that they take the plagiarism issue seriously.

If you suspect plagiarism, follow through on the situation. Your best tactic is to gather documentary evidence, alert your department chair, and then have a conference with the student in which you draw out the critical facts. If you calmly point to the evidence most students will admit their guilt. Be prepared, however, for some students to refute your accusation, perhaps angrily. If the evidence you have gathered is not yet sufficient, or if the student challenges what you have found, let him or her know that you will continue to pursue the matter and communicate your findings.

If ethical students in the class know you are checking for plagiarism, they will appreciate and sometimes reinforce your efforts with their peers. Honorable students are rightly frustrated by the cheating of others, but perhaps even more so when a professor fails to enforce ethical standards, especially when those standards were made explicit (Lyons, McIntosh, & Kysilka, 2003).

TEACHING ONLINE: WHOLE OR IN PART

Fully web-based classes are becoming popular and competitive. Tens of thousands of adjunct professors are facilitating those courses, typically from their home offices. A look at the return on investment of such higher education companies as the Apollo Group, ITT Educational Services, the University of Phoenix Online, and others (*The Chronicle of Higher Education Almanac*, 2002) demonstrates the growth in this arena. Some universities now offer entire programs through the Web, in spite of the higher student attrition rates when compared with traditionally delivered sections of the same courses. The added access to higher education that distance learning provides time-and-place–challenged students and the cost savings it provides to institutions seem to be strong incentives for the future growth of distance learning. The population growth among college-age citizens, coupled with the mushrooming growth of the Internet, indicates that, for the foreseeable future, significant investment dollars will continue to flow into the further development of distance learning technology. In addition, many governors and state legislators and their economic development-minded constituents view distance learning as a viable tool for improving access to higher education and increasing the degree completion rates among citizens who reside in remote areas or travel widely as a function of their work. Various stakeholders expect distance learning to increase the productivity of publicly funded systems and expand the economic base of their respective states.

Thus, colleges and universities can expect to see companies developing more increasingly student- and professor-friendly software programs and customer support systems for distance learning. You would do well to follow this growth and continually look for ways to integrate evolving strategies into your instruction. Also be aware that with their mandates for inclusion, many state legislatures and additional funding sources are creating incentives for you to add technology to your kit of teaching tools. However, in doing so, you will probably not be limited to delivering instruction by distance learning only. Realizing that some students' learning styles, technology skills, or other factors make them unlikely to succeed in distance learning–only education, many institutions are experimenting with various forms of "blended" or "hybrid" courses that provide many of the conveniences of distance learning while maintaining the high-touch aspect of traditional teaching.

Although many see value in this mode of program delivery, the adjunct professor should not enter into web-based instruction lightly. The dynamics of teaching online are very different from traditional classrooms and require much training to be successful. Some institutions recognize that and provide first-rate, continuous training of their online faculty; others do not. In addition to the higher expectations facing facilitators of online courses, administrators monitor retention rates closely to ensure they mirror those of traditionally delivered courses. If students become disenfranchised on the Web, it is much more difficult for professors to encourage their recommitment since they have typically not met face-to-face. Also, faculty members are usually clued in faster about potential dropouts in face-to-face situations than in a web-based class, where students can "hide" from the professor and thus stifle early intervention.

Adjunct professors who choose to deliver their courses fully on the Web need extensive planning time to rethink, restructure, and redesign their courses, and then time to develop the course website and its learning activities. Most institutions employ program management software such as WebCT or Blackboard, but be sure to ask many questions before signing up. While online teaching is not place-bound from the instructor's perspective, it is far more time consuming and time intensive than traditional teaching methods. Those who venture into delivering other forms of distance learning (e.g., video broadcasting or interactive television teaching) also have to think in entirely new ways. Teaching students who are seen on a small screen or not at all is very challenging, to say the least (Sanders, 2001).

If you choose to go the route of teaching at a distance, you will need to learn much more than I can share in this book. Be prepared for an entirely new way of thinking about how and what you teach and willing to invest considerable time rethinking your courses in the medium employed by the institution. In this, as in other areas of your teaching, it is very important to recognize that technology is only a tool. It cannot substitute for genuine concern about the complex needs of your students. If you rely too heavily on technology while ignoring the personal touch, you may fail to foster the type of learning that today's society demands, and you may lose more of your students than is acceptable. Because retention is an increasingly critical issue, it is imperative that you use technological tools appropriately and remain sensitive to the needs of your students.

As technology continues its proliferation within higher education, it will become increasingly critical that those facilitating technology-enhanced instruction, especially distance learning, sensitize themselves to the psychological and emotional needs of students. Professors must be consistently mindful of the high-tech/high-touch paradox. Those most successful at employing technology will be able to view their strategies continually through the eyes of those with whom they are interfacing at a distance.

An interesting example comes to mind. A colleague is currently enrolled in a graduate-level course in statistics, delivered by the Internet. An intelligent person with some degree of experience in statistical concepts, the colleague has been appalled by the terseness of the course facilitator's communications and frustrated by the lack of commitment to provide feedback on assignments submitted. Frequent technical difficulties prevent the students from receiving communications as intended, and the result is that the students do not understand the professor's policies or procedures. One must ask if this professor anticipated the range of challenges that would be faced in facilitating this course, and/or received the comprehensive training required to be successful.

In contrast, a team of physics professors at the U.S. Air Force Academy, Indiana University/Purdue University at Indianapolis, and Davidson College have collaborated to develop what they call just-in-time teaching (JiTT). JiTT employs the Web to deliver multimedia curricular materials and manage communications between faculty and students while emphasizing personal teacher-student and student-student interactions in the course. By increasing interactivity and offering rapid responses to students' problems, the strategy increases students' engagement with material often regarded as of secondary importance. The professors firmly believe their strategies can be employed in courses that are taken largely to satisfy requirements and those taken by part-time students (Novak, Patterson, Gavin, & Christian, 1999).

SUMMARY OF KEY POINTS

- The use of technology can be an asset to both the professor and the learner.
- There is a growing array of ways in which professors can use technology to enhance their course organization, presentation, and assessment.
- Technology provides students with multiple opportunities to enhance learning.
- Technology engages students in their learning and increases their opportunities to develop higher-order thinking skills, including problem-solving and critical-thinking skills.
- Technology can improve your communication with your students markedly.
- Technology has increased student access to material, with both positive outcomes and negative temptations.
- Distance learning is a growing area of higher education that holds great potential but also presents many challenges.
- Ineffective use of technology can dramatically affect the retention rate in your classes, particularly if students see it (and thus you) as impersonal and uncaring.

THE FINAL WORD

"By completing much of my doctoral coursework online and now teaching through that medium, I have learned that technology, especially distance education in its array of forms, allows students greater flexibility and choice. The international students enrolled in my online courses add a perspective that enriches the education of my North American students markedly. If most colleges and instructors continue as they are in their twentieth-century educational processes, they will become more distant from the students and organizations that they serve."

—Johnny Morris, PhD, Banner Elk, North Carolina

CHAPTER 10

MANAGING THE EXAMINATION PROCESS

"I consider any quiz or exam to be an opportunity to reinforce the importance of the material I have tried to convey to my students. Therefore, I try to structure the exam around those few elements that I know they will absolutely need at the next level. I regularly experiment with new ways of assessing learning, using computer technology, and giving my students the opportunity to impress themselves, their peers, and me."

—Marcia Andrews, Salem, Oregon

FOCUS QUESTIONS

- What are the characteristics of an effective examination?
- How is an effective examination constructed?
- What are the best procedures for administering an examination?
- What follow-up activities are essential to the administration of an examination?

Adjunct professors often say that among the most daunting tasks they face is the development of examinations that they feel good about administering. "Fending for yourself" often goes hand-in-hand with the adjunct experience, but developing effective examinations focuses students' and potentially instructional leaders' attention in an especially scrutinizing way. Those who have taught for very long can likely cite an especially uncomfortable situation in the administration or review of the results of an examination that will stay with them throughout their teaching careers. With today's emphasis on accountability however, a faulty test can create an array of challenges that are well worth the effort to prevent. This chapter is designed to provide you the insights and skills needed to develop examinations that challenge and assess students appropriately while reinforcing the professionalism that you have invested so much energy to develop during the term's first crucial weeks.

As you approach developing your examinations in an increasingly accountable manner, keep in mind not only your stated learning objectives but also the varied perspectives of those besides yourself and your students, who have a stake in your examination—students enrolled in other professors' sections of the course, professors who teach other courses from which or to which your students matriculate, and your instructional leaders. Refocus on our suggested tactic of developing your examinations early in your instruction and then allowing the examination to help guide your management of the material on which students will be evaluated.

Students and other stakeholders rightly expect your test items to accurately reflect the content and logic articulated in the course textbook and other instructional materials you have used in class. A significant disconnect between the texts and the examination will contribute to confusion and frustration, stymie learning, and foster ill will among students and other stakeholders. Increasingly time-conscious students expect an examination that provides a fair opportunity to demonstrate their knowledge of material in which they have invested precious hours studying. When their expectations are not met, today's students are typically not shy about expressing their concerns on end-of-course evaluations, whose content is fed back in a communications loop to those with the authority to evaluate your effectiveness and continued employment.

Although both students and instructors typically associate one overriding type of decision with examinations—grade determination—tests have at least two other important functions as well. First, examinations should help students assess for themselves their progress toward achieving their educational goals. Second, tests should help professors make better instructional decisions such as how much class time and which instructional resources to dedicate to teaching particular concepts. With so much riding on the results, the test items you develop must be grounded in sound pedagogical principles and must take a perspective sensitive toward students.

QUALITIES OF AN EFFECTIVE EXAMINATION

Traditionally, experts in educational testing have emphasized the importance of the following three attributes of an effective examination:

1. *Reliability* refers to the consistency of students' scores. A very important concept for those who are concerned about accountability issues, reliability comes in two forms. First, if a test does not produce consistent results at different testing times with the same group of students, then it is not a reliable measure of student learning. This form of reliability is referred to as *stability*. Second, some professors typically design two or more versions of a test to be administered to multiple sections of a class or to be used as make-up tests. If you do this, you need to be certain that the

different versions are equivalent, so that students should not be able to score better on one version than another. The term used to describe this type of consistency is *alternate form reliability*. This term is most often associated with high stakes or standardized tests.

2. *Validity* is focused on the *inferences* educators make from test scores about student achievement or status in class. High scores lead to one type of judgment, low scores another. Validity, then, "hinges on the accuracy of our inferences about students' status with respect to an assessment" (Popham, 1999, p. 43). You need to be extremely conscious of judging students according to their performance on a single test. Even a well-designed test will lead to invalid inferences if it is given to an inappropriate group of students. Do not use the same test each semester without considering the nature of your students and the content you addressed. In an age of accountability, you need to be certain that you are making valid inferences about your students. Thus, you need to be conscious of how well your tests *measure the content* that was taught. Validity is a filter through which we seek to answer the question, "Does the test reflect the content and skills emphasized in the process of teaching the course?"

3. *Absence of assessment bias* refers to a score flowing primarily from students' mastery of course learning objectives rather than from the idiosyncrasies of the developer of the test items. In other words, is the test free of bias? Test items worded as if they were fact, when they are actually the opinion of the test item developer, lack *objectivity*. Some test items can even *offend* test takers. Angry, upset, or frustrated students cannot be expected to do their best; their scores are probably not an accurate reflection of their mastery of the concepts addressed on the examination. The reading level and vocabulary of tests should fit the level of the students taking the examination, otherwise it becomes an exercise in something other than mastering the material. With the increased diversity of students in college, the use of unbiased language in examinations has become critical. Many English words are open to multiple interpretations, so test items must be written as unambiguously as possible. Nonnative speakers of English may not understand idioms, colloquialisms, or slang for example.

These three general test properties (reliability, validity, and absence of bias) should undergird your test development. You should also observe the following principles:

- An effective examination should be a learning experience, and an evaluative one. It should serve as a thorough review that enables students to deepen their mastery of the concepts included and to signal test takers on standards expected throughout the remainder of the course.

- Each examination should be a "win/win" proposition for students and the professor, not a battle of wits. Effective test items are written in a clear and concise manner and are subject to a limited interpretation.
- An effective test item should evaluate the understanding of the most critical concepts rather than the rote memorization of trivial factual data.
- An effective test differentiates degrees of mastery by addressing the various levels of Bloom's Taxonomy. Always test at the level instruction was delivered. Including questions at varied yet appropriate levels will help you analyze which students are developing *grounded* rather than *surface-level* knowledge.
- An effective examination should have no significant surprises for the well-prepared student.
- A well-developed examination should reflect the class time spent on all significant ideas and concepts taught. A student should never exit from taking a test thinking its contents did not assess ideas that were conveyed as highly relevant, that too many items were focused on a narrow range of concepts, or that class time dedicated to specific topics was not appropriately reflected.
- Consider *test banks* provided by publishers of the textbooks of your courses as a *starting point* in the development of items for your examinations.

James Popham (1999) has developed five general item-writing commandments that apply to any type of test you develop:

1. Thou shall not provide opaque directions to students regarding how to respond to your assessment instruments.
2. Thou shall not employ ambiguous statements in your assessment items.
3. Thou shall not provide students with unintentional clues regarding appropriate responses.
4. Thou shall not employ complex syntax in your assessment items.
5. Thou shall not use vocabulary that is more advanced than required. (p. 112)

Typically, introductory college courses and their adopted textbooks focus on students' achieving learning objectives at the *knowledge, comprehension,* and *application* levels of Bloom's Taxonomy. Subsequent courses within a curriculum and their textbooks tend to focus on a middle range, while capstone courses focus on the *synthesis* and *evaluation* levels.

The various test formats lend themselves to evaluating student learning at different levels of Bloom's Taxonomy. Introductory courses typically employ *selected response* test items (e.g., true/false, multiple choice, and matching). The terms *selected response test* and *objective test* are often used interchangeably with *forced-choice test.* These issues will be addressed more fully as this chapter progresses, but it is most important to recognize the need to ensure that the majority of questions in your test are at the level your teaching and the textbook address. Among students' greatest test frustrations is to be *taught* at Bloom's knowledge and comprehension levels and then to be *tested* at the application and analysis levels or higher. That is not only unfair and demotivating to students but also inherently ineffective in achieving teaching and learning objectives.

DEVELOPING EFFECTIVE SELECTED RESPONSE ITEMS

Unseasoned professors often wonder about the best format for their tests. What is best, however, depends on the level at which instruction took place, the nature and complexity of the learning objectives, the pre-existing level of students' knowledge and experience, and other factors. Selective response items provide ease of scoring and quick turnaround, enabling timely feedback to students, which fosters rapid advancement up the levels of Bloom's Taxonomy. The major types of selective response items will be addressed in the following subsections.

True/False Items

On the surface, true/false items seem to be easy for the instructor to develop and employ in a test. However, to make true/false questions the least bit challenging, the professor must be highly focused while avoiding tactics that students might regard as tricky or deceptive. Most adjunct professors seek to minimize heated discussions when scored examinations are returned and reviewed in class. Being perceived as a professor who includes tricky questions establishes an undesirable adversarial relationship with students. Regardless of how well or how poorly they are written, true/false items give students a 50 percent chance of success, even without reading the question. Although not as effective in most college course environments as other types of test items, true/false questions lend themselves to evaluating the lower levels of Bloom's Taxonomy. They can work well for evaluating knowledge of definitions; comprehension of the characteristics of key entities (especially when those characteristics are quantifiable); and applications of terminology (e.g., x is an effective example of y), but are otherwise limited. In evaluating at the upper end of Bloom's Taxonomy, true/false items must be written at a level of complexity for which they are not designed, and therefore phrasing them in a way that is easy for students to decipher is nearly impossible.

In summary, the following tips can help you develop effective true/false questions:

- Focus them at Bloom's levels of *knowledge* or *comprehension*.

- Keep their wording concise, focused on a single issue, and free of unnecessary detail.
- Use quantifiable terms—that is, words and concepts than can be measured precisely.
- Construct true items so that they are completely true, false items so that they are totally false.
- If *no*, *not*, or some other negative word is used, italicize or underline it.
- Avoid using the words *never* and *always*, which usually render an item false.
- For each examination, include true and false questions in roughly equal numbers.

Matching Items

After the true/false format, most test developers would consider the matching format the next most sophisticated of forced-choice test items. Matching exercises typically employ two vertical lists: a left one, in which items are numbered, and the right, in which items are preceded by letters. The student is expected to enter the correct letter in a blank beside each number. One set—usually the right column—is comprised of terms or names to be defined, and the other provides definitions or descriptions. Since the matching format does not easily lend itself to machine scoring, it has become nearly obsolete for large classes. Some publishers no longer use this format for questions in their test banks. However, well-written matching items can be more challenging and effective than true/false items for evaluating students' mastery of vocabulary words or basic definitions of key concepts. Like true/false items, matching items fit Bloom's *knowledge, comprehension,* and *application* levels and are not effective for more sophisticated levels of learning.

The following tips should be followed in developing effective matching items:

- Focus them at Bloom's *knowledge, comprehension,* or *application* levels.
- Ensure that directions are very clearly stated.
- Position the descriptors (defining phrases or sentences) in the left-hand column and designate them with numbers.
- Alphabetize the terms or names in the right column, and designate them with letters.
- Develop an easily recognizable theme common to all items in the matching exercise.
- Ensure that none of the definitions could match two terms.
- Develop extra names/terms for the right-hand column that do not match any descriptor in the left-hand column, thus avoiding a situation where a student automatically misses two questions by answering one incorrectly.
- Avoid using *clangers*, or clues that facilitate guessing a correct answer.

Completion Items

Completion items, sometimes called *fill-in* or *short answer* questions share a number of features with matching items. The key difference is that the student calls to mind a word or phrase and then enters it in a blank within a statement or sentence, in the process making it complete and accurate. Some professors employ a hybrid format, between matching and total recall items, in which they provide a list of terms at the beginning of a testing exercise or enter them on the board before the examination. Students are then directed to select their answers from the list provided.

In addition to most of the tips in the preceding matching section, the following apply to completion items:

- Provide sufficient and precise details in the sentence so that there is only one correct answer.
- Eliminate unnecessary detail that might serve as a barrier to students' achieving a clear focus on the issue to be decided.
- Avoid using phrases verbatim from the text, unless it is your goal to evaluate students' recall of a famous passage.
- Avoid clangers in the sentence, such as, "The rather bald and plump movie maker who directed *The Birds, Psycho,* and *North by Northwest* was _____.
- Place the blank to be completed either first or last in the sentence in order to focus the student's decision-making effectively.

Multiple-Choice Items

With increasingly larger class sizes and stakeholders' demands that professors turn around test results quickly, multiple-choice items have become the favorite testing format for most college instructors today. These items are not only relatively easy to develop but also lend themselves to being machine-scored and analyzed. When well-constructed, multiple-choice items can be valid, reliable, and unbiased in situations that address Bloom's *knowledge, comprehension, application,* and *analysis* levels.

The following are tips for creating effective multiple-choice items:

- Ensure that correct answers are facts, rather than opinions, unless you clearly indicate which famous person or recognized body held the opinion.
- Provide four or five response options to each question, ensuring that distracters (wrong answers) are plausible responses rather than throwaways.
- Arrange the question so that the stem (opening statement) includes all necessary qualifiers and that the response options are relatively brief.

- Ensure that both the correct response and distracters are approximately the same length, with similar amounts of detail and levels of complexity.
- Avoid clangers such as having only one option whose verb agrees with the subject in the stem or having only one response begin with a vowel when the last word of the stem is *an*.
- Ensure that none of the distracters could be considered correct by someone truly knowledgeable in the field.
- Omit nonfunctional words and trivial facts from both the stems and the options.
- Avoid negative phrasing in the stem. For example, rather than, "Which of the following is *not*," use "All of the following are true, *except*."
- Limited use of options such as "both *a* and *b* are correct," "none of the above," or "all of the above" might contribute to the effectiveness of a test, but be careful that such questions are not disproportionately reflected in your inventory of questions for each chapter. Too often, "all of the above" is the correct answer.
- Avoid response options that overlap or include each other. For example, "less than 25 percent" is included in "less than 50 percent."
- Whenever possible, use scenarios to which students can easily relate as the focus for application and analysis questions, thus encouraging immediate clarity and longer-term retention.

Although the task of incorporating the above advice into the development of your test items might seem a little overwhelming, you likely enter this activity more experienced, and better-equipped, than you might recognize. As suggested earlier, *test banks* provided by publishers of textbooks vary greatly in their quality. Review closely any of their items before including them in your examination. Some test bank items are perfectly acceptable as written, others may need editing, and some may be totally invalid or trivial. Ultimately it is your examination, not the textbook publisher's, so invest the time to do it right. In the long run, you and your students will be glad you did.

DEVELOPING EFFECTIVE ESSAY TEST ITEMS

Forced-choice test items are convenient to score, but many stakeholders in higher education claim that their overuse has contributed to a marked decline in the writing and critical-thinking abilities of college students. Their concerns have led to a resurgence of essay items on examinations, even in introductory-level courses. Essay writing is widely viewed as an effective strategy in the development of students' higher-level thinking, because they can be written to encompass Bloom's *application, analysis, synthesis,* and *evaluation* levels. More specifically, essay questions are useful in helping students in the following ways:

- Establish connections between theoretical principles and real-world situations
- Compare and/or contrast two or more approaches to an issue
- Explain the range of factors that contribute to a particular situation
- Integrate information from several sources to explain a particular situation
- Propose and defend a grounded solution to a problem
- Evaluate the quality or appropriateness of a product, process, or action

Besides requiring a great deal of time, scoring essay questions holds several other challenges for professors. First, students often have been conditioned to equate "quantity of words" with "quality of response," a perception that unfortunately has been reinforced in some classrooms. Second, essay question responses require psychic energy to score. Finally, scored essays may contribute to uncomfortable dialogue between professors and disagreeable students when results are shared. To combat these challenges, effective professors employ *rubrics*. Rubrics are well recognized for their ability to focus student thinking while increasing objectivity and reducing time in scoring. The rubric might be as simple as the following:

Opening: Provide clear introduction/restatement of the key issue   2 pts. possible

Body: Provide sufficient, correct detail and logical reasoning   5 pts. possible

Conclusion: Provide effective summary and application   3 pts. possible

TOTAL POINTS POSSIBLE   10

In summary, the following tips can help you develop effective essay items:
- Include clear parameters within the directions and/or the essay question itself so that students will not be tempted to write unfocused or unnecessarily long responses.
- Provide precisely identified elements to which you expect students to respond.
- Avoid starting an essay question with *how, why,* or *what.* Instead use a descriptive verb such as *explain* or *describe.*
- Provide students a scoring rubric that will be used to guide your evaluation.

FACILITATING STUDENT SUCCESS

Adjunct professors and their students have a major stake in being successful in the examination process. There are proven steps that you can take to increase the probability of such "win-win" outcomes. First, students should not enter a testing situation without knowing what to expect. Your students deserve to know in advance exactly what content is going to be assessed, and the type of items you will include on the test. The best way to provide this information is to provide a review session at the class meeting before the examination. How you conduct the review will depend on the nature and experience of your students and the material addressed. If your examinations will be comprised solely of selected response items, you might for the first examination provide students with sample questions. Knowing how you construct multiple-choice distracters, phrase true/false items, or structure matching items can help them avoid confusion and anxiety during the test. Consider showing them samples from a previously administered examination, having them work in small groups to answer the questions, and then reviewing the answers as a class. Students need to be reassured that questions will not be tricky, and that they will be relevant to the content that has been addressed. For the first examination in your course especially, you might provide a study guide that lists the most important ideas on which the examination will be based. The key is to assure students that the examination will be a fair assessment of your expectations of the students' learning, thus encouraging their thorough preparation.

In addition to reviewing content and test formats, you might also want to review your administration procedures. The following are some suggestions:

- Identify the "supplies" the students should bring (e.g., Scantron sheets, blue books, pens/pencils).
- Explain any special seating arrangements you intend to employ for the examination and why you will institute them.
- Explain the schedule to be followed for the examination. Tell students when the test will begin and end and whether class will resume after its administration. The latter would be particularly important for classes that only meet once a week for an extended period.
- Explain when and how they can expect to receive their scores.
- Reiterate the penalties for missing the examination and review make-up procedures if applicable.

Since the first examination is such a critical milepost in retaining students throughout the entire term, go the extra mile to give students every chance of success on it. Depending on the level of your course, the nature of your students, the difficulty of the subject matter, and other factors, you might want to (1) host extra study sessions, (2) post mock questions to your course web page, (3) agree to stand by your computer to respond to e-mail questions the evening before the examination, and (4) place old examinations in binders and make them available through the reserve room of the campus library. Fostering the best results on the first examination is a "win-win" strategy for you and your students.

ADMINISTERING THE EXAMINATION

When the examination is to be administered, arrive early and have all the materials ready for distribution as soon as the class is assembled. Arrange the seating and check the lighting and temperature of the room. Provide a special seating area near the door for students who might arrive late. Proofread your examination one last time and correct any errors on your key. Greet students as they enter the room and try to orchestrate a comfortable atmosphere. Avoid joking about the difficulty or simplicity of the test.

When the class is fully assembled, ask if anyone has a question regarding the procedures. Keep responses brief. Have students clear their desks of all items except the materials needed to take the examination. Identify where they should place their completed examinations and answer sheets, and remind them what time the class will resume if that applies. Distribute the examination and bring to students' attention immediately any errors you found while proofreading it, both orally and by writing the correct construction on the board. Remind them of the time allocation for the examination and wish them good luck.

Although you may have brought your own work to do while the students are taking the examination, do not get so involved in it that you lose sight of the dynamics of the classroom. A few minutes into the test, circulate the room quietly; it is imperative that the students recognize your attention to their behavior during the examination. Respond quickly to raised hands, wandering eyes, or puzzled looks. Since it discounts the importance of the test and your standing in students' eyes, avoid having someone else proctor your examinations. Be aware also that observing your students take an examination can be very revealing; their comfort level or frustration with the content and approach can help you make better decisions about subsequent teaching and examinations.

DEALING WITH STUDENT CHEATING

According to several recent reports, cheating among college students is becoming more widespread (McCabe & Drinan, 1999). The majority of this dishonesty takes the form of plagiarism (see Chapter 9), but cheating on examinations is also a concern. Most professors want to believe that the care they have taken in constructing their examinations should preclude any cheating. The reality, however, is that some students continue to peek at other students' papers, whereas others use crib sheets and other methods of cheating during examinations. Technology, larger classes, machine-scored answer sheets, and the risk-taking mind-set of many students have evoked brazen methods of cheating, including:

- Storing potential answers on calculators, microcassette recorders, and other electronic devices
- Recording answers on a duplicate answer sheet that is then given to a friend as the prepared student leaves the classroom
- In large classes, having another student take their examination for them
- Accusing the instructor of losing an examination that was never submitted
- Sending nonverbal clues to friends, not readily recognizable by the instructor, to indicate correct choices (e.g., rubbing the nose indicates answer *a*, scratching the head means answer *b*)

Students who perceive that their peers are cheating and getting away with it often lack the self-discipline to resist cheating themselves. They may also be reluctant to alert the professor to the cheating of others, for fear that they will be identified as snitches. Clearly, the best strategy to minimize cheating is to be proactive in its prevention. Disbursing students throughout the classroom, checking materials on students' desks, and moving throughout the classroom all stifle cheating. More fundamental, however, is establishing a trusting relationship between you and your students, designing tests that are perceived as fair, and preparing students adequately.

If a student does come forward and indicates that cheating occurred during the examination, take the complaint seriously. Carefully analyze the answers on the test, and look for patterns in grades (e.g., a failing student abruptly scores very high). If you can identify an individual as likely having cheated, ask him or her to see you privately and pose some nonthreatening questions like what they are doing differently to account for their success. Unless you have absolute evidence, however, avoid accusing a student of cheating. Often the best you can do in this case is put the student on notice through your behavior. The next time a test is administered, be sure the suspected cheater is more isolated within the classroom and observe him or her carefully.

SCORING EXAMINATIONS

Earlier in this chapter, you were given some guidelines for scoring answers. Traditionally, professors constructed scoring answer keys that could be positioned next to the examination to highlight erroneous responses, which were then marked by hand. Through technology, however, this task has been simplified. Among the makers of scoring machines and specially designed answer sheets, the most familiar is the Scantron Corporation. For a given examination, Scantron machines are programmed by inserting a correctly marked answer sheet. As each student's answer sheet is fed through, the machine marks incorrect responses and prints the total number of correct responses on it. Machines of the most recent technology will also provide item analyses—that is, they can calculate the number of times each question was missed, mean scores, medians, ranges, and other descriptive analyses.

Machine scoring can save you time, which you can then invest in making your test items more reliable, valid, and bias-free. If the item analysis indicates the vast majority of students missed an item, you might examine it thoroughly and consider dropping that item from the number of scored items. If other items do not indicate quality or level of learning (i.e., everyone got them right) you might consider restructuring those items the next time you employ the examination.

REVIEWING RESULTS OF EXAMINATIONS

In today's accountability environment, students increasingly expect quick feedback on their examinations. Although using selected response items can help you provide it, be sure to budget sufficient time to score the more grounded essay items, especially if you have large classes. Nevertheless, you should make every attempt to return examination results to the students by the next class.

To foster grounded learning in your students, you must review scored examinations thoroughly with them. Try to ensure that any makeup tests are given before the session at which the examination results will be reviewed so that those students can also participate in the review. The most effective way to review a selected response examination is to first distribute the test itself and discuss the correct responses before returning the answer sheets to students. This encourages students to focus on each question and better understand the concepts addressed rather than spend time justifying incorrect answers to questions they missed. If your item analysis identified questions you have decided to delete, explain your rationale in terms of their ineffective construction, not the fact that too many students missed them. Then explain how you recalculated scores. This tactic and your refusal to curve the examination scores (explained in Chapter 6) will demonstrate your fairness and reinforce your high standards.

After all questions are reviewed, write the scores on the board in descending order and provide the calculated average score in the class. Only then should you distribute the students' answer sheets. They can then look at their test scores, compare their results to those of the class as a whole, and analyze the questions they missed. Giving the students ample information about the test results typically prevents anyone from becoming unruly during the review. Solicit questions but do not engage in arguments over particular test questions. Invite any especially distressed students to stay after class, and encourage others to see you later to talk about their specific test results. Quick attention may not only alleviate students' frustration but may also mitigate what might be an irrational decision to drop the class. Remember, many of your students are trying to balance school with other obligations, so they may need some time to accept the poor results of a test. Keeping the door open to conversation is very important to helping students properly assess and manage their progress.

Reviewing the results of essay items during class time is a little more difficult, but using scoring rubrics greatly helps objectify the discussion and reduce students' emotionality. You might also provide examples of high-quality responses so that students understand your expectations on subsequent examinations. Again, inviting students to talk after class is likely to be useful, especially for those whose writing skills might benefit from further coaching.

Our entire society increasingly relies on examinations to sort out those who have mastered skills and concepts from those who need further development. The strategy you employ in managing examinations in your classes will serve to provide a lasting statement about your integrity as a learning facilitator. Commit yourself to continually improving your abilities in this critical area.

SUMMARY OF KEY POINTS

- Examinations contribute to the students' overall perceptions of the professor.
- Examinations measure not only student learning but also effective teaching.
- Construct drafts of examinations as you plan your instruction.
- Ensure that your examinations are reliable, valid, and unbiased.
- Test items should reflect a variety of levels of Bloom's Taxonomy and emphasize the levels as presented in class.
- Popham's commandments for constructing good test items include giving clear directions, avoiding ambiguity, not giving clues to answers, keeping syntax simple, and using appropriate vocabulary.
- Tests should be constructed to make judicious use of selected response items and essay items.
- Prepare your students for your examinations by keeping them informed of your expectations and providing appropriate review time.
- Administer your examinations in an organized way yourself, rather than through a proctor.
- Analyze the results before returning the examinations to your students. Be prepared to explain any anomalies to them and what your plans are to accommodate those anomalies.
- Return examinations promptly, preferably at the next class meeting, and review results in a systematic manner.
- Demonstrate sensitivity to student anxiety before, during, and after examinations.

THE FINAL WORD

"After 29 years of full-time teaching at two very different colleges, I'm now teaching as an adjunct. One thing that experience has taught me about student learning is how very critical it is to require them to write, not just in their communications classes, but 'across the curriculum.' I am passionate about the fact that the incorporation of writing in the learning process motivates students to become more active learners and promotes their critical and creative thinking. The assignment of research papers and reports, and administering essay exams may more effectively display what has been learned than the quick and easy multiple-choice exams. Unfortunately faculty not teaching English have, for a number of reasons, moved away from giving essay exams, as I was reminded on a recent flight when I overheard two professors talking on the subject. One stated that he gave an essay exam once and it took him a week to correct it. The other agreed that essay exams were too time consuming, so she never gave them either. I wouldn't be surprised if both regularly bemoan the deteriorating intellectual skills of their students in discussions with their colleagues. All during their conversation, I sat behind them correcting papers, resisting the urge to give both a lecture on the benefits of students' writing – even if it must be limited to a single question on each of their exams. A combination of essay questions with other question formats would allow for the evaluation of students' knowledge of information, as well as encourage creative, critical thinking."

—Agnes J. Robinson, M.A., Austin, Texas

SELF-ASSESSMENT

Directions: For each of the following potential questions, explain why it would be inappropriate for inclusion on an examination. (Analyze items 7 to 16, the Matching section, individually and as a whole.)

TRUE/FALSE

_____ 1. The climate of Georgia is *humid, subtropical.*

_____ 2. The "father of American education," John Dewey, taught for many years at the University of Michigan.

_____ 3. The two elements that comprise CO_2 are carbon and oxygen.

_____ 4. Washington, D.C., has always been the capital of the United States.

_____ 5. When he gave his *Ich bin ein Berliner* speech, John F. Kennedy was not in Germany for the first time.

_____ 6. The U.S. Supreme Court hears only cases whose decisions have been appealed from lower courts.

MATCHING

_____ 7. Dwight D. Eisenhower   a. A state senator

_____ 8. Joseph McCarthy   b. Wrote books used in American schools

_____ 9. Harry S. Truman   c. President of Columbia University

_____10. Sandra Day O'Connor   d. World War II hero

_____11. J. Edgar Hoover   e. Critic of prayer in school

_____12. Franklin Delano Roosevelt   f. Civil rights activist

_____13. Admiral Hyman Rickover   g. Critic of progressive education

_____14. Madeline Murray O'Hare   h. Authorized use of atomic bomb

_____15. Robert Dole   i. A zealot anti-Communist

_____16. Medgar Evers   j. President of the United States during World War II

COMPLETION

17. Winston Churchill was_____.

18. During World War II, George C. Patton, the _____ was the first militarist to use _____ during wartime.

19. During World War II, Iosif Dzhugashvili led _____.

MULTIPLE CHOICE

20. Which of the following is not true of an effective course syllabus?
   a. It serves as a contract between the instructor and the student.
   b. It includes a "tentative schedule" that the instructor should expect to change.
   c. It provides answers to most questions students are likely to have about the class.
   d. It is especially clear on the issues of grading and attendance.
   e. None of the above.

21. During the first class meeting:
   a. Distribute your syllabus, but don't review it until the second meeting.
   b. The classroom and your handouts should create a positive visual impression.
   c. Wait ten minutes before starting to allow latecomers to arrive.
   d. Take about fifteen minutes to review your professional and personal background.
   e. Be sure to tell the students if the class was assigned to you on short notice.

22. Which of the following is the most important reason to conduct an icebreaker?
   a. To break down barriers between students who are likely to be reserved
   b. To give students a chance to have fun as a balance against "heavy stuff"
   c. To provide students a chance to satisfy their need to fit into a new group
   d. To foster a positive learning atmosphere
   e. To encourage students to begin relationships that might launch study groups

23. Which of the following is true of learning domains?
   a. The *psychomotor* domain refers to the thought processes.
   b. The *effective* domain refers to attitudes and appreciation of artistic work.
   c. The *cognitive* domain refers to physical skills and dexterity.
   d. All of the above are true.
   e. None of the above are true.

24. Which of the following provides the correct sequence of Bloom's Taxonomy?

    a. Application, analysis, knowledge, comprehension, evaluation, synthesis
    b. Knowledge, comprehension, analysis, application, synthesis, evaluation
    c. Analysis, knowledge, comprehension, application, evaluation, synthesis
    d. Knowledge, comprehension, application, analysis, synthesis, evaluation
    e. Comprehension, knowledge, analysis, application, evaluation, synthesis

25. When a college professor is urged by instructional leaders to employ cooperative learning practices within his/her classroom:

    a. Students work in small groups to process information or solve problems.
    b. Groups work best when members are alike in age, gender, and ethnicity.
    c. Students should work with the same group of students throughout the term.
    d. Groups should include no more that five students so that everyone can contribute.
    e. Both *a* and *d* are correct.

Essay

26. What did Jesus mean when he said, "Blessed are the meek, for they will inherit the earth"?

Key

  1. Which Georgia, the state in the United States or the former Soviet republic, which is now an independent nation? Reword to: "Using the Köppen classification system, most of the southern U.S. state of Georgia has a *humid, subtropical* climate," or include a section heading or similar element that indicates the geographic range of the question.

  2. Two thoughts are included, one arguably true, the other false. Reword to: "The renowned American educator John Dewey taught for more than thirty years at the University of Michigan." (The answer would be false; Dewey taught at the University of Chicago.)

  3. The stem contains a clanger, CO_2. It would be difficult to make this a valid true/false question; a completion or multiple-choice item would work better.

  4. The words *always* or *never* should not be used in a true/false question because doing so makes the answer disproportionately false. Reword to: "Washington, D.C., has been the capital of the United States since the country's founding." (The answer would be false; Philadelphia and New York City were each once the capital.)

5. The word *not* should be underlined or italicized. I would ask, however, what knowledge the question is designed to elicit. Do you want students to recall that JFK had visited Germany as a journalist just before World War II, or that he did in fact make the speech mentioned, or that his use of the German language was flawed?

6. As it reads, the question is *nearly always* true. However, the seldom-used *writ of certiorari* empowers the Supreme Court to recall cases for review whose decisions have not been appealed. This item should be reworded so that it does not appear to be a trick question. For example, "The vast majority of cases heard by the U.S. Supreme Court are ones that have been appealed from lower courts." (True.)

The matching exercise illustrates an array of problems. First, the names should be positioned in the right-hand column and alphabetized for easy identification. Several extra yet logical choices should be added to the mix so that students who make one inaccurate match will not be locked into missing two questions automatically. The phrases used to describe the activities of the individuals listed are not of equal quality in that some refer to major activities and others are trivial. For example, Dwight D. Eisenhower is far better known for his military accomplishments and his role as president of the United States than for his presidency of Columbia University. Likewise, J. Edgar Hoover's role as director of the FBI is much more significant than his authoring a social studies textbook used in American schools. There is also a problem in that several descriptors fit several names. There are four persons on the list who were U.S. senators, two presidents who served during World War II, several World War II heroes, and at least three persons who could be described as staunch anti-Communists. Clearly, there are questionable matches on the list. (As given, the "correct" answers might be: 7c, 8i, 9h, 10a, 11b, 12j, 13g, 14e, 15d, 16f.)

17. Insufficient detail is provided in the stem for students to determine what is requested about Winston Churchill. Churchill was prime minister of Britain from 1940 to 1945 and again from 1950 to 1955, but he was also a well-known author, a leader against Germany during the Battle of Britain, and a British statesman. Any of these answers could be considered correct or incorrect, depending on the professor's perspective or whim.

18. In this question, any of several descriptors could be used in the first blank: general, commander, leader of the Third Army, or leader of the African Campaign. The use of the article *the* before the blank would indicate that the answer should be a phrase, but only one blank is given, which suggests that the answer should be a single word. The second blank is very ambiguous. The desired word is *tanks*, but any of a large number of words would seem to make sense.

19. This question is focusing on relatively trivial information. Unless students knew that Iosif Dzhugashvili is the transliterated name of the person we know as Joseph Stalin, they would have no clue as to what to provide in the blank. Furthermore, the question is structured for many different responses. The teacher may have been looking specifically for "the Soviet Union," "the USSR," or "Russia," but without more context, students could identify any number of correct answers.

20. While *b* is the "correct" answer, students must employ some convoluted logic to arrive at that choice. Especially troublesome is the relationship between the stem's use of the word *not* and choice *e*, "None of the above." The stem of the question should be rephrased to read "All of the following are true of an effective course syllabus except" and by making choice *e* a true statement.

21. The stem lacks a phrase that would focus the respondent's search for a correct answer. A better stem would be: "During the first class meeting, an effective instructor should:". The correct answer to the ineffectively written stem is *b*, but notice that it is the only option that begins with a word other than a verb, providing the respondent with a "clanging" clue to the correct answer.

22. The correct answer to this question is a matter of opinion; different people could see different reasons as the "most important." Any of the answers could conceivably be correct.

23. The definitions of choices *a* and *c* are juxtaposed, and thus both are incorrect. Choice *b* looks correct on the surface, but the word *effective* should actually be *affective*, making the "correct" answer *e*. This item would be interpreted as mean-spirited by anyone answering it. "All of the above" and "None of the above" are clearly space takers.

24. Did you look back in the book to find the correct answer? Whether this question is effective depends largely on the level at which the course is delivered. If it is an introductory course, choice *b* is probably too similar to the correct answer *d*. If the question is for an advanced course in educational psychology, the question might be fine, although one could make the case that an essay item would work better than a multiple-choice item for such a key concept.

25. The stem has too much unnecessary detail. Reword stem to: "Which of the following is correct about the effective use of cooperative learning?"

26. Theologians have written volumes on this question. The stem needs boundaries so that respondents can give focused responses.

ESSAY QUESTION EXERCISE

Directions for Students: Score the two responses to the question below, using the criteria provided.

Question: Explain what you learned about yourself from completing the Decision Style Inventory. Address your typical problem orientation, information orientation, management style, and organizational preference. Also explain how your weaknesses are likely to appear to others.

Scoring Criteria:		*A*	*B*
Opening provides context and overview?	2 points	__	__
Body provides sufficient, correct detail?	5 points	__	__
Conclusion makes application to your management career?	3 points	__	__
TOTAL POSSIBLE POINTS	10 points	__	__

RESPONSE A

The Decision Style Inventory was very useful. It identified me as having a *behavioral* style. I like people and make decisions that tend to make others happy. I support people because they need that in order to stay motivated and continue to learn. I prefer to work in companies that demonstrate the same concern for others that I have. As I start my management career, I will become the kind of manager that others will always want to follow.

RESPONSE B

The Decision Style Inventory is a tool to help us better understand how we typically go about making decisions, how our decisions are likely to be perceived by others, and the types of organizations in which we are most likely to be successful. Completing the inventory identified my dominant decision-making style as *behavioral*.

I tend to make decisions that stress the human aspects. I gather information by having empathy toward others, listening, and reading others' body language effectively, and tend to see things in right-or-wrong terms. My management style is supportive, encourages team building, and avoids conflicts. I prefer to work in environments that are well-designed to support members of the team, like having open-door policies. Some people are likely to see me as overly sensitive and unable to make hard decisions, such as disciplining wrongdoers.

Being a behavioral decision maker can be very effective at times, but I will also need to demonstrate an understanding of the financial and technical aspects of getting the job done. It seems few top managers have my style and may well regard me as a pushover unless I can develop these other skills.

■ ■ ■ ■ ■

CHAPTER 11

ALTERNATIVE METHODS OF ASSESSING STUDENT LEARNING

"Don't bore me," I tell my students. "Tell me something new. If you're bored by your own paper—bored with writing about the same old boring topics in the same old boring way—then I am bored ten times over. Surprise me. Tell me something new, and tell me in a new way."

—Ali Lichtenstein, Marlborough, New Hampshire

FOCUS QUESTIONS

- Why should you invest the extra effort required of authentic assessment?
- What types of learning lend themselves to being assessed in alternative formats?
- How should oral presentations be managed so that students' learning is maximized?
- What are the advantages of student journal writing and portfolios?

Can you recall a time when you came out of an examination thinking any of the following:

- "I knew so much more than what this test will show!"
- "Why didn't the test include more about _____, instead of asking for so much trivial information?"
- "This test only covered a very small part of what we've studied, but it's going to count for 25 percent of my final grade! That's crazy!"
- "The professor keeps talking about critical thinking skills, but then tests us with true/false and multiple-choice questions. Does that make sense?"

Years later, these sentiments are still being expressed on campuses across the country, largely because busy professors take their eye off of the real goal and allow it to be supplanted by responses to other pressures. A growing number of educators, including adjunct professors, are realizing that assessment should promote learning rather than just measure it (Wiggins, 1993).

Chapter 10 focused on helping you understand and develop more effective written examinations, an extremely valuable set of skills for a multitasking adjunct professor. However, the reality is that many of our courses' learning objectives are not assessed effectively through examinations, such as those within the affective and psychomotor domains and in many advanced courses that focus on the highest levels of Bloom's Taxonomy. Concurrently with the growth of the quality movement in business circles in the 1980s, leaders in higher education began to challenge traditional testing as disconnected from the ultimate goal of education to prepare students for real life (Huba & Freed, 2000). In real life, they say, graduates are seldom expected to choose from someone else's options but instead to identify their own options, analyze solutions from several perspectives, and orchestrate multidimensional strategies designed to solve those problems nearly every day of their lives (Brookhart, 1999).

In the past few years, consequently there has been a mushrooming interest in developing more genuine and effective ways of assessing student learning. Advocates of alternative assessment, sometimes called *authentic* or *genuine* assessment, view their approach as focusing more on student learning, rather than on teaching techniques. Chapter 8 addressed the paradigm of constructivist learning (i.e., rather than passively receiving knowledge from their professors, students are actually trying to make sense of new material by linking it with knowledge they already possess). Said another way, students *construct* new knowledge on the foundation that already exists within their individual learning systems. Advocates of alternative assessment speak of introductory courses developing a "scaffold" on which more advanced learning is built; they also speak of the need to link courses so that students avoid both gaps and excessive overlaps that foster demotivation to learn. All students, they say, should be encouraged to demonstrate their learning frequently, through a variety of authentic means in either real or realistic (simulated) settings. Alternative assessment attempts to place learning within a systems context, in which courses in a curriculum dovetail smoothly with each other, a perspective students often see and appreciate more readily than do professors invested in developing and refining a single course or two (Darling-Hammond & Falk, 1995).

To demonstrate the importance of the concepts in this chapter, I present you the following exercise, in which I ask you to actively take part rather than just reading the words:

1. Think about there being two kinds of knowledge, *declarative* and *procedural*. Declarative knowledge can be thought of as information that has component parts, or facts, concepts, ideas, and principles that students need to know. Its name is derived from the fact that students can declare it. A student might be able to declare names and dates pertinent to a period of history or definitions of words related to a course in biology. In an

economics course, he or she might be able to declare five reasons why the gross national product (GNP) could decline. Thinking of the discipline you teach, list in the box below some examples of declarative knowledge that your students need to know on completion of your course.

2. The second type of knowledge (for our purposes) is procedural knowledge, which can be defined as *skills, strategies,* and *processes* that students need to know *how to do*. Because it focuses on *procedures* that students must execute, it takes the name *procedural knowledge*. Examples of procedural knowledge would include the ability to deliver a persuasive presentation, calculate the force of an object of a given weight traveling at a stated speed, and so on. Focusing on your course, identify some examples of procedural knowledge that your students must master by the conclusion of your course.

3. In the matrix below, list the courses you most commonly teach, along with the approximate ratio of declarative knowledge and of procedural knowledge (those two columns should total 100).

   Now look at the last column and focus on the *assessment* you do in each class. What is the percentage of declarative knowledge assessed versus the percentage of procedural knowledge assessed? Enter this ratio in that last column.

Course Number/ Name	% Declarative Knowledge	% Procedural Knowledge	Assessment Ratio (Declarative:Procedural)

4. In the numerous workshops in which she has conducted this activity, Meggin McIntosh has found that most professors discover a major mismatch between what students need to know and how their learning is assessed. For example, a professor who teaches lower-division under-graduate courses commonly finds that his declarative percentage is 70 percent and his procedural percentage is 30 percent, but that his assessment ratio is 100:0. An upper-division professor might list her intended declarative knowledge as 40 percent and procedural knowledge as 60 percent and then find that her assessment ratio is 90:10. In both these cases, and the majority of others, there is too much assessment of declarative knowledge at the expense of the procedural knowledge that students most need from the course. Said another way, there is usually too much reliance on objective, easy-to-score examinations and too little demonstration of mastery of key processes by students (Lyons, McIntosh, & Kysilka, 2003).

Traditional paper-and-pencil objective tests are often quite appropriate for measuring students' learning of declarative knowledge and should be used for that purpose. However, if you, like most professors, are teaching to help students learn procedural knowledge as well as declarative, then you know the folly of genuinely measuring this on a selected response test.

Incorporating alternative assessment into your courses achieves the following objectives:

- Assesses student learning relative to critical objectives, particularly procedural ones, which are not measurable through traditional paper-and-pencil examinations
- Provides students alternative and often richer means to examining their own learning
- Helps students discover connections between what they are learning and real-world applications

- Fosters creative thinking and collaborative learning with their peers
- Increases the retention of learning because the performance is done in context
- Encourages self-reflection and self-evaluation

So, what alternatives do you have? There are many, but the ones featured in this chapter are performance assessment, oral presentations, writing assignments, portfolio assessment, and individual learning agreements.

PERFORMANCE ASSESSMENT

Across all disciplines, being able to "perform" is a major predictor of success, and is especially critical in an era of accountability. Professors working to prepare students for the knowledge age would do well to measure and most importantly provide genuine, specific, and timely feedback on their performances. Performance assessment can be defined as "an activity in which students construct responses, create products, or perform demonstrations to provide evidence of their knowledge and skills" (Hibbard et al., 1996, p. 277). Be aware, however, that constructing responses, creating products, or making demonstrations alone does not constitute performance assessment. Only when you build in an assessment tool and a feedback process do you have an alternative form of assessment (Macmillan, 1997).

What you might use as a focus for performance assessment is limited only by the nature of your discipline and your imagination. Students can write, draw, act, create, interview, dance, propose, prepare, build, evaluate, exhibit, and so on. Performance may also include providing assistance to a person or group in the community (e.g., service learning that was discussed in Chapter 8). Projects observed by the author include a videotaped orientation program for new employees in a human resource management course; a mock education summit with presentations by various stakeholders in a curriculum development course; and a costumed, choreographed skit in a leadership course. In each case, the students attained high levels of content mastery because of their voluntary investment of creative energies in a synergized effort with others (Danielson, 1996).

When designing a performance assessment, you should ask yourself the following:

- What do I want students to know and be able to do? (Review your course's learning objectives and identify those that cannot be measured using traditional examinations.)
- How will I know if they know and can do these things? (List the behaviors, the indicators, and/or the skills that you need to see in their performances.)
- Can I design an assessment for a real-world situation, or will I need to set up a mock situation? (Can marketing students design an advertising campaign

for a real community organization, or do you need to hypothesize an artificial company? Can engineering students build and patent an invention, or do you need to have them build a model of an existing invention?)

■ What are the standards by which I will judge the students' performance? (List the measurable criteria by which you will evaluate the students' work. What will be considered superior performance? Satisfactory? Unsatisfactory? The more specific you can make this, the better the work you will receive from students and the easier it will be for you to grade.)

■ What weight will I give each of the criteria? (Will the *content* of a writing assignment be worth more than the *conventions?* The design specifications worth more than the actual object? The number of people interviewed worth more than the depth of the interviews?)

Once you have resolved these questions, you can design the assessment instrument. Most important is to create a meaningful context for the assessment task, one that is based on the real experiences, issues, or problems that students face now or likely will in the future. Walvoord and Anderson (1998) recommend the use of the acronym AMPS when writing your assessment:

■ A = Audience. (Whom are the students to focus on as they do the work? Disadvantaged children living in government housing? Executives of global manufacturers of machine parts?)

■ M = Main point and purpose. (What is the reason for having students do this particular assessment task? Your main point may be defined in one sentence or a whole paragraph.)

■ P = Pattern and procedures. (What processes, steps, or parts do students need to include as they work through the assessment task? You want to be quite explicit on this portion. Do not assume that students know what you want. Tell them what you want and you are much more likely to get it.)

■ S = Standards and criteria. (Write a description of the ultimate product. Let students know how you are going to evaluate their work and at what level.)

James Popham (1999) identifies several factors to consider when determining which tasks you intend to use as performance assessment tasks:

■ *Generalizability.* Will the performance on this task be applicable to other tasks?

■ *Authenticity.* Is the task similar to what students might encounter in the real world rather than just a "classroom" task?

■ *Multiple foci.* Does the task measure more than one instructional objective?

■ *Teachability.* Will the students increase their proficiency in completing the task as a result of the teacher's instruction?

- *Fairness.* Does the task avoid bias based on student characteristics such as race, gender, socioeconomic level, or age?
- *Feasibility.* Can the task be reasonably accomplished with respect to time, cost, space, and/or equipment?
- *Scorability.* Will the task elicit student responses that are measurable?
- *Significance of the skill to be assessed.* Is the skill worth spending the time required for adequate performance assessment? (pp. 165–166)

An alternative form of assessment requires alternative modes of evaluation. Chapter 8 introduced the concept of *rubrics* as evaluative tools for student presentations. A rubric, you will recall, is a scoring device that lists and weights the criteria on which an activity will be evaluated. An effective rubric distinguishes between unsatisfactory, satisfactory, and excellent quality. The criteria on the rubric should address both content and presentation skills. Recall also that you must *share* your rubric with your students before they engage in their projects. Many professors find that it is valuable to have the students evaluate themselves using the rubric before submitting their work. Mature students' self-assessment is often quite close to the professor's assessment; less mature students often are not as clear on how they are performing relative to a standard.

Rubrics work best when they are appropriate for the task, easy to understand, and focused on the most important aspects of the project. When students understand your expectations, they can strive for quality rather than spending time guessing what you want. With a rubric, they can constantly evaluate their progress toward the known goal as they prepare their work.

From a more personal viewpoint, having your criteria clearly delineated in a rubric will usually prevent students from questioning their grades. Also, the rubric will help you focus your energy during scoring, fostering greater consistency of grading across projects and reducing total scoring time. Developing an effective rubric requires an initial investment of time, but you can leverage that investment by creating a template on which subsequent rubrics can be built. The consistency you gain, the time you save, and the trust you build with your students will make the effort to design the rubric more than worth it.

ORAL PRESENTATIONS

Perhaps one of the most wasted opportunities in higher education is the area of student oral presentations. Living it every day, we understand the inherent benefits of preparing a convincing argument, presenting it to others, and responding to their signals and questions. As a means of alternative assessment, oral presentations allow students to develop an array of other life skills that seemingly can be mastered through no other vehicle. Many professors do require students to make presentations, but unfortunately they provide such muddled expectations of student performance that they set some students up for failure. A few students will thrive in spite of their professors' poor handling of the process; many others, however, will become so unnerved that they will literally become sick. How can you make sure that you do not waste the opportunity to help students be successful?

First explain to students that they already do oral presentations every single day of their lives—presentations that are called by such innocuous names as *conversations*, *discussions*, and *interviews*. Second, to help students deliver a solo performance in front of the entire class, you can stair-step them to that point rather than tripping and shoving them into what they often perceive as a lake filled with alligators. For the first step, start small, by having students interview a single other student and then report the results, while seated, to the rest of the class. Move up to panel discussions, in which each student is expected to present a specifically selected portion of a broader topic. Spiral further upward by having students deliver an extemporaneous thirty-second response to a course topic drawn from a hat or shoebox. Finally, if you have provided ample verbal feedback (not just numerical scores) throughout the preliminary activities, and have given students a clear rubric well in advance, they can reach the high point of giving a short presentation in front of the class. Even those few experienced, high school debate team members you may have who are capable of delivering a moving presentation on the first day of class will benefit from the preliminary activities.

Some students seem to believe that oral presentations should be limited to speech classes, but the reality is that being well prepared to make presentations to others is an increasing requirement for success in today's society. This applies to health care professionals, administrators, training officers, managers, and so on. To leave your students unprepared would be to shirk your responsibility as an educator. With the development of students' speaking skills, as you well know, comes their growth in self-esteem, poise, and leadership. Appendix 11.1 provides a very basic rubric for guiding the planning of a presentation, delivering it effectively, and providing useful feedback. Think about using it to guide your development of a rubric that is a tighter fit with your students' learning objectives.

WRITING ASSIGNMENTS

One group of stakeholders increasingly significant in higher education is the employers of students, both before and after their graduation. Employers who reimburse students for their educational expenses and/or invest large sums of money to recruit the most capable graduates expect their employees to be able to write position papers, reports, and an array of other documents that communicate complex situations succinctly and accurately. One of employers' greatest criticisms of recent years has been that student writing skills have declined. Professors in fields other than the humanities often say, "Teaching students to write is the job of the composition instructors, not ours." The composition instructors say, "We do the best we can, but many students come to us with base-level writing skills far below what they need to be." With the challenges that elementary and secondary schools now face, students entering college in the foreseeable future are not likely to exhibit writing skills any better than those of the past decade. Admitting that students' writing skills have received less instructional attention than they should, many leading institutions are putting new emphasis in this area (Bartlett, 2003).

Over the past few years, a movement called *writing across the curriculum* has taken hold in some colleges and universities. Research in this area promises to help professors outside English departments attack the problem of poor student writing skills. In short, writing across the curriculum aims to have professors in all fields integrate more writing opportunities into their courses. In Chapter 10, I emphasized the inclusion of essay items on course examinations. This would be a start, but all professors must give additional writing assignments if students are to master the writing skills employers and other stakeholders expect.

As with oral presentations, you can build your students' writing skills step by step. "One-minute papers," in which students respond to one or two questions at the end of a class session, are recommended strongly by Robert Boice (2000) and others. Such brief writing assignments:

- Require students to reflect critically on content to which they have been exposed during the class session, perhaps synthesizing it with another concept
- Prompt students to pay closer attention and pose more pertinent questions
- Provide prompt feedback to the professor on the comprehension level of students

Journaling is an especially effective strategy for engaging students more deeply in writing and thinking activities. Since its emphasis is placed on depth and breadth of content written, rather than adherence to formal rules of writing, student journal writing is by nature more nonthreatening to students than their other writing assignments. In fact, students are encouraged by this activity to truly learn from their mistakes and underdeveloped responses to arrive at solutions that work for them. This strategy is especially effective with those whose development of language and critical thinking skills has lagged, including those whose first language is not English. In order to promote the steady acquisition of those skills, students' journal writing should be assessed frequently, but on its positives, not its shortcomings. Those who have researched the use of student journals differentiate several specific types.

Dialogue journals provide students the opportunity to have an ongoing conversation with the professor or perhaps another individual capable of modeling thinking and writing skills that would benefit the student. Students write journal entries about issues of personal concern; submit their journal for review and response; and then benefit from the personalized feedback, questions that spur further thought, and writing techniques by the more mature writer. Students typically improve their formal writing skills markedly and deepen their analysis of logical arguments through the nonjudgmental coaching approach that is inherent in this strategy.

Literary journals require students to maintain a written record of personal responses to key passages of assigned literature. This strategy encourages students to read more actively, respond to developments throughout the piece, and articulate those responses in personalized, coherent entries. They might write about their analysis of characters and those within their lives of whom they are reminded, connections between themes and exemplars in today's society, or even about the writer's style.

Subject journals foster students' mastery of key terminology and concepts. They might, for example, be encouraged to cite the differences between their understanding of what the textbook says about a particular topic with the explanation made in the professor's lecture. When submitted for review, the professor could help clarify the writer's questions but also monitor the totality of entries to identify patterns with the content with which a number of students are having difficulty. Clarification through appealing to different student learning styles might then be addressed at the following class meeting (Cobine, 1995).

Reflective journals are used by professors to foster stronger connections between course content and outside activities of students' lives (e.g., employment, service learning experiences, internships, and so on). An effective tool to jumpstart awareness of self-concept and the connection-building dynamic is the "I am from" exercise, popularized by Beverly Tatum, which is provided in Appendix 11.2. An approach to the reflective journal that the author has employed with meaningful success in leadership and management courses is requiring students to (1) reflect on a critical event related to the course, (2) identify a thought triggered by a theory or approach discussed in class, and (3) compose a two- to three-paragraph response that requires the student to more deeply integrate the issues. Mature students invariably resist the assignment initially but by halfway through the course begin to value the experience.

Regardless of the format, student journals help students see the larger picture, make connections between courses, and apply learning attained outside the classroom. If you experiment with employing student journals as a strategy, expect the unusual and be careful not to judge the students' reactions but to understand their feelings and interpretations. Although journaling between the student and the professor can be very revealing and meaningful in helping you understand your students, be aware that it requires time when done properly and thoughtfully by both the student and the professor. This can be mitigated however by providing a rubric to which entries should adhere and limiting the length and number of responses. Because what gets scored gets done, evaluate journals on an acceptable/unacceptable basis and the number of acceptable entries, (e.g., 15 acceptable entries out of 20 required equals 75%).

Many adjunct professors assign the types of papers that they experienced in their student days. Keeping with the same theme expressed earlier, always ensure that you develop measurable performance standards and provide students a rubric that weights those standards in a logical way. Not only will this approach save you time in scoring, but it will also lessen the chances of students' challenging their grade. In reality, can we truly say that a B+ we awarded last term would be exactly a B+ this term?

Students today are time pressured, so consider helping them develop their knowledge/process base by dividing major writing assignments into smaller segments. For example, you might require students to submit a proposal or a position statement, followed by an annotated bibliography, then a first draft. You would then score each component as a percentage of the overall grade of the entire assignment. This process enables you to not only provide feedback to your students in a timely and meaningful manner that they can use to make adjustments and improve the quality of their work but also saves you from having a mountain of unfamiliar papers to read and score within a short period. At each juncture, a section of the overall rubric should be employed to focus student efforts and more meaningful feedback. Improving students' writing deepens critical thinking skills—the mission of all in higher education.

PORTFOLIO ASSESSMENT

The use of portfolios in higher education is not a new phenomenon, at least in some fields. Having students create portfolios to present their ideas and accomplishments to prospective clients or employers has been standard practice for art departments, journalism schools, and marketing programs for decades. These portfolios are a means of demonstrating the quality and range of work produced by the student, just as a working artist or an advertising executive's portfolio showcases the quality and range of work he or she has produced.

In other fields, however, the use of portfolios is much more recent. Insightful educators in academia have realized that the portfolio concept is not just for artistic work, so they have come to use various types of portfolios as assessment tools in many areas of the curriculum. Portfolios can provide a professor with a body of student work that shows growth in performance, illustrates a range of quality, or demonstrates achievement of specific skills. Three basic forms of portfolios in use in higher education are working portfolios, showcase portfolios, and assessment portfolio (Danielson & Abristyn, 1997).

Working Portfolios

Working portfolios are designed to be ongoing interchanges between you and your students. Based on specific learning objectives, they serve as "holding tanks" for student work. By frequently examining their working portfolio, you can diagnose students' strengths and weaknesses and provide guidance for the students in how to improve or perfect their work. Working portfolios can also show you what you might need to emphasize in your teaching. Term papers or research projects are ideal candidates for inclusion in a working portfolio.

However, the main audience for the working portfolio is the student. With feedback from you, students can develop their reflective skills and learn to be self-evaluative by working on the projects within the portfolio. The substance of a working portfolio is specific content related to course learning objectives. As students complete their projects, they can move some of the pieces from the working portfolio to a showcase portfolio, discussed in the next section.

Working portfolios allow for iterative processes of instruction—that is, students complete an assignment, get feedback from you, make alterations, and resubmit the assignment for your input. This cycle can be repeated as often as necessary within your given time constraints. Ideally, each cycle increases the students' learning and their perceptions of their growth, both of which are important. Students usually view this iterative process as much more personalized than grades on a test, general statements made during a class about writing skills, and so on.

As you might imagine, reviewing working portfolios with students is a time-consuming process, and this must be taken into account before implementing this form of alternative assessment. I recommend that you use the working portfolio first with a very small class or a subset of a class who wants to explore this level of interaction and feedback. As with so many instructional techniques, this one will become easier as you gain experience with it.

Showcase Portfolios

Compiling a showcase portfolio is an especially rewarding experience for students involved in ongoing creative work. Including their best work in a showcase portfolio enables students to define who they are in terms of their culture, learning, experiences, and beliefs. Showcase portfolios can be used in just one class or an entire program. The latter case allows students to have a collection of their best work developed over several months or years. A program showcase portfolio can serve as a culminating activity for the program in lieu of, or in addition to, comprehensive examinations.

The audience for showcase portfolios includes the student, the faculty, and potential employers. The content may include projects created in class as well as projects done outside of the classroom environment, maybe for a part-time job or a volunteer experience. The main advantage of a showcase portfolio is that the students can select their best work from a variety of experiences to demonstrate their learning.

In addition to sharing showcase portfolios with potential employers, you can, with students' permission, display them to potential donors, prospective students and their families, or accrediting agencies. In imagining how to demonstrate what students have learned, contrast the impact of displaying a showcase portfolio to that of displaying student test scores. You will clearly appreciate the difference.

Assessment Portfolios

A third type of portfolio is the assessment portfolio, whose primary purpose is to document what the student learned during the course. Items in an assessment portfolio must be designed to help the student manifest learning related to specific course objectives defined in the syllabus. Assessment portfolios can be used to demonstrate mastery of both skills and content. The specific audience for the assessment portfolio is the teacher. The items in the portfolio must show that the student has achieved the intended learning outcomes of the class. An assessment portfolio can include lab activities, notes taken in class, artwork, drafts, book reviews, audio/video productions, or whatever else the teacher and student together feel serves to document learning of the course objectives.

The following three steps need to be followed when using assessment portfolios:

1. Identify what forms of procedural knowledge will be assessed through the portfolio process.
2. Design assessment tasks for the identified learning objectives.
3. Identify the criteria for each assessment task.

As with all types of assessment in the strategic classroom, students need to know the target—that is, they need to know what your standards are and how their work will be measured against those standards.

GENERAL SUGGESTIONS REGARDING PORTFOLIOS

James Popham (1999) suggests five steps necessary to assure quality portfolio assessment:

1. Recognize that students own their portfolios—that is, the material in the portfolios belongs to the students and is not merely "stuff" to be graded by you.

2. Help students determine what should be included in the various types of portfolios and clarify which type is being used, why, and how it will be used.
3. Select the criteria by which you and your students will judge the quality of the products within the portfolios.
4. Require students to continually evaluate their own products. One of the values of portfolio assessment is student self-reflection.
5. Schedule portfolio conferences with your students in which you can provide feedback on both the products and the self-assessments by the students.

Through portfolio assessment, students gain a more positive perception of themselves as learners, individuals, and ultimately, professionals ready for the world of work. As you examine individual portfolios, you get a more complete picture of your students as persons who are unique and have lives beyond the classroom.

Another important benefit of portfolio assessment is that, because they are participants in their own assessment, your students *share* in the responsibility for their learning. In this age of accountability, shared responsibility is a must. As students assume more of the responsibility for their own learning, you will have more time and energy to devote to other aspects of your instruction. Therefore, portfolio assessment can be a "win-win" situation for both you and your students.

Some of your students will have had experience with developing portfolios, but for others, it will be a brand-new experience. They will grow through the discomfort, but too much discomfort is counterproductive. Therefore, provide adequate explanation and support for students as they embark on this contemporary form of assessment.

Portfolio assessment is labor intensive and time consuming, so you may want to start on a small scale. Once you become comfortable with the process, you can expand your portfolio activities. It is much better to grow with the process than to start on a large scale, become frustrated, and then vow never to try it again. In many courses, it is too valuable an assessment tool to avoid.

Portfolios are one of the types of authentic assessment that do not just measure learning but also promote it. Wright, Knight, and Pomerleau and his colleagues (1999) posit that "professors and students are entering the age of 'portfolio careers,' in which continuing employment depends on the evidence that we provide of our wide range of skills, understanding, and qualities" (p. 89). It behooves us all to prepare our students to live in this age successfully.

INDIVIDUAL LEARNING AGREEMENTS

In Chapter 3, we addressed learning styles and generational influences that affect the capabilities of students within a given course section. If your ultimate goal is to maximize student learning, you should probably offer structured learning opportunities for doing so within each class you teach. I have successfully implemented Individual Learning Agreements as an assessment tool that contrasts with the contract grading approach that many professors have employed for years. Contract grading typically focuses on the quantity of work to be performed by students (e.g., reading a certain number of books or journal articles, writing a certain number of reviews) without measuring learning achievement (McKeachie, 2001). In contrast, Individual Learning Agreements provide options for achieving specific course learning objectives, consistent with students' unique learning strengths and interests.

An Individual Learning Agreement (a sample of which appears in Appendix 11.3) requires linkage with one or more objectives from the course syllabus, and then places the responsibility for proposing a suitable product on the student. Because students are empowered to use their own creativity, the energy they invest in the project will typically exceed that which they would apply to traditional textbook reading assignments and professor-constructed examinations. The Individual Learning Agreement approach emphasizes the "win-win" or "no deal" paradigm of Stephen Covey (1989). Attuned to this approach, students are encouraged to look for opportunities that not only satisfy a portion of their course grade but also provide potential benefits for their employer and their own career development, the interests of an organization to which they belong, the status of a relationship within their lives, and/or other areas of their lives. The "no deal" aspect of the paradigm requires the student and professor to arrive at a final agreement on the project through a set of proposals and counterproposals. It might seem that this process could become somewhat convoluted, but it rarely does.

The Individual Learning Agreement is usually designed to assess only a portion of a particular traditional or distance learning class, but it might be expanded to address the full range of learning objectives. The instructor should build in multiple opportunities for feedback to the student throughout the term, with the number of sessions dependent on the array of objectives and related factors of complexity. Individual Learning Agreements offer a significant opportunity to demonstrate accountability to a wide variety of stakeholders in the success of a particular student.

In *Millennials Rising: The Next Great Generation,* Neil Howe and William Strauss (2000) express great optimism about the most recent generation of students to enter college. Members of this generation, they say, will embrace strong values and thrive on giving back to their communities. Concurrently, the United States has failed to solve many of its problems to the satisfaction of those who remain marginalized by poverty, racism, homophobia, and so on. Professors in nearly any college course have a great opportunity to embrace service learning in a successful way. John Dewey (1916) viewed education as the most critical vehicle for the advancement of empowered citizens within democratic society. Why not research the needs in your area, connect with a community service organization that is doing really good work, and develop some opportunities for synergy that make a difference?

SUMMARY OF KEY POINTS

- Alternative assessment supports and reinforces student-directed learning.
- Alternative assessment is a strong bridge between schooling and real-world application.
- There are three major categories of alternative assessment—performance assessment, portfolio assessment, and Individual Learning Agreements.
- Genuine learning is achieved when students have choices in the development of assignments and the evaluations of those assignments.
- Portfolios can serve three different purposes: working, showcase, and assessment.
- Rubrics are effective tools to evaluate alternative assessment strategies.

THE FINAL WORD

"A part-time instructor for thirty years, I noticed long ago that most students just turn in their assignments to the instructor and let him or her decide what kind of grade to give it. Most of the time, students have no idea what the criteria are for any given graded item. After explaining the learning goals and completing instruction, I now have the students create a list of the criteria that will be used in the evaluation of their project. I believe that a good teacher doesn't always give students the correct answer, but gets students to ask the correct question. The students then participate more in their education, and after all, that is what being an educated person is all about."

—Raymond Lillback, Kirtland, Ohio

ORAL PRESENTATION RUBRIC MODEL

Student _____

Key dimensions of audience:

Goal of the presentation:

Opening *(___ points possible)* *Earned:*
Effectively gained audience attention? How?
Established common ground with audience? How?
Topic framed effectively? How?

Body of presentation *(___ points possible)* *Earned:*
Logical points developed to support goal of presentation?
Presentation remained focused on goal?
Presentation followed a logical sequence?
Sufficient evidence provided to support goal?

Closing *(___ points possible)* *Earned:*
Essential points summarized?
Audience asked to take a specific action?

Vocal qualities *(___ points possible)* *Earned:*
Volume? Rate?
Tone? Vocal variety?
Articulation? Energy?

Nonverbal qualities *(___ points possible)* *Earned:*
Facial expression? Eye contact?
Posture? Gestures?
Use of notes? Appropriate props, visual aids?

Additional comments:

I AM FROM EXERCISE

First paragraph focuses on things around the formative house and neighborhood.

Second paragraph focuses on those who helped shape values and beliefs in childhood.

Third paragraph focuses on food and its preparation methods within the formative home.

Fourth paragraph focuses on core beliefs and how, where they were honed.

I'm from haircuts sitting on books piled on the toilet and scootching my butt against the door while dad marks how much I've grown with a pencil. I'm from playing baseball for six straight hours and havin' so much dirt in my socks that the bath water got brown really quick, but Dennie had had his bath. I'm from cuttin' grass when it's 90 and sweltering, from stringin' beans while mom's cannin', and from playin' horse in the backyard 'til it gets cold and dark.

I'm from Uncle Ernie and Aunt Nan, and the Martins and their shiny cars. I'm from the Millers and the Powells and growing up on Savage Drive. I'm from the American Legion Post, cigarette smoke, and the talc on the bowling machine. I'm from Miss Leona, Miss Anderson, Miss Clary, Miss Kennedy, and the warehouse that was high school. I'm from teen club and cruising through Frisch's and hangin' out in front of the cafeteria before school.

I'm from fried chicken with mashed potatoes and milk gravy on Sunday afternoon. I'm from spaghetti and meatballs, chili with spaghetti, green onions from a glass of cold water in the middle of the table, meatloaf and corn on the cob, and fried pork chops and fried potatoes with onions. I'm from ice cold watermelon on the picnic table in the backyard, covered with this morning's paper.

I'm from say your prayers, tell her thank you, and hold the door for ladies. I'm from Onward Christian Soldiers and Jesus Tells Me This I Know. I'm from a Methodist mom and a Catholic dad, and I don't understand. And I'm from oh-so-close to Vietnam and how did I deserve to miss that plane?

LEARNING AGREEMENT PROPOSAL

Student _____

In satisfaction of the required project weighted at 20 percent of the final course grade in MAN 2021, during the Fall 20— term, I propose the following project that satisfies learning objective(s) _____ of the course syllabus:

Product to be delivered (e.g., videotape, written plan):

Approximate length:

Resources on which the development of this project will rely:

Detailed outline of project:

Due date of final project:

_____   _____
Student   Date submitted
____   I have reviewed and approve the project with conditions noted above, with
        the understanding that the student will schedule a progress meeting for the
        week(s) of _____, by returning a photocopy of this proposal.

____   I will accept the following counterproposal:

_____   _____
Merriam B. McAllister, Ph.D.   Date approved

CHAPTER 12

BRINGING YOUR COURSE TO AN EFFECTIVE CONCLUSION

"Today I will say good-bye to 75 students. But instead of closing the course, I have lately been trying to make the last session an opening, by emphasizing that the course content, pedagogy, and ideology will shape and feed students' future experiences, in academics, the workplace, and other aspects of their lives. As the term concludes, each course we teach should become a metamorphosis, an opening up, a new beginning, a fresh way of knowing, a revision of life."

—Greg Grewell, Tucson, Arizona

FOCUS QUESTIONS

- How do you maintain enthusiasm as the term draws to a close?
- How do you energize a class that seems to be losing its momentum?
- How do you manage the critical questions related to final student grades?
- What end-of-term procedures can you expect?

As discussed at the outset of the book, a growing number of stakeholders in higher education are emphasizing the need for colleges and universities to retain students throughout each course and on through completion of their degrees to employment and/or acceptance into higher levels of education. College graduates tend to lead far more productive lives than those who fall by the wayside. In the process, graduates contribute more significantly than noncompleters to the prestige of their institutions, as well as to the leadership and economic well-being of their communities. Education's stakeholders are coming to recognize that the success of individual students can be traced to individual classrooms, led by individual professors (Moxley, Najor-Durack, & Dumbrigue, 2001). It is incumbent on adjunct professors, fair or not, to be at least as, if not more, successful in this effort than faculty members who are protected by tenure.

Even if you have been careful to manage effectively the key retention mileposts within the term class—the first meeting, the first examination, and the midterm meeting—toward the end, you will most likely experience some loss of momentum. Given your and your students' multiple responsibilities outside the course, along with all the tasks, assessments, and projects related to the course, it is no wonder that mental fatigue starts to creep in. Your students need extra attention and support to ensure powerful sessions near the end of the semester. Blaming students for slacking off only tends to alienate them. Instead, work to remain on common ground with students, bring them in as problem solvers, and offer regular encouragement. This chapter will help you deal with issues that frequently arise as you seek to lead the class to the finish line.

ENERGIZING YOUR CLASS AS YOU APPROACH THE END

As you enter the last few weeks of the term, it is common for some students to demonstrate telltale signs of fatigue. These include:

- Expressing frustration over the collective demands of their professors
- Arriving late to or not showing up at all for class sessions
- Submitting assignments late and/or below acceptable standards
- Exhibiting a lack of mental engagement and/or participation in class discussions
- Demonstrating a decline in spontaneity and sense of humor

As in personal or work relationships, the key to solving this situation is proactive, positive communication. Assuming you have done most of the things previously recommended in the book, you are reasonably well positioned to achieve success if you will simply make it a point to talk with students.

If the problem is widespread, you might want to talk to the entire class at the beginning of a session. Otherwise, you will probably achieve better results in addressing students individually, before or after class. Be careful to use a constructive approach and a nonjudgmental tone of voice. Negative statements might create a self-fulfilling prophecy.

Straightforwardly share your concerns, identify some of the behaviors you have observed, and then provide students the opportunity to respond. They may tell you how much they enjoy the course and your instruction, but then describe the challenges they are experiencing. Demonstrate clearly again that you believe in "win-win" relationships and remind them of the goals you established together at the beginning of the course. Reinforce their commitment to those goals and confirm your determination to orchestrate a valuable learning experience for them. At the same time, let them know you are especially energized and will exceed their expectations if they will agree to finish the course strongly. If you are so inclined, share a motivational story or videotape clip, relative to the positive rewards that accrued to someone who overcame challenges to see a goal through to its conclusion (Duffy & Jones, 1995).

After the midpoint of the term, it is not uncommon for one or more students to stop coming to class altogether. Initially, you may want to just write these students off as having lost their commitment, but try to remember that they probably became overwhelmed by the multiple demands on their time. We suggest you telephone such students at home to encourage them to return and finish the course. Be prepared to hear a wide variety of excuses and comments, from the trivial to the serious. Listen genuinely and try to understand the students' perspectives. Quitting may be a pattern in their lives, a tactic often modeled for them. Be willing to offer some specific type of relief such as an extra tutoring session or an extension on an assignment, as well as some level of extra performance you would expect in return. Follow up with an e-mail message to reassure the student of the sincerity of your concern. Offering a lifeline to students demonstrates a level of concern, perhaps unexpected, to which many will respond in a very positive way.

In your closing class sessions, use the following responsive teaching techniques to energize the course:

- Adapt the learning environment by taking the class to a new meeting place: outside under a tree, to the student union, or someplace else that lends itself to rich communications.
- Shorten the length of lecture segments.
- Employ more cooperative learning activities, engaging students in the application of concepts addressed earlier in the course.
- Use appropriate audiovisual materials and action-based activities, which engage the minds of students.
- Schedule an upbeat guest speaker who will tie together several key concepts of the course, emphasizing the *analysis, synthesis,* and *evaluation* steps of Bloom's Taxonomy.
- Provide positive, timely, and specific feedback to students collectively and individually, as often as possible.

NOTE: The investment you make will counteract any drain you would feel at the end of the course if you did nothing.

One of the most effective ways to assess the energy in your classrooms, throughout the semester but particularly at the key retention mileposts, is to employ the Energy Quadrants strategy developed by Meggin McIntosh and displayed in Figure 12.1 (Lyons, McIntosh, & Kysilka, 2003).

High positive energy is present when both you and the students are in a state of upbeat, active involvement. Anyone who walks into a classroom that is in the high positive energy quadrant knows it; the overall feeling is, "Wow! There is great

FIGURE 12.1 Energy Quadrants

High Positive	High Negative
• Lots of involvement • Lots of productive interaction • Purposeful movement • Lots of learning	• Sarcasm • Frenetic, unorchestrated movement • Anger and resentment • Little desired learning
Low Positive	**Low Negative**
• Little movement or active involvement • Pondering and introspection • Focused energy • Learning can occur	• No energy • No movement • No thinking • No learning

stuff happening here." Students in this quadrant are intensely involved in a lab exercise, a small-group project, or experiential learning. The instructor strategically plans for this quadrant, although there are those rare, serendipitous occasions when high positive energy emerges seemingly on its own.

Low positive energy is present when the students and the instructor are engaged in thinking, working, reflecting, listening, observing, and so on. Observers who come into a classroom that is in the low positive energy quadrant may say, "Hmmmm, these students are 'into' what's happening here. This professor has really drawn them in." The strategic professor plans for periods of low positive energy that allow students to reflect on the learning, listen carefully to a musical piece or a literary selection, work intently with a partner on finding an answer, and so on. Low positive energy must be managed carefully, as we will discuss.

Low negative energy is likely to display itself at midterm and/or at the end of the semester. It generally appears when students are exhausted from staying up late working on projects, studying for tests, or working at outside jobs that leave them little time for rest or balance in their lives. Professors who sense that students are in the low negative energy quadrant must be proactive; otherwise no deep learning occurs. The strategic professor might elect to have students stand and do quick stretches or even sing and exercise, "Head, Shoulders, Knees, and Toes." Getting students to move and laugh helps bring up everyone's energy level. Knowing that students tend to fall into this quadrant during predictable times of the term, the strategic professor will plan for learning experiences that inspire more energy and movement than usual. It is also wise to increase the use of change-ups, as discussed in Chapter 7, during periods of low negative energy.

The last quadrant, which can appear at any time but which is to be guarded against at all costs, is the high negative energy quadrant. In this quadrant, students are mad, frustrated, and contentious; it is not a pretty sight. This quadrant can rear its ugly head in the following situations: (1) a project or examination is returned and the overall grades were far lower than students expected; (2) a cohort of students has just received bad news from another class or on another issue; (3) some type of bad news has just been delivered to a large group of students (e.g., a favorite professor has resigned, a key course has been eliminated, a new class has been added to the requirements). The best direction for a professor to take when a class is in the high negative energy quadrant is *out*. Get the students out of that quadrant as quickly as possible because teaching and learning cannot occur. One technique is to ask students to write a complaint on a piece of paper, then crumple it up, and throw it at the professor. The sight of a classroom full of paper wads being thrown at the professor is enough to make almost everyone laugh and to break the tension, which is the point. Another strategy is to give students each an envelope, ask them to write their concerns on a piece of paper and seal it inside, and then take up the envelopes, telling students you will return them at the end of class. Assure them that their concerns will still be there but that you need them to focus on what you are trying to teach them at this juncture. If you have established a proactive working relationship with your students, these sorts of techniques will work to refocus them on the task at hand—learning the content of the course.

Although some would read the description of the high positive energy quadrant and think, "That's what I want all the time," it quickly becomes apparent that neither the professor nor the students can maintain high positive energy throughout a whole class period and certainly not throughout an entire term; it would be too exhausting. Therefore, it is best to plan for periods of high positive energy interspersed with periods of low positive energy. Picture in your mind's eye undulating waves of high positive energy, low positive energy, high positive energy, and low positive energy, and you will get the desired rhythm. Early in the term, when students' energy is fairly high anyway, it is possible to spend long periods in low positive energy. Later in the semester, however, it is best to plan for fairly short periods of low positive energy along with fairly short periods of high positive energy.

If you embrace the concept of energy quadrants and are strategic in your management of these quadrants, you and your students will benefit from productive teaching and learning situations.

SUPPORTING YOUR STUDENTS' TIME AND PROJECT MANAGEMENT SKILLS

Having retained most of your students so far, you should be proactive in ensuring their completion of the course. As the term winds down, students are likely to find themselves overloaded with more than they can manage. Teaching your students basic time and project management skills will serve them not only in your course but also in other courses and throughout their lives. Here is one activity for guiding your students to a productive course conclusion:

1. Ask students to bring their calendars or planners to the next class, along with copies of their various course syllabi. Tell them that you are going to help them become more successful and less stressed as they complete the term.
2. At that class meeting, have each student make a master list of every single project that still needs to be completed before the end of the term. The list may include daily assignments, tests, lab reports, and papers. Some students may experience minor (or major) panic when they see everything written down, but assure them that the first step to getting the projects completed is to understand them more completely, in context.
3. Next, have them look through the list and determine the order in which the projects are due. They can put a "1" next to the first one that is due, a "2" next to the second one, and so on. At this time, there is no need to rewrite the list in order. Suggest, however, that they later redo their list on their own computers so that they can manipulate the projects easily; they can move the first one to the top, deleting it as it is completed, and so on.
4. Once each student has determined the order of the due dates, they need to look at the first project and list all of the tasks that comprise it. For example, if they have a paper due, they should write down the steps of choosing a topic, gathering research materials, and so on. Encourage them to break the project into small, bite-size pieces—the smaller the better.
5. Now it is time to schedule work on the individual tasks. Tell students that just as they schedule time for appointments (haircuts, visits to the doctor, and so on), they must also schedule time for the tasks they have listed. They should look at their calendar for the following week and make sure that every single "appointment" is scheduled in: classes, work, sleep, group meetings, and so on. Then they need to schedule their project tasks in the hours between the appointments. Tell them to schedule the first task of the first project first, the second task of the first project second, and so on.

There is no magic bullet for time management, but the process outlined above does give students a handle on what might otherwise be overwhelming at the end of a term. If they can get in the habit of listing all their projects, breaking the projects down into manageable pieces, scheduling the first ones first and the last ones last, and then start to work straight through their list and calendar, they will be amazed by their accomplishments and motivated to continue. One can hope that this motivation then carries them into future terms in which they manage their time well, right from the beginning.

DETERMINING FINAL COURSE GRADES

One of the thorniest challenges facing adjunct professors is the awarding of final course grades. On the one hand, most seek to establish and maintain a standard of true excellence for their courses, to motivate students to produce their best work, and to demonstrate traditional values to their colleagues. On the other hand, they know that students feel enormous pressure to get high grades. These pressures may come from family members, employers (many of whom offer tuition reimbursement but only if above-average grades are received), coaches who want students to maintain eligibility, or organizations that fund scholarships. Meanwhile, institutional leaders concerned about maintaining enrollments may, tacitly or explicitly, promote a "recruit, retain, and satisfy" mindset that puts pressure on adjunct professors to award higher grades than they believe are justified (Burke, 1998).

In recent years, grade inflation has permeated American higher education. External stakeholders perceive that they had to work harder to make a good grade than today's students do. Some college and university administrators have sought to curtail grade inflation, but others have turned a blind eye, believing it has at least a short-term positive impact on the retention of students. Many who study the situation agree that grade inflation is most prevalent at highly selective private colleges, although grades at public universities and less-selective institutions have risen also (Gose, 1997). Still, some adjunct professors bring to their teaching the grading standards they experienced as students, sometimes decades earlier. Against all of the factors in this contemporary context, it is critical to analyze your grading practices and adopt a strategy that is in the best long-term interests of students.

At many institutions, professors receive mixed messages about determining final course grades. A college may have a formal, written statement of academic freedom that says a professor is free, within reasonable parameters, to deliver instruction and assign grades according to his or her personal standards. Yet at the same time it may monitor final course grades. Instructors who assign a disproportionate number of low and/or high grades may be required to fill out a "grade justification" form on which they explain how they arrived at the range of scores within each class section. Instructors new to an institution would do well to investigate, understand, and adhere to the formal grading protocols of their institutions.

In addition, each institution—and often each department within the institution—has an informal grading system based on historical precedent, the philosophy of its leaders, the nature of the student body, and the philosophy of institutions to which students might matriculate. Expectations of parents and other stakeholder groups can contribute to this culture of grades. Whatever the pressures they feel, adjunct professors must think strategically and maintain long-term integrity. The new adjunct professor would be wise to solicit input on grading from a variety of sources.

After developing a full understanding of your institution's formal and informal practices, you must deal with the dynamics of your students in each particular class section. Many younger students were conditioned in high school to expect ample opportunities for extra credit, curving of grades, and in general, receiving higher grades than they might deserve. They may object to receiving low grades, yet may not invest the energy required to attain higher ones. It is your legitimate role to consistently explain your performance standards. Older students may take more responsibility for their grades and will often exert a great deal of effort to achieve one more point on a test or project. Invest the time to understand the range of attitudes on this critical issue.

Your personal discretion has been historically recognized and you are ultimately the standard setter for each course you teach. But always be able to justify your decisions logically. The key to managing final course grades lies in being consistent in your practices while remaining focused on the best long-term interests of your students and the communities to which they will advance.

CONDUCTING EFFECTIVE CLOSING CLASS MEETINGS

Nearly as much as the first class meeting, the final session or two can markedly affect the overall success of your course. The final examination and the course evaluations will reinforce each student's sense of personal achievement, attitude toward you, and valuation of the total learning experience. If you started your class with a bang, you certainly want to end it on an upbeat note. With so much riding on the outcome, it is critical to effectively manage each aspect of the closing class meetings. Be sure to:

- Prepare in advance an agenda of items you should address prior to final examination and course evaluation.
- Create a professional image within the classroom; students should see clean chalkboards, appropriately arranged desks, and orderly materials.
- Reduce the predictable tension of test taking by greeting students by name as they enter the classroom; be relaxed, but also be careful not to discount the importance of the examination.
- Thank students for their effort and reassure them that the energy they invested in the course will pay off; be as specific as possible about the likely benefits.
- Review key items from your agenda, such as the status of projects and papers students may have submitted, and when/how examination scores and final grades will be available.
- Encourage students' progress toward their educational goals by identifying the next logical course they should take within the curriculum. Be specific about course numbers, dates, time, and instructors.
- Identify the next course you expect to be teaching for the institution, provide a short overview, and encourage students to enroll. Provide a syllabus if possible.

- Outline the procedures for the course evaluation (your institution may require you to leave the room as students complete these; be sure to follow that and other rules).
- Ask for last-minute questions before distributing the final examination.
- Specify the procedures for submitting the examination, along with directions for picking up graded assignments.
- Note any typos or faulty language you may have caught in your final review of the examination.
- Avoid saying much more; students are usually anxious about the final examination and want to get on with it.
- Say a warm good-bye to each student as he or she leaves. If you can do so without disturbing any remaining test takers, share some bit of personalized, positive feedback about a well-done project or contribution to the class and wish the student well in future courses and beyond (Lyons, Kysilka, & Pawlas, 1999).

Former students tend to remember disproportionately the first thing we said to each of them individually and the closing statement we made as they left our class. Therefore, before your final class meeting, jot down one or two positive experiences or thoughts about each student (using your class roll as a guide). As individual students gather their belongings and bring you their final examination, check your notes, approach them, and warmly shake hands. Deliver the essence of your thoughts in a sincere, positive way. Some students may make wisecracks or express disdain (more out of discomfort than malice), but keep your own comments positive. If possible, walk them to the door and wish them well. Your sense of professionalism will likely make a lasting impression and contribute to your gaining a reputation that any adjunct professor would be proud to have circulating the campus.

Students vividly remember professors who go the extra mile to ensure they learned not only the subject matter but also the context into which that subject matter fits. By managing the last moments of the course effectively, you increase the likelihood that your students will be encouraged to pursue their educational goals even more passionately than before they enrolled in your course.

Once you have graded all assignments and final examinations, consider sending an e-mail to all students in each course section you teach. Your message might:

- Summarize the major accomplishments of the class in its entirety
- Present the range and average scores on the final examination and/or the overall course grades while guarding privacy (see the following section)
- Remind students of the logical courses for them to take next, as well as those that you will be teaching the following term.

- Invite them to continue to regard you as a mentor and to tell you, in person or through e-mail, about their challenges and progress
- Wish them well in their future endeavors

Often those in education, at all levels, celebrate the completion of a term with a social occasion of some sort. You should support such events and attend them, albeit briefly, when appropriate. However, as we noted earlier in this book, be leery about participating in any function whose activities might jeopardize your position (e.g., those at which alcohol is served). Seek to move end-of-course celebrations to places or times that can include everyone; most students will appreciate your integrity.

In the days following the conclusion of the course, do not be surprised if some of the more engaged students seek you out by telephone, e-mail, or in person to bring to closure their feelings about their experience with your course. Maintain a professional stance, but be assured that most efforts of students are genuine. Such encounters are among the most gratifying within the overall teaching experience, and they go a long way to helping you build a following that helps you achieve improved enrollments in future course sections.

SUBMITTING END-OF-TERM REPORTS

By the end of the term, your institution or department will have given you a final grade roll and most likely some standard report forms. Plan accordingly to submit these materials as early as possible; the last thing you want is for your reputation to be tainted by failing to "dot your i's." If any procedure is unclear, consult the faculty handbook, an office manager or secretary, or your instructional leader well in advance of the deadline.

A word about confidentiality: professors in the past commonly posted the names and final course grades on their office doors or some other accessible area. As noted earlier, the Federal Educational Rights and Privacy Act (FERPA), sometimes referred to as the *Buckley Amendment*, requires professors to maintain the privacy of information related to students, including grades. Grades, attendance records, and so on should be shared only with the student and those at your institution with a *legitimate* need to know. Make yourself aware of both your institution's policies and the law and then demonstrate that understanding while being firm and professional in dealing with requests for confidential information about individual students.

SUMMARY OF KEY POINTS

- Look for telltale signs of the loss of student momentum.
- Expect to invest class time into energizing students' progress toward the conclusion of your course.

- Remind students of the learning objectives you established together early in the course.
- Telephone students who stop coming to class.
- Calculate and monitor students' overall grades throughout the course.
- Become familiar with your department's and your institution's formal and informal policies regarding grade distribution.
- Carefully plan and conduct the closing meetings of the class.
- Submit end-of-term reports on time.
- Celebrate the achievements of your community of learners.
- Consistently maintain the confidentiality of students' grades and related information.

THE FINAL WORD

"I strive to conclude my courses on a celebratory note. On many levels, college classes are difficult and demanding, and my classes are no exception. If my students and I feel that they accomplished any degree of learning or growth, then we have just cause for celebration. Throughout the semester, I hold periodic check-ins with individual students who may be struggling or who may have incomplete or missing work. During those check-ins, I offer students serious, ongoing motivation and suggestions to ensure that work is completed. Similarly, I encourage and offer strategies to those struggling students who need to face and address their barriers to success. By doing whatever I can to reasonably meet their individual needs, concerns, and educational goals, I am able to facilitate student learning and success. On the last day of class, students bring food to share, and I sincerely congratulate them on their accomplishments. Often students report to their coursemates their surprise at how much they learned. These instructional strategies help ensure that the course comes to a natural and indeed celebratory close."

—Lori Schroeder, St. Paul, Minnesota

CHAPTER 13

EVALUATING
THE EFFECTIVENESS
OF YOUR TEACHING

"In any given course, there will likely be a student or two who knows as much or more than you about some critical topic. Telling your ego it's OK not to be the expert on everything will not only make the term go much smoother but helps you build a community of true learners within the class."

—Sarah Alden, Lebanon, New Hampshire

FOCUS QUESTIONS

- Why should you evaluate your performance informally throughout your courses?
- How can you effectively solicit meaningful feedback from students and colleagues?
- How should you manage the common procedures for end-of-term evaluation?
- Why should you cycle feedback into your continuously developing teaching style?

A major theme throughout this book has been that an adjunct professor's commitment to excellence is the single most important key to success. Such excellence requires careful planning, a thorough understanding of today's students, creativity, a willingness to try new teaching and learning methods, and consistently communicated high expectations of students. It also requires, as this chapter will address, continuous gathering of feedback and its objective analysis. Some adjunct professors feel threatened by many factors within the culture of higher education, and the increased call for accountability perhaps seems especially daunting to them. However, readers who have gotten this far in this book likely realize that continuous self-improvement is critical to success, whether you are an *aspiring academic, freelancer, career ender*, *specialist, expert*, or *professional*. Assuming ownership of one's own development is far preferable to expecting it to be enforced by others and lessens the chances of being blindsided by criticism of one's teaching. The expanding range of stakeholders in higher education in North America, focused on a global society and marketplace, has become increasingly concerned about effective, lifelong learning. As the business community has embraced a "quality movement," an array of governmental entities and the regional accrediting associations have mandated more genuine measurements of the output of higher education. Colleges and universities must—sometimes over the objections of academic traditionalists—be prepared to convincingly document the learning of their graduates. This emphasis has an effect on every professor—new or veteran, full time or adjunct. Readers of this book are likely to be the opinion leaders among their adjunct colleagues, so you might want to think through your possible response on this issue now.

Virtually all institutions of higher education now employ formal instructor evaluation procedures. Because they work more independently than most other categories of professionals, adjunct professors must "own" the process of ongoing data collection, analysis, and effective response. The best professors improve the outcomes of their teaching by continually focusing on which concepts or skills are most essential for students, regularly assessing student progress and identifying ways to more effectively facilitate student learning. Waiting passively for the end-of-term formal student evaluations or classroom observation by an instructional leader is quite risky. In nearly every case, employing proactive measures early in the term could have uncovered and led to corrections of ineffective practices and negative student perceptions (Diamond, 1998).

The literature of education differentiates *formative* from *summative* evaluation. For professors, *formative evaluation* provides immediate feedback while the course is still in progress and allows them to change their performance to increase effectiveness. Typically, formative evaluation methods are unofficial—that is, they are not recorded, made public, or used in formal decision making. Conversely, *summative evaluation* takes place at the conclusion of a course and thus gives professors no opportunity to improve performance within that particular term. Summative results are recorded and made known to appropriate officials for use in official decision making and are too frequently the sole basis on which an adjunct professor is assigned subsequent courses to teach. As originally conceived, the course evaluations that students completed were intended to be *formative* in nature. However, in recent years, they have become increasingly official. In fact, at some institutions, they have even been published for distribution to students and increasingly appear on one of the growing number of websites that respond to the consumer orientation of many students (Vargas, 2001).

CONDUCTING INFORMAL STUDENT EVALUATIONS

Most people are of two minds about being evaluated. They want genuine feedback to affirm their efficacy and provide data on which to strengthen their performance, but they also resent being judged. Those who have previously been disappointed by evaluative feedback and those who are new to a particular endeavor usually are the most resistant to initiating informal assessments. Thus, veteran adjunct professors who have read students' derogatory comments on formal evaluations sometimes find it easy to discount any form of feedback gathering and often declare that since students are incapable of providing meaningful feedback their input should have no impact. New professors, who often perceive great risk in asking for help from any stakeholder, are equally reluctant to solicit feedback proactively. Paradoxically, they are the ones who might benefit the most from being assessed several times, using different methods, because their teaching styles are still under development. On the opposite side, students completing evaluations are often reluctant to provide meaningful evaluative data for fear of being penalized in future dealings with the professor. Therefore, always make informal evaluations optional and anonymous, and you will find participation usually quite high.

If evaluation in your classroom is a natural, informal, ongoing component of your regular practices, the official ratings at the end of the term should hold no surprises when they are read. Most students will respond very positively to being asked to provide feedback on your teaching, so consider strongly adding this strategy to your practices. Even a good thing can be overdone (e.g., evaluating every class meeting), so think carefully about how often and in what forms to gather informal feedback. There are several key mileposts during the term, however, when evaluation is especially valuable and a natural fit with the rhythm of the course. These include the following:

- At the end of the first class meeting
- At the end of the third week of class
- At the time of, or immediately after, the first examination, or submission of first project
- At midterm
- Several weeks before the end of the term, when a formal process will shortly follow (Lyons, Kysilka, & Pawlas, 1999)

You probably noticed the high correlation with the retention mileposts discussed earlier. Gathering data at these times will enable you to discover problems before they become too difficult to overcome and identify where an extra investment of your classroom energy might have its greatest impact. Furthermore, it will encourage students to give you additional individualized feedback more frequently and reduce the chances that a student harboring malice will dump it on the end-of-term evaluation. In the following paragraphs, we will look more closely at each of the evaluation points suggested above.

The suggestions for conducting an effective first class meeting in Chapter 5 were also designed to engender an environment in which students feel comfortable providing useful feedback. Some additional ways to garner feedback at the end of the first class meeting include the following:

1. Ask students to respond to the following four stems:
   - I came expecting...
   - I got...
   - I am looking forward to...
   - I am hoping...
   You can imagine the wealth of information and insight that you will gather from the students! You are likely to feel affirmed and alerted, both of which are important as you make early adjustments.
2. Give students an index card and ask them to write down a question they wish you had answered in the first class meeting or a point that is still "muddy" to them (Angelo & Cross, 1993).
3. Put a "so far" graph on a piece of chart paper on the wall. Just before the end of class, give students colored adhesive dots and ask them to put their dots at the appropriate places on the graph. Mark off six to ten categories: "I love this class," "I am anxious about keeping up with the workload," "I am nervous about the content," "I think I already know most of this stuff," and so on. Because students are doing this as they leave, you can be attending to business at the front of the room and gather the chart paper just before you depart.

After the first three weeks of class, your students will have gotten a better sense of the class and how they can accommodate its demands into their lifestyles. They will have had an opportunity to see you in action, and they will better know you and your expectations. They also will have seen how the class typically flows, so their feedback at this point can be much more directed and specific than it was at the first class meeting. The following are some ideas you might use at this point:

1. *Thumbs up/thumbs down.* List aspects of the course that students will have experienced so far (e.g., small-group work, homework problem sets, guest speakers, lectures, textbook, and readings). Ask students to give each of the aspects a rating. A thumbs up is positive; a thumbs down is negative. You can compare and contrast the responses that you get and gain an overall sense from the class about what is going well and what is not going so well. You can always come back to the class for clarification if ratings were mixed.
2. *A mock evaluation.* Ask students the questions (or at least a few of the ones that you are most concerned about) that will appear on the end-of-term formal evaluation. Tell them that you are working to make this the best class possible and that their feedback is critical to your being able to accomplish your goal. Provide some instruction on the kinds of responses that are helpful.

3. *Learning logs.* Learning logs are full- or half-size sheets of paper with one question at the top. I use questions such as "What do you think the professor of this class believes about teaching and learning? How do you know?" and "What is the most surprising thing you have learned so far this semester? Explain." Immediately after students complete the learning log, the professor collects them to read for the feedback provided. In some cases, you may write comments on them before returning them to students, but most often, you are keeping them for the information provided and they are not returned to students.

Another natural milepost for seeking evaluation from students is either the session during which the first examination is administered or the first major assignment is submitted. The evaluation can be conducted during that class meeting or the one after when the graded items are returned. The former will tend to provide better feedback on the nature of the assignment, whereas the latter will yield more information on your grading procedures, so identify your objective clearly before conducting the exercise. Employing the same index card procedure used at the end of the first class meeting, write several items on the board, such as the following:

- What was your biggest challenge in completing this assignment (or preparing for this examination)?
- What would you do differently on this assignment (or test) if you could?
- Which resource (library, fellow student, other teacher) did you most rely on for help?
- How, without being shorter or easier, would you make the assignment (or test) be even more worthwhile?

You may get some creative excuses for what turned out to be less than exemplary work but as with the first informal evaluation, you probably will be surprised by the quality and quantity of feedback that this activity elicits. Having asked students for their feedback, you are obligated to do something with it, such as responding to their comments in an e-mail summary or opening the next class meeting with summary feedback and an opportunity for questions. While resisting the fleeting temptation to lower your standards, you might want to consider implementing some of the suggestions when you assign the next project or as you clarify expectations for the following examination.

The next strategic milepost for gathering informal feedback is at midterm. By that point, students likely will have completed several out-of-class assignments, one or more tests and/or quizzes, and several in-class activities. Having established a precedent through the first two informal evaluations, you are likely to sense that students are increasingly comfortable sharing their deeper feelings.

Employing a similar procedure as before, ask students to respond to several of the following:

- How do you feel about the learning environment created within the class?
- What have you most *benefited* from in the course to this point? Why?
- What could have been left out, and what could be added or modified? Why?
- How would you assess your own efforts to this point?
- On a scale of 1 (poor) to 10 (outstanding), what score would you now give the course? Why?

These questions should elicit your most detailed and deeply grounded responses to date, providing you with meaningful data on which to base changes in class procedures for the remainder of the term and for the next time you teach the course. Again, you should respond in some way to demonstrate your commitment to the concept of continuous improvement. You should also expect some critical comments by this point, which can be interpreted as strength as much as a weakness (your students are being honest with you). Resist the urge to strike back at the class over such comments or to single out a person who might have made them. Protect the integrity of the process by demonstrating a constructive attitude.

Stephen Brookfield (1995) suggests using a method called the *Critical Incident Questionnaire (CIQ)*. You can ask the following questions at most any point in the term from beginning to end. Brookfield suggests compiling the answers and sharing them with the class, in addition to using them for your own personal use:

1. At what moment in the class this week (term) did you feel most engaged with what was happening?
2. At what moment in the class this week (term) did you feel most distanced from what was happening?
3. What action that anyone (teacher or student) took in class this week (term) did you find most affirming and helpful?
4. What action that anyone (teacher or student) took in class this week (term) did you find most puzzling or confusing?
5. What about the class this week (term) surprised you most?

In addition to periodic feedback sessions, I have found it useful to solicit conversational feedback from key students throughout the term. The results of your first examination, coupled with volunteered student feedback, will help you identify those who are most invested in the course's outcome and most able to provide you effective feedback on your teaching performance. (In most classes, several students will fit these criteria, providing breadth of perspective that reduces the chances of making changes based on too small a sample.) Several times during the middle of the term, ask this group to stay at the end of class and help you assess your teaching strategies—that is, what worked especially well for them, and which, if any, created learning obstacles. Those teaching especially large classes have formalized this process somewhat by instituting "teaching circles," similar to focus groups, comprised of diverse student volunteers who meet with the professor at several junctures throughout the term.

Gathering feedback informally throughout the term will enable you to produce an ever richer learning experience for the overwhelming majority of your students and will make teaching far more rewarding for you. In addition, it will likely reduce the amount of negative feedback you would have otherwise received on the formal, end-of-the-term student evaluation that is so important to your career success and will put an upbeat tone in the voice of your instructional leader.

ARRANGING INFORMAL ASSESSMENTS BY COLLEAGUES

Another extremely valuable activity that you might employ is to invite an experienced instructor with whom you have developed rapport, perhaps your mentor or peer, to attend your class, observe your teaching, and give you feedback. You might ask your colleague to use a form such as the one in Appendix 13.2, or the official one from your department or institution, but be aware that some colleagues will resist such a degree of formality and would prefer to give you general written or verbal feedback.

Note that there is significant risk in this process unless you are absolutely comfortable with the person observing your teaching and that person likewise is comfortable playing this role. If the person you chose declines for perfectly understandable reasons, resist applying pressure of any kind. The simple fact that you invited him or her to participate in the process might plant a seed that will bear fruit at some later time. Such an informal assessment may be especially useful when there is a formal observation that you must respond to later; your colleague's observation can serve as a trial run. Therefore arrange it far enough in advance so that you have time to make changes based on its feedback (Chism, 1999).

VIDEOTAPING A CLASSROOM PRESENTATION

Having gathered data from students and perhaps a peer, you have no doubt begun to identify several significant tendencies in your teaching style. As a way of confirming these initial findings and/or gaining additional insights, you should consider viewing yourself in action—that is, on video. If your institution has a *teaching and learning center* or other faculty development entity (discussed in more detail in Chapter 14), you should to find out whether its staff can assist you in this. If you decide to videotape yourself, I would make several recommendations. First, be aware that the tape may give you more information than you can digest. You might therefore want to approach this self-assessment incrementally, by first audio-recording a session. An audiotape presents a narrower set of data; you can focus on your vocal style, timing, and ease in making transitions between segments of the class meeting. Reviewing this data first may enable you to focus more objectively on other components of your teaching effectiveness when you view the visual component.

For a videotaping session, you will need to recruit a camera operator in advance. I suggest you find a person somewhat familiar to your students but not a member of the class. A colleague from your department or a former student would be two possibilities. Tell your students about videotaping the class session in advance. Orchestrate it as a learning opportunity for them by explaining that you are dedicated to continually improving your performance, just as you hope they will be when they enter their professions. If students who normally sit on the front row are uncomfortable about being in the video, allow them to change seats. At the same time, you do want to have some student faces in your tape, so invite others to move up for this single session. Set up the camera and accessories well in advance of the class starting time and check that the lighting, sound, and framing will give you the quality of finished product you will need to assess the activity thoroughly. To minimize the impact on your students, you will not want to make more than one video during a given course, so make sure you get it right the first time.

You will probably want to view the finished video by yourself, at least the first time. I suggest that you use the self-assessment form in Appendix 13.1 to maximize your objectivity and minimize the emotionality of your review. Regardless of your perceptions, congratulate yourself on your courage in conducting an activity that many would not attempt; it says a great deal about your professional dedication. Keep the videotape and review it later, perhaps with the input of a colleague or mentor. After you have reflected on this first effort, consider conducting a second videotaping session in a different class.

GATHERING THE OFFICIAL RATINGS

At nearly every college and university, it has become common practice to ask students to evaluate instructor and course effectiveness at the conclusion of each term. Many adjunct professors dread this experience and make their negative opinions on the issue known to their peers and sometimes even to students. Remember, however, that your earlier efforts at informal evaluation—student input, peer review, self-assessment by audio- and videotape—have provided you a significant edge.

Although admittedly imperfect, the practice of conducting student evaluations is likely to take on even more significance to the marketplace and external stakeholders of your institutions. Instructional leaders rely on the results to make their best decisions, so to openly fault the process can set up some unhealthy interpersonal dynamics that you want to avoid. As stated earlier, the process especially affects course assignment decisions for adjunct professors. Therefore, I encourage you to view student evaluation in its most positive light—an opportunity to gain feedback that will enable you to improve the quality of your instruction in succeeding terms.

Most official student rating processes employ some type of standardized form, unique to a particular instructional unit or to the institution as a whole. The form typically contains a series of statements such as the following:

- The instructor was knowledgeable in the subject area.
- The instructor was well prepared for each class meeting.
- The instructor presented the material in a clearly understandable manner.
- The course examinations and other evaluative measures fairly and accurately assessed students' mastery of the course material.
- The methods of instruction were effective and appropriate for this course.
- The instructor used class time wisely, including starting and ending on time.

Typically, accompanying these is a Likert scale, which encompasses a continuum of agreement from perhaps *strongly agree* through *strongly disagree* or some similar system, to which numerical values can be applied. Such a design enables the calculation of an overall score and allows instructional leaders to make comparisons (e.g., an individual's score to the average within the department, the average of one instructor's scores within an academic year to another instructor's, and so on). It would be nice to say that all of these comparisons are made objectively and in a spirit of professionalism, but that statement cannot be defended. Most forms also include several open-ended questions that enable students to provide comments on a range of issues. Because the results of student evaluation are so critical, you would be very wise to obtain a copy of the form used in your teaching situation well in advance of its administration date and review it closely (Scriven, 1995).

To protect the anonymity of students and validity of results, most colleges and universities have developed strict procedures for administering student evaluations. These typically include:

- The scheduling of the activity at the close of the term
- The administration of the evaluation, and transport of forms, by someone other than the instructor (an administrator, peer teacher, or student)
- The instructor's leaving the classroom during the administration of the evaluation

- The availability of the completed forms for the professor to review only after the submission of final course grades or after a specific date

Many administrators view taking liberties with these procedures, even unintentionally, as a breach of ethical standards. Therefore, make sure you know exactly what to do before administering official student evaluations.

To achieve the goal of improving your teaching effectiveness, you must manage the evaluation session carefully. First, give students enough time to complete the form thoughtfully. Scheduling the evaluation as the last activity of a given class meeting or immediately before a timed final examination is likely to reduce the quality of student input. Introduce the activity professionally and emphasize its value. Finally, review the evaluation forms as soon as possible while the issues they raise are still fresh in your mind (Hilt, 2001).

You may be surprised the first few times you read the official evaluations. Students will sometimes rate your performance below what you believe it should be, or they may write comments that are blatantly unfair and perhaps not even true. This is one of the reasons it makes sense to help students understand which kinds of comments are constructive and which are not. Help them understand that critical statements should be delivered in the spirit of being helpful. Mean-spirited statements make it difficult for the professor to sort out his or her reaction to being attacked from any legitimate complaints or concerns (Weimer, 1990).

Another troubling aspect you may find is that different students' comments sometimes seem to be in direct conflict with each other. One student may praise your anecdotes as good ways of emphasizing points, whereas another may criticize them as tangential and irrelevant. There is no way to guarantee that all students will perceive your class the same way, so accept the process as useful while being less than perfect. The simple fact that students get such a significant voice makes a powerful statement about the culture of higher education in our society. Again, your efforts to informally gather evaluative data throughout the term will markedly reduce the type of negative feedback that sometimes overwhelms the unprepared adjunct professor.

Few people really enjoy being judged. However, your openness to student voices in the instructional process creates a positive dynamic that, when fully understood and appropriately managed, provides you the most effective and consistent source of data on which to improve your instruction (Marincovich, 1999).

PREPARING FOR FORMAL OBSERVATION/EVALUATION BY A DISCIPLINE LEADER

Although far less frequent than student evaluations of adjunct professors' teaching, observations by department chairs and instructional deans are being implemented at a growing number of colleges and universities. Although the disruptive nature of such observations makes it a less than perfect practice as well, you can manage it to effect beneficial outcomes, if you maintain a constructive perspective and employ sound strategies.

First, you must thoroughly understand the process employed in your teaching situation. Gather answers to as many of the following questions as possible:

- Who conducts the observation? Does the observer prefer to be introduced to the students or treated as a "fly on the wall?"
- Are the observations scheduled in advance, or are they spontaneous?
- If spontaneous, do they normally begin with the start of a class period?
- Do you have any say about which particular class meeting will be observed? For example, can you give the observer a list of classes when examinations or other activities that would create an inappropriate atmosphere are scheduled?
- Is a form used to guide the observation? If so, is a copy available for you to review in advance? (A copy of a typical observation form is found in Appendix 13.2.)
- What are the unwritten factors that contribute to the particular perspective of the person most likely to observe your teaching?
- How do the observation results factor into decisions that affect you later?
- Is a follow-up meeting with an instructional leader standard? How is it managed?

Besides helping you develop a grounded strategy for achieving success in the observation, knowing the answers to these and related questions will likely reduce the anxiety you may experience, as will having conducted other forms of assessment earlier.

Regardless of the combination of methods your institution uses to evaluate teaching performance, it is critical to demonstrate to instructional leaders that you are continuously improving your classroom performance. Even if you are not required to do so, seek a brief appointment to discuss results of formal procedures annually. If you are able to speak with your instructional leader, listen carefully to his or her counsel. In a professional manner, express your responses to the formal evaluation procedures, and to feedback gathered through the informal methods you used. Highlight some of the changes you intend to incorporate into future courses you might be assigned. Keep the session brief and focused, with the goal of simply reinforcing your commitment to excellence.

CONDUCTING A SELF-ASSESSMENT

The professor who regularly engages in systematic self-evaluation will unquestionably derive greater reward (and/or potentially less damage) from his or her institution's formal methods of evaluation. Regular self-evaluation is especially important early in your career as you seek to develop insights and skills to improve your teaching style (Centra, 1993).

One method for providing structure to an ongoing system of self-evaluation is to keep a journal, handwritten or electronic, in which you reflect on your teaching experiences. Regularly invest fifteen or twenty introspective minutes following each class meeting to process and write down the techniques and activities that drew a positive response from students. Word-processing software is especially convenient and effective in helping you get the words and tone just right and for making sure you can connect with what you have written later. Begin by reviewing the SWOT analysis and Personal Philosophy of Teaching that you developed earlier and note any significant changes in the perspective you held at that time. As the term evolves, proceed to focus on the strategies and events in class that students have indicated were especially effective. Focus especially on the key student retention mileposts and identify specific students that dropped your course. Ask yourself if there were reasons behind their decisions that you could have influenced more effectively. Examine your grade distribution on examinations. At the end of the term, seek data that would help you compare your final course grades to your past results or to the department average. Putting your thoughts into words and editing them to reflect your precise ideas and emotions enables you to develop more effective habits and in the process build confidence in your teaching performance (Fisch, 1996).

Invest the time to conduct a self-audit at the midpoint of your course, much the same way a business conducts an audit or a college conducts a self-study as a component of the accreditation process. As noted earlier, Appendix 13.1 is an instrument for guiding a self-assessment. Depending on your discipline, institution, or other circumstances, you might want to modify the instrument to more effectively target your goals. The key is to begin your self-assessment early in the term and to synthesize your findings with informal inputs from students and peers to develop a valid assessment of your strengths and needs at any particular point (Chism, 1999).

As you strive to help students master your course material, regularly query yourself using the following questions:

- Am I open to new ways of seeing issues, or do I have all of my answers already?
- Am I trying new things, or am I limited by old paradigms?
- Do I inspire my students or limit them?
- Do I validate others and myself, or do I disparage?
- Do I actively seek challenges, or am I comfortable with the status quo?
- Am I tenacious, or do I give in or give up?

- Am I described as enthusiastic or bland?
- Do I regularly demonstrate that I am a learner as well as a teacher?
- Am I setting new goals or wishing things would be different?

Consider asking yourself these questions at least once each term, and if significant, record your responses in your journal as a future reference. Decide whether you need to change direction or stay on course (Fink, 1995).

Finally, reflect on your experiences from the nonacademic world, in which motivated and competent young professionals sometimes see their careers stall in their tracks or even come to a crashing end. Often their downfall is due to a single offhand remark they made at a company function, or to an inappropriate tone of voice they used with a client who was unknowingly connected in some mysterious way to an executive of the company. Early in your adjunct teaching, you enter a new fishbowl. Unfortunately, you may at some point be judged by a remark or action taken out of context by an observer who communicates it through his or her personal filter to a key decision maker. I once knew a promising adjunct professor whose teaching at one institution was quietly terminated due largely to a harshly derogatory comment made in class about the local public school system. Unknown to the instructor at the time, the class included the spouse of a system administrator. The learning objectives of her course had nothing at all to do with the school system or anything else that justified the comment. To co-opt a familiar expression, adjunct professors were provided with two ears and only one mouth for a very good reason.

SUMMARY OF KEY POINTS

- Conduct informal student evaluations at these milestones: the end of the first class meeting, following the first examination or major assignment, and at midterm.
- Informal student evaluations provide you significant data on which to build your teaching style.
- Informal evaluations reduce potential problems that would otherwise show up in the formal end-of-term evaluation.
- Ask open-ended questions likely to solicit grounded responses.
- Involve peer instructors or your mentor in observing, videorecording, and evaluating your teaching.
- Early in the term, obtain copies of the student evaluation form and observation criteria form from your instructional leader.
- Follow guidelines precisely when administering formal student evaluations.
- Maintain a journal to self-evaluate your teaching experiences.

THE FINAL WORD

"Rather than measuring success by how much money I am paid, I evaluate success by the feedback my former students provide, especially those who go on to teach. Telling me how much they learned about themselves, about life, about teaching, as well as how much they use works read or insights and skills gained from their courses with me in their own teaching reminds me why I teach. There is no better affirmation or confirmation of success as a professor."

—Melinda Haag, Indianapolis, Indiana

CLASSROOM MANAGEMENT SELF-ASSESSMENT FORM

Recognizing that self-assessment is likely to be more deeply internalized than other forms of evaluation, I recommend that you periodically respond to the following questions and contemplate the impact of your answers on your classroom success.

1. How do I typically begin a session of my class?
   Possibilities: By reviewing key points from the previous session? By posing a rhetorical question? By citing a current event or telling a story?
2. How/where do I position myself within the classroom?
   Possibilities: Behind a lectern at the front of the room? Near a student's seating position? Against a table near the front of the room?
3. How do I typically move within the classroom?
   Possibilities: Not at all? Back and forth in front of the room? Around the perimeter?
4. Where are my eyes usually positioned?
   Possibilities: On my notes? On the board? On the back wall? Into students' eyes?
5. How do I facilitate students' visual processing of course material?
   Possibilities: Using PowerPoint or other presentation software? Writing key phrases on the board or on an overhead transparency in advance? As they are spoken? By displaying appropriate props?
6. How do I ask questions of students?
   Possibilities: Ask individual students likely to know the answer? Those unlikely to know the answer? To the class as a whole, deliberately selecting a random student to respond?
7. How often do I chuckle or smile in class?
   Possibilities: Seldom? When a student initiates something funny? Frequently?
8. How do I respond when students are inattentive?
   Possibilities: Lose my temper? Ignore it and plow on? Pose a non-judgmental question that engenders focus on the content issue?

9. How do I respond when students express opinions different from those I have expressed?
   Possibilities: Discount their opinions? Ask them to explain themselves so that I can find error in their logic? Orchestrate it into a teaching and learning moment?
10. How do I typically end a class session?
   Possibilities: Abruptly? By summarizing key points? By providing an overview of the following session?

MODEL TEACHING
OBSERVATION WORKSHEET

Professor: Date: Room:

Course Title: Time:

Course ID#:   Number of Students Present:

Enter objective observations that address each of the following questions:

1. Visual impact created?

2. Devices/techniques used to introduce the lesson?

3. How was student participation elicited?

4. How was the professor's expertise demonstrated?

5. Teaching methods used?

6. How did the professor contribute energy to the class?

7. Methods of verbal communications?

8. Nonverbal communications?

9. Classroom management techniques?

10. Nature and amount of support materials employed?

Comments on factors other than those above:

CHAPTER 14

MANAGING YOUR ADJUNCT CAREER

"Make managing your career job #1, and take advantage of any and all training opportunities offered by the institutions where you teach. Especially helpful are opportunities that lead to certifications and mentoring, which provide you with strategies for managing classroom and organization challenges, including how to locate resources for your students and your courses."

—Joan Gilson, PhD, Overland Park, Kansas

FOCUS QUESTIONS

- How can you keep your teaching focused?
- What are some specific steps you can take to set yourself apart from others?
- How can you effectively leverage your teaching success for greater rewards?
- How do you define success within the adjunct teaching environment?

Ideally you approach the conclusion of this book with a renewed sense of yourself as a significant contributor to the learning of your students and a refreshed sense of the possibilities for genuinely excellent teaching. I also hope that you have acquired some new insights and strategies for recruiting students who might not otherwise enroll in your class sections, more effectively retaining those who do enroll, and playing a proactive role in helping students complete their degrees and move to the next level such as graduate programs or careers that dovetail with their academic work. Again, stakeholders of your institution expect no less. Improved results in each of these arenas will markedly improve your career success as an adjunct professor (Vargas, 2001).

It would be wonderful if those things alone were enough to achieve the mission for your teaching that you developed earlier. They are not. Many aspiring academics and other adjunct professors report that they have done most of those things but have fallen short of their dreams about teaching college. Like our great grandparents told us about using the hand pump on their farms, we cannot stop pumping just as the desired reward is about to make it to the surface or else all of our earlier efforts are lost. This final chapter seeks to provide you the insights needed to close the circle and achieve your dream. We will approach that objective purposely, through evaluation and analysis.

REVISITING YOUR MASTER STRATEGY

Chapter 1 highlighted research on adjunct professors, largely through the typology of Judith Gappa and David Leslie (1993) that yielded *aspiring academics, freelancers, career enders, specialists, experts,* or *professionals.* Your were likely able to identify with this grouping quite well, but also realized that your current type is perhaps no longer what it once was or what it might be in the future. You hopefully proceeded to develop a mission statement and personal philosophy of teaching and assess your individual teaching style before developing a grounded master strategy to direct your career. (If you did not do one or more of these, you might see value in doing it now.) The simple truth is we cannot judge where we are effectively if we do not lay out a destination and itinerary for getting there (Haugen, 2000).

At this point, it would be useful to ask yourself some additional reflective questions, including, but certainly not limited to, the following:

- What additional advantages or obstacles to teaching as an adjunct professor have surfaced in your mind since developing your master strategy?
- Does your master strategy look more or less attainable than when you developed it?
- Assuming you have taught between starting your reading of the book and now, do you perceive that your rewards have been different since then? How?
- To what factors is that change attributable?
- Do you need to modify your master strategy? Toss it out and start again? Move ahead as it is, even more confident that you are on the right path for you?

Some very individualized responses will arise, as will clustered responses for specific categories. For example, many *aspiring academics* might well note that their earlier career goals were unrealistic in today's environment and that for their own well being, they need to stop viewing themselves as victims of the system. Many *career enders* might well note that their expectations before beginning their teaching were not proving to match the reality of the classroom, and thus a very different paradigm must be adopted (Longmate & Cosco, 2002).

Through interviews with hundreds of adjuncts across all four of the categories I, however, have discovered more commonalities than differences between adjunct professors who achieve their teaching objectives. This closing chapter will focus in depth on each of those common areas.

BUILDING A FOLLOWING AMONG STUDENTS

Professionals in most fields have long recognized the rewards of networking with a broad spectrum of other professionals. Often because of inherent shyness, some academics, both full- and part-time, decry the strategy of building strong interpersonal relationships as being ingenuine, and link such efforts closely with unscrupulous businesspeople. No one would argue that authenticity is rare in many arenas of our society today, but recent research builds a strong case for viewing a lack of authenticity with professional networking as stereotypical (Goleman, 2002).

In interviews with successful adjunct professors, I have found that those who report the greatest personal rewards regularly focus on and make continuous progress toward building a following among present and prospective students, as well as those with the influence to direct students toward their courses. If implementing some of this book's recommendations has already helped you improve the quality of your relationships with students, you have taken the first step in this process. Without that quality, additional strategies will be extremely limited in their potential impact (Wellman, 2000).

Reputations are important and get built whether you want them to be or not. To foster the type of reputation you desire and one that genuinely reflects your character, regularly conduct the sorts of self-analysis discussed at several points in this book, then consistently manage your teaching activities to foster the trust and dependability that most good students want. If you teach in a behemoth department on a large campus, it may take some time for you to build your reputation, but at a medium-size or small campus, it is remarkable how rapidly you can become known. Negative reputations are built very quickly and students love to feed the rumor mill about ineffective professors, so always be careful about taking shortcuts. Your excellent teaching will slowly but surely result in tales that become part of your department's culture—a very special reward for any adjunct professor. You can continue to build your student following by taking some of these positive steps:

- Underpromise and overdeliver. Return graded assignments by the following class meeting whenever possible, which means carefully planning your schedule to allow for grading time soon after assignments are submitted. Tell students that telephone calls will be returned within forty-eight hours but get back to them sooner. Send helpful e-mail messages and include links to helpful on-line resources. Attend your students' performances (theater, sports, music) and congratulate them on their successes.

- Come to class impeccably organized and prepared, belying the stereotype students have unfortunately developed of professors. You will immediately distinguish yourself in the students' minds, and they will remember.
- File your completed student profile forms and refer back to them both during and after the course to refresh your recall of names and faces, identify recruits for courses you might be assigned, and so on. Being known as "the professor who remembered my name when she saw me at the supermarket" is a powerful tool for building your student following.
- Become involved, if only in a small way, in some aspect of student life on campus. Choose an area in which you have expertise to share, in which you would like to become more knowledgeable, and/or in which a large number of your students are involved. The possibilities include sports teams, arts organizations, student chapters of professional associations, and others. Once involved, remain involved for the entire academic year, then evaluate your rewards afterward. Such involvement fosters a broader, deeper knowledge of students, perhaps over generations. Students who have a positive experience often encourage younger siblings and friends to attend the same school and become involved in similar aspects of campus life, so your sphere of influence may very well expand exponentially.
- Become involved in your community, outside the institution. Some adjunct professors tie such involvement to their discipline, whereas others pursue their avocations. As you participate, people learn about you in a richer way and you develop connections to all sorts of potential rewards. When they hear you speak informally about your teaching, they may begin to refer students to you. Over time, if you are perceived as approachable and invested in others' success, your influence will expand.
- Volunteer to speak at meetings of civic and service organizations, which love to showcase such expertise at their meetings. These groups include among their members professionals from an array of fields who generally like to serve as contacts to a larger portion of the community. Volunteer for your institution's speaker listing that is sent to service clubs and the local media. If such a listing is not available, contact the clubs in your area individually, letting them know the range of topics you feel comfortable addressing at their meetings.

Although some of these suggestions might lie outside your comfort zone, consider that the zone of discomfort is where the real learning begins. Your reward will come not only from the activities themselves but also from the following you will build. It is not unlike starting an exercise program, which may cause aches and provide only limited benefits at first but will soon show itself to be making huge contributions to your health. Eventually, you would no more miss your regular exercise session than you would miss eating an elegantly prepared meal or taking part in some other rewarding activity. Once you begin to have students drop by before class to tell you that they have heard good things about you, the parade will become a steady one. Someone in the community may seek you out to tell you about her son, who was one of your students and now recommends your class to his friends.

In formulating a longer-term strategy for building a following, choose one or two local schools from which your institution draws its students. Through your growing campus contacts, identify some of the leading teachers at those schools and call or e-mail them to see if it would be possible for you to visit in the near future. When making presentations, ask the teacher about serving as a judge for a public-speaking contest, a scholarship competition, or some other activity that is a close match with your expertise. Afterward, be sure to send the teacher a thank-you note with a reminder.

Developing a following among students is less about "popularity" than it is about professional respect. As an adjunct professor, you largely teach others who you are. When people do your position justice, word gets around, as it should. You must be especially vigilant regarding your teaching reputation—the portion that spreads the fastest around campus and is noted by members of the public, who often are unaware of all the other contributions you make. View yourself as a teaching professor at all times and be watchful of the messages you are sending. The result will be a professional following based on respect.

LEVERAGING YOUR INSTITUTION'S FACULTY DEVELOPMENT RESOURCES

At least partly due to the burgeoning calls for accountability from stakeholders, an increasing number of colleges and universities have initiated some type of faculty development entity on their campuses, often under the mantel "teaching and learning center" or a similar title. They range from small, part-time, shoestring-budget efforts managed by one or a few faculty members with a keen interest in teaching, to large, substantially funded ones managed by a full-time director with an array of additional staff members. Regardless of the size, these programs are worth exploring, both as a client of services and a contributor to their offerings. If a faculty development program is available at your campus, investigate it and consider making a commitment to it for at least one year so that you can experience the wide range of activities it offers and find a good fit for your expertise.

The first step will be to contact the program (many have websites) to find out what it encompasses. Most teaching and learning centers offer classes and workshops for professors that run the gamut from informal, brown-bag lunch sessions on a variety of topics to week-long, or even semester-long, sessions on specific topics related to instruction. You may be the only adjunct professor in attendance, but remember, you will always learn something of value to your teaching. Although it requires an investment of time to participate in these activities, there will always be a return in new skills and new colleagues.

After taking part in one or more of the classes, volunteer to offer one yourself for other adjunct professors. Are your student retention results significantly better than the institution's as a whole? Why? Others would like to know. Do you have good organizational tips from which others could benefit? Do your students consistently comment on how difficult, but fair, your tests are? Have you achieved a high degree of active student participation in your cooperative learning sessions? Think about something you do that others could learn from and offer to share your skill or knowledge, either in a workshop, during a brown-bag lunch session, or as part of a panel program on good instruction.

Often centers promote collegial relationships where members serve as consultants to each other in a topic of their greatest expertise. By participating and having a faculty consultant observe your class and introducing the person and explaining why you have asked him or her to visit, you demonstrate to students that you are focused on your instruction and that you want to do the best job possible. Many students are quite surprised by this, and your stature increases in their eyes. After the consultant's initial visit, you might want to record a teaching demonstration or two and debrief it afterward as suggested in Chapter 13.

Find out if your teaching/learning center has a professional library, a sort of one-stop shop for books, journals, and articles focused on teaching college. In addition to checking out the materials, it is often wise to ask someone in the center for recommendations in a particular subject area. Your use of the services of your teaching/learning center will be repaid many times over, both because you can become more efficient at what you do and because your impact on students is multiplied as you become more effective.

DEVELOPING MUTUALLY BENEFICIAL MENTORING RELATIONSHIPS

As much as you may want to keep your own counsel related to your teaching, it is valuable to have at least one trusted colleague with whom you can regularly discuss issues related to instruction. A few teaching and learning centers sponsor these, but most do not, so initiate an informal relationship yourself, with a veteran adjunct professor or a full-time professor whose background fits well with your course assignments. Talking of each other's successes with another professor can help you identify ways in which to grow your career.

Likewise, you will have frustrations and disappointments with which nonprofessors cannot empathize. It is important to have someone who knows the frustration that comes with teaching when it feels as if no one wants to learn— someone who can offer a supportive, listening ear while you vent but who can also help you figure out what your next step will be. While there are some who will listen to the venting and join right in—eventually putting all the blame back on the students—there are others who will help you get to a more constructive place so that you stay positive in your determination to help students learn.

The person who shares your interest in teaching might be in your department or college, across campus, or elsewhere in the country or the world. In this age of around-the-clock communication, it really does not matter where the person is located. You can e-mail professors around the world or join listservs that will help generate new insights and build collegiality (Baiocco and DeWaters, 1998).

You should let one of these informal relationships develop further. *Mentoring* can be defined as the process, formal or informal, in which a knowledgeable, skilled veteran (usually not a direct supervisor) guides a relative novice through the maze of an organization. Thus the *mentee* or *protégé* develops self-confidence and develops productivity faster and more effectively than he or she could do alone. Mentors provide growth opportunities unavailable anyplace else. Instructional leaders at an increasing number of institutions see mentoring as a critical tool for maximizing the effectiveness of adjunct faculty members and have developed formalized programs. Although there is a variety of roles that a mentor may serve, for the purpose of this section, we are focusing on a mentoring relationship concentrated on improving instruction by the professor, thereby resulting in increased learning by students.

A successful mentoring relationship must be built on common interests, be nurtured by both parties, and offer mutual benefits. The common benefits to the protégé typically include the following:

- A grounded orientation to the institution, division, or department
- Information for developing an enriched perspective of the organization's mission
- Encouragement at critical times
- An effective model for accepted organizational behavior
- Introductions to others, both on and off campus, who might provide insights and support
- Increased exposure and visibility
- Support during critical situations
- Increased self-awareness
- Feedback on teaching performance without the judgment associated with the formalized work relationship (i.e., supervisor/subordinate)

For the mentor, potential benefits include the following:

- Developing a dependable, crucial support resource
- Achieving vicariously through the accomplishments of the protégé

- Being valued as a knowledgeable person
- Receiving a fresh, grounded perspective on key issues
- Gaining the opportunity to repay past debts
- Developing a replacement when career advancement is sought

In short, an effective mentoring relationship must provide benefits that are perceived as equitable and significant to both parties. Long-lasting mentoring relationships are built on mutual respect and positive interdependence. Stephen Covey (1989) refers to this as maintaining a positive "emotional bank account," and creating "win-win or no deal" interactions.

Effective mentors are invested in developing the potential of others. They are open-minded, patient, nonjudgmental, and unselfish. Perhaps most important, they are effective listeners. They understand the need for their institution to invest in its future, and they are comfortable with giving the credit for success to the *protégé*. They understand that the *protégé* is likely to need help when they themselves are busy, but they are willing to subordinate their own needs at such times. They avoid giving advice and instead simply emphasize their more grounded information and different perspectives on key issues. Mentors realize their role does not include rescuing the *protégé* from his own folly.

Effective *protégés* reflect many similar characteristics, including being open to constructive feedback (i.e., being a bit thick-skinned), willing to critically examine old beliefs and try new ideas, and able to accept full responsibility for their own success. They view their mentors as resources with whom they must initiate communications and do not expect mentors to rescue them. They regularly demonstrate appreciation.

That being said, I would also encourage you to extend yourself somewhat by not trying to link up with a mentor or a *protégé* who is just like you. Since your goal in fostering the relationship is to grow professionally, you should seek out someone who is quite different from you in age, culture, national origin, perspective, or some other significant way. This means there will be times when the two of you butt heads on issues, but when you work through this confrontation, the result is growth for both of you.

To manage that growth and ensure that unreasonable expectations are avoided, develop a written agreement that addresses your individual and mutual needs. A model for your consideration can be found in Appendix 14.1. If you find that model too legalistic, consider a didactic e-mail decision that begins with a proposal of expectations of the mentoring arrangements. Through the interchange, you can hammer out an agreement with your potential partner that provides the psychological boundaries your relationship is likely to require as it evolves.

Mentoring is only one tool within a comprehensive program of professional development. Research shows that effective mentoring must build on an existing knowledge base held by the *protégé*. In other words, the mentor cannot be successful and feel rewarded when mentoring is the only tool being employed by the *protégé* (Lyons, 1996). Still, it is a powerful tool. The highs and lows of teaching require reflective brainpower. In this case, two heads are better than one (Zachary, 2000).

AVOIDING CAMPUS POLITICAL CONFLICTS

The history of higher education is replete with stories of politicized relationships between academics from the turn of the nineteenth century until today (Kors & Silverglate, 1999). In recent years, adjunct professors on some campuses have found themselves in an increasingly volatile maelstrom with traditional, tenured professors and administrators. In their landmark book *The Invisible Faculty* (1993), Judith Gappa and David Leslie cited their finding of a two-tiered faculty structure at the institutions they studied, in which tenure track faculty are treated as partners, and adjunct faculty members are denied privileges and are subject to closer supervision. Since their research was published, the periodicals of higher education have featured frequent stories of legal actions and other conflicts involving adjunct faculty members, in California, Michigan, New Hampshire, and Washington state, as well as other locations within North America (Fogg, 2002; Smallwood, 2002). As is often the case, polarization has set in between some adjunct faculty members, especially *aspiring academics* that are most dependent on their teaching salaries to sustain themselves and tenured faculty who choose to discount their role and standing.

On some campuses the relationship between those who should ideally treat each other as colleagues has evolved into an adversarial culture. In those cases, a number of adjunct professors have perceived widespread unprofessional treatment from their tenured colleagues (Carroll, 2001a), and have come to feel marginalized and even victimized (Dubson, 2002). Those factors have fueled in some the determination to build and present their case for legitimacy and fair treatment to those with the power to make changes. At the same time, leaders at a growing number of institutions have looked ahead, more precisely identified the issues involved in assimilating adjunct faculty members, and begun to move their cultures toward greater collegiality (Lyons, 2001).

Sometimes related to the larger issue, sometimes not, adjunct professors have at times become actively involved in institutional and departmental politics—perhaps more involved than was prudent. Although individual activities are very much a personal matter, adjunct professors must be vigilant in evaluating the potential benefits and losses from involving themselves in campus political actions, especially when there appear to be some indicators of break-throughs in the treatment of part-time faculty members. By nature, adjunct pro-fessors are vulnerable. At most colleges and universities, their greatest security lies in the ability to foster the same or higher level of learning in students as their tenured colleagues, provide a breadth of understanding for which tenured faculty are ill-prepared, and achieve a following among students that "wow" everyone. Until a revolution occurs, the wisest strategy might lie in achieving small victories, and avoiding those political minefields that have the potential to sabotage your teaching (Greive & Worden, 2000).

DEVELOPING A COLLECTION OF TEACHING AND LEARNING RESOURCES

Facing fierce market competition, vendors of all sorts of educational materials are providing valuable resources (many online) to support the professors and students who use or might someday use their products—most free of additional cost. Many of these resources are developed using contemporary pedagogical research and can contribute much to the adjunct professor's effectiveness and students' achievement. Besides discipline-specific materials however, you owe it to yourself and your students to also stay current with teaching methods and strategies, as you are doing by reading and completing the exercises within this book.

Twenty years ago, a professor had to scrounge around to even *find* books and articles about college teaching. Today it seems that a new one is published each week and the choices are excellent. Although there may be a bit of hyperbole in that claim, the truth is that the growing emphasis on good instruction in higher education, not coincidentally related to the growth in the accountability movement, has spawned a proliferation of publications supporting instruction at the college level (Ruben, 2001).

Some of these books are meant to be read cover to cover, whereas most others are designed to allow the busy professor to delve into one chapter or topic at a time. Keep resource materials of interest on a nearby shelf so that if you have a spare moment (waiting for a student to show up for an appointment, standing by on hold during a phone call) and you need a burst of inspiration or if the answer to a difficult teaching problem is eluding you, you can grab a book or article to read for ideas. There will be some books that you eventually decide to purchase for your own library, but most college and university libraries are pleased to purchase materials on request. If you have not done so already, let Amazon.com, BarnesandNoble.com, or your local bookstore know that you have an interest in college teaching, and you can be alerted to new books by e-mail. The bibliography in this book provides an excellent starting point for your reading list.

An exploding amount of free teaching and learning information has become available online. Websites are being launched daily by individual institutions that offer useful information to the continuously developing learning facilitator. An array of resources also can be accessed through my website at http://www.developfaculty.com.

DEVELOPING YOUR TECHNOLOGICAL SAVVY

Throughout this book, especially in Chapter 9, I have emphasized the importance of infusing technology into your instruction to better engage students in their learning. The key to doing so is becoming as technologically savvy yourself as possible and then staying current. Those professors who have stayed relatively current in technology know even better than the rest of society that they are, in fact, behind and that almost everyone is. The growth in technology's uses, applications, nuances, and challenges has been unfolding faster than anyone could have predicted, and if you are not constantly upgrading your skills in this area, you are at risk of lagging dangerously behind.

Legislators who are asked to increase technology budgets for institutions in their city or state, regents or trustees who are expected to oversee expenditures at colleges and universities, students who pay technology fees, donors who give money to expand the technology capabilities of institutions, and other stakeholders in higher education expect all professors to learn and use the best of what is available. They do not expect to walk by a classroom that is outfitted with a document camera, a high-speed Internet line, and a high-tech projector and see the professor standing at the front of the room, reading from lecture notes while students madly attempt to write down the words verbatim.

To increase your technology proficiency to improve student learning, you must take advantage of every means imaginable, including every training opportunity from your own institution, at retail computer outlets, or at other places that offer them at a time and level that is appropriate for you. Think also about enrolling in an online class (many of which are free) through your own institution or through such entities as BarnesandNobleuniversity.com. Let me repeat: to keep your own competitive edge, you must become and stay technologically savvy.

DEVELOPING A TEACHING PORTFOLIO

The concept of the professional portfolio as a tool for student development was discussed thoroughly in Chapter 11. It should not come as a surprise then that portfolios hold great potential for helping adjunct professors, especially *aspiring academics*, develop their teaching skills. Peter Seldin (1999) defines a teaching portfolio as "a factual description of a professor's teaching strengths and accomplishments, which includes documents and materials that collectively suggest the scope and quality of a professor's teaching performance" (p. 110).

The first step to creating a teaching portfolio is to develop your philosophy of education, as discussed in Chapter 2. Then articulate the purpose of your portfolio and the questions you want your portfolio to answer. A single, carefully crafted paragraph usually is enough. Decide whether you are focusing on your growth as a professor in the classroom or whether you want to focus on just one aspect of your teaching. Focusing on the area of your greatest strength, for example, will help you figure out why you are so good in one setting or with one kind of student. Or maybe you want to focus on the area that is giving you the most difficulty because you want to ameliorate the situation. When using your portfolio to help maintain your edge, focusing both on what you are doing well and what you are struggling with will help answer some questions you have about your teaching (Murray, 1997).

Next, you need to begin to collect *artifacts* that demonstrate your philosophy and fit with the purpose of your portfolio. Artifacts might include a course syllabus, a sample of student work, a letter from a colleague who visited your class, comments from student evaluations, and so on. As you select an item, do not just stuff it in the binder or folder but also reflect on it in writing. Why have you chosen this item? What does it say about your teaching? How does it reflect your philosophy? What have you learned as a result of the experience that this item represents? Without the reflection on the artifacts, the portfolio becomes nothing more than a scrapbook, and although scrapbooks have value in some arenas, they will not help you advance in your career or improve your skills.

Creating a teaching portfolio is an ongoing process. Some people devote a whole weekend to start and then continue on a regular basis after that. Others set aside an hour each week to add to their portfolio, making a selection from some student work, from an assignment given, from a note received, and then writing about the selection and reviewing other pieces already included. Over time, patterns emerge, but that takes a while. Some faculty eventually share their portfolios with a trusted colleague who can help them identify the patterns presented. Start working on yours as soon as possible and let it grow into a dynamic document that serves you in your quest to keep your edge.

FOCUSING ON THE DIFFERENCES YOU ARE MAKING

As your teaching evolves and your relationships with students mushroom, you will receive cards, letters, and e-mail messages that warm your heart. Knowing that there will also be miserably frigid days in the future, begin now to start a "warm fuzzy" file of all of those positive messages. Sometimes we need to be reminded that we are making a difference so that we can muster the emotional energy to get in front of a class that simply has not responded (Palmer, 1998).

In addition to thinking about the difference you are making to individual students, you can also think much more globally about the impact of your teaching. Are you helping to create scientists? Writers? Thinkers? Problem-solvers? Are you helping to create better teachers, better statisticians, better doctors, better policymakers, better journalists? You *are* making a difference in what and how you teach. Remind yourself of the potential repercussions of what you do since the lives you touch through your teaching are never the same. Because you change brains, chemically and physically, through your instruction, students are literally not the same when they leave your classroom, lab, or field site as they were when they arrived. That is both an awesome responsibility and a jolt of reality.

You will need reminders of this responsibility and reality on a regular basis, in some terms more than in others and at some institutions more than at others. The cold, prickly truth is that good adjunct teachers are not always universally adored, most notably not by their "colleagues." Sadly, some people still think they are living in a "zero-sum" world—that is, a world in which the pie is only so big, if you get more of the pie, they think, then I get less. These are the professors who, when they hear students sing your praises, will denigrate you in a covert (or not-so-covert) way. These are the professors who, when you gain some recognition, will pointedly not congratulate you. It is on these days that you need both your warm fuzzy file and your focus on the real difference that you are making. There are few professions that allow you to have the impact that teaching does. Channel your attention on this impact on a regular basis. It helps keep you going in the positive direction that you desire and know is right.

TAKING CARE OF YOURSELF

Teaching is a physically, emotionally, intellectually, and sometimes even spiritually demanding profession. You will spend a great deal of your time around people who expect you to be a certain way. They need you as a colleague, teacher, speaker, adviser, and so on. All of these interactions take energy, and if you do not keep your energy supply replenished, then you will have none to pour into your teaching (or into your personal life). So practice moderation in all things that comprise your professional life (Boice, 2000) and balance in your daily lifestyle.

For many adjunct professors, solitude helps to replenish the supply. You will have to make an active decision to find solitude, and you will have to make the appropriate space. Today's adjunct professor teaches in a classroom anywhere from three to fifteen hours each week; invests hours preparing for the classroom time; advises students on some very weighty issues; conducts research on the Internet or in the field; answers e-mail and returns phone calls for minutes that turn into hours each day; and more. Nearly all of these commitments happen in the company of others or involve interactions with others. Finding time alone is essential for refueling your energy reserves.

Throughout this book, I have written from the perspective that, in today's world, adjunct professors are being held increasingly accountable for their work and the learning of their students. Some readers may feel guilty about taking time for themselves, whether in solitude or for other renewing endeavors. A healthier perspective is that you must take this time to keep yourself balanced so that you can do your job better. Students cannot benefit from your instruction, if you have become so surly or so drained of energy that you are operating far below your potential.

In today's society, the term *role model* is heard often, as is the wish that we had more of them. Many professors disdain that term when it is applied to their profession. Yet, just as many public servants have become elevated to the status of role model, regardless of their desire or willingness to hold that position, professors will increasingly be viewed as people to emulate. You will be asked by a student to serve as a reference in a job application, to write a letter in their pursuit of a scholarship, and so on. The idea may cause you some discomfort, but try to say yes as often as possible. Although it may feel like a burden at times, it is really a privilege you have been accorded. A guiding question is, "What kind of people do you want your students to grow up to be?" Once you answer that for yourself, you will realize what to model for them.

It is essential that you regularly sharpen your teaching edge because it will become dull almost without your noticing it. Your students will notice, however, and eventually so will you. The edge becomes especially difficult to sharpen if you ever lose the passion, the momentum, and the currency within your teaching (Massy, 2003).

A Hindu proverb states, "There is nothing noble in being superior to some other person. The true nobility is in being superior to your previous self." In this age of accountability, I challenge you to be superior to your previous self. You, your students, your institution, your community, and an increasingly global society will be well served.

SUMMARY OF KEY POINTS

- Higher education has changed and will continue to change; you must change to thrive and, in many cases, to survive.
- Develop a following among students by being an excellent teacher; word of mouth spreads quickly among students and colleagues.
- Network on campus and within the community to grow your following.
- Avail yourself of the resources of your institution's faculty development initiative.
- Find a colleague with whom you can work closely on your teaching and consider developing a mentoring relationship.
- If you get a mentor, become one for a newer adjunct professor.
- Study your own teaching so that you can increase your talents and help others be more successful.
- Read outside your discipline area about effective teaching and learning practices.
- Work continually on developing your technology skills.

- Leverage the free resources provided by publishers of your textbooks and other vendors.
- Maintain a teaching portfolio, not only for official reasons but also for the reflection opportunities it will provide.
- Keep the passion, desire, and quest for excellent teaching alive; the strength of your enthusiasm will inspire others.
- Because the strength of this enthusiasm will inspire others, *invest* time in yourself.
- Stay focused on the difference you are making in the lives of the students.

THE FINAL WORD

"Throughout my career, I have focused on the importance of each of the things that I enjoy in life. What I've learned is that life can become even richer through a managed combination of planning, effort, and good luck. It's very important to maintain a balance in my life between work and all the other things that enrich my life."

—Jack McElwee, Reno, Nevada

"So often I hear professionals at one level of education criticize those at another for not having prepared adequately the students they receive or taking proper care of those students that they send forward. For example, college professors discount the efforts of high school teachers, without understanding the range of pressures upon them. Or high school teachers criticize college professors for failing to properly challenge or nurture one of their high potential graduates who gets off track and drops out to play in a band. Having taught social sciences concurrently at a high school (full-time) and as an adjunct college professor for eight years, I am regularly reminded of how much more we could do for each student if we would support each other in our missions. When was the last time you spoke with a high school teacher whose discipline dovetails with yours? We have much more in common with each other than we have differences and we are really 'all in this together.'

—Toby Edwards, Louisville, Kentucky

MODEL MENTORING AGREEMENT

Realizing that an ongoing mentoring relationship between veteran and adjunct instructors can provide benefits to both, as well as to Wilmington College, Chris Smith, Associate Professor, and Tony Barkwell, Adjunct Professor, enter into the agreement below to enable Mr. Barkwell to:

1. Plan and launch his course consistent with accepted practices.
2. Develop, debug, and analyze results of course examinations.
3. Retain students within his course, and recruit students to future courses.

During the Fall 200- semester, Dr. Smith agrees to:

1. Meet with Mr. Barkwell alternate Friday afternoons for approximately one hour to review Mr. Barkwell's experiences and provide other information as needed.
2. Speak with Mr. Barkwell as needed by telephone, at 462-9999, between 1:00 and 4:00 P.M. any weekday afternoon.
3. Allow Mr. Barkwell, upon a day's notification, to visit regular class meetings of any evening course being taught by Dr. Smith.
4. Unless agreed otherwise by Mr. Barkwell in advance, treat all communications with Mr. Barkwell as confidential.

Mr. Barkwell agrees to:

1. Accept Dr. Smith's coaching as nondirective, realizing that academic freedom and other professional practices require his acceptance of ultimate responsibility for all decisions discussed with Dr. Smith.
2. Serve as a guest speaker, on a mutually agreeable topic, for a segment of one of Dr. Smith's class meetings, and review that activity immediately afterward.
3. Submit small developmental activities, such as creating several test questions, no later than the prescribed deadline set by Dr. Smith.
4. Serve as a substitute instructor for the Wednesday, October 1, meeting of Dr. Smith's class (5:30 P.M., room 118, Gore Business Building).

5. Unless agreed otherwise by him in advance, treat all communications with Dr. Smith as confidential.

It is agreed upon that this arrangement will remain in effect throughout the 200-/0- academic year only. Any extension will need to be negotiated in May 200-. Either party may terminate the agreement, without reason, at any point, by e-mailing the other party and cc-ing Dr. X. Brands, at xbrands@wcslc.edu.

_____   _____

Dr. Chris Smith   Mr. Tony Barkwell

_____   _____

Date   Date

BIBLIOGRAPHY

■ ■ ■ ■ ■

Ailes, R. (1995). *You Are the Message*. New York: Currency-Doubleday.

Angelo, T. & K. P. Cross (1993). *Classroom Assessment Techniques: A Handbook for College Teachers*, 2nd ed. San Francisco: Jossey-Bass.

Astin, A. W., L. J. Vogelgesang, E. K. Ikeda, & J. A. Yee (2000). "How Service Learning Affects Students," Higher Education Research Institute, Los Angeles: UCLA Graduate School of Education & Information Studies.

Ausubel, D. P., J. D. Novak, & H. Hanesian (1978). *Educational Psychology*, 2nd ed. Austin, TX: Holt, Rinehart & Winston.

Baiocco, S. & DeWaters, J. (1998). *Successful College Teaching*. Boston: Allyn & Bacon.

Banta, T. W. & V. M. H. Borden (1994). "Performance Indicators for Accountability and Improvement." In V. M. H. Borden and T. W. Banta, eds., *Using Performance Indicators to Guide Strategic Decision Making*. New Directions for Institutional Research, no. 82. San Francisco: Jossey-Bass.

Bartlett, T. (2003). "Why Johnny Can't Write, Even Though He Went to Princeton." *Chronicle of Higher Education*, 49, no. 17 (January 3), pp. A39-40.

Basinger, J. (2002). "Casting a Wider Net." *Chronicle of Higher Education*, 49, no. 16 (December 13), pp. 32-33.

Benvennto, M. (1999). "In an Age of Interactive Learning, Some Students Want the Same Old Song and Dance." *Chronicle of Higher Education*, 45, no. 39 (June 4), p. B9.

Berk, R. (1998). *Professors Are from Mars, Students Are from Snickers*. Madison, WI: Mendota Press.

Berne, E. (1964). *The Games People Play*. New York: Ballantine.

Birnbaum, R. (2000). *Management Fads in Higher Education*. San Francisco: Jossey-Bass.

Bligh, D. A. (2000). *What's the Use of Lectures?* San Francisco: Jossey-Bass.

Bloom, B. S., ed. (1956). *Taxonomy of Learning Objectives: Cognitive Domain*. New York: David McKay.

Blythe, H. (1998). *It Works for Me*. Stillwater, OK: New Forums Press.

Boice, R. (2000). *Advice for New Faculty Members*. Boston: Allyn & Bacon.

Borrego, A. (2001). "A Wave of Consolidation Hits For-Profit Higher Education." *Chronicle of Higher Education,* 47, no. 48 (August 10), pp. A42-43.

Bowen, R. (2001). "The New Battle between Political and Academic Cultures." *Chronicle of Higher Education,* 47, no. 41 (June 22), pp. B14-15.

Boyle, R. & R. Dunn (1998). "Teaching Law Students through Individual Learning Styles." *Albany Law Review,* 62, no.1, pp. 213-255.

Bridges, J., writer and director, (1973). *The Paper Chase* [film]. Beverly Hills, CA: Twentieth Century Fox.

Brookfield, S. (1995). *Becoming a Critically Reflective Teacher.* San Francisco: Jossey-Bass.

Brookhart, S. M. (1999). *The Art and Science of Classroom Assessment: The Missing Part of the Pedagogy*. ASHE-ERIC Higher Education Report, 27, no. 1. Washington, DC: The George Washington University, Graduate School of Education and Human Development.

Brown, D. (2001). "Faculty Practice: The Power of E-Mail." *Syllabus,* 14, no. 12 (July), p. 26.

Burd, S. (2002). "Accountability or Meddling?" *Chronicle of Higher Education*, 49, no. 4 (September 20), pp. A23-25.

Burke, J. C. (1998). "Performance Funding Indicators: Concerns, Values, and Models for State Colleges and Universities. In J. C. Burke and A. M. Serban, eds., *Performance Funding for Public Higher Education: Fad or Trend?* New Directions for Institutional Research, no. 97. San Francisco: Jossey-Bass.

Buscaglia, L. (1990). *Living, Loving and Learning.* New York: Fawcett Books.

Carlson, S. (2001). "A Web Site of Reviews of Instructors Faces Challenges." *Chronicle of Higher Education,* 47, no. 29 (March 30), p. A46.

Carroll, J. (2002). "Don't Go the Extra Mile, Except . . ." *Chronicle of Higher Education Career Network.* http://chronicle.com/cgi2-bin/printable_verity.cgi.

Carroll, J. (2001). *How to Survive as an Adjunct Lecturer.* Houston: Adjunct Solutions.

Carroll, J. (2001a). "Being a Professional in an Unprofessional Climate." Chronicle of Higher Education Career Network. (October 5). http://chronicle.com/cgi2-bin?printable.cgi?article= http://chronicle.com/jobs/2001/10/2001.

Centra, J. (1993). *Reflective Faculty Evaluation.* San Francisco: Jossey-Bass.

Chism, N. V. N. (1999). *Peer Review of Teaching: A Sourcebook.* Bolton, MA: Anker.

Chronicle of Higher Education, (2002). Almanac Issue, 49, no. 1 (August 31).

Cobine, G. (1995). *Effective Use of Student Journal Writing.* ERIC Clearinghouse of Reading, English, and Communication Digest #99. Bloomington, IN.

Colberg, J., P. Desbery, & K. Trimble (1996). *The Case for Education: Contemporary Approaches for Using Case Methods.* Boston: Allyn & Bacon.

Covey, S. (1989). *The 7 Habits of Highly Effective People.* New York: Fireside.

Cox, A. M. (2001). "The Changed Classroom, Post-September 11." *Chronicle of Higher Education,* 48, no. 9 (October 26), pp. A16-18.

Cranton, P. (1989). *Planning Instruction for Adult Learners.* Toronto, Canada: Wall and Emerson.

Danielson, C. (1996). *Performance Assessment: A Collection of Tasks.* Princeton, NJ: Eye on Education.

Danielson, C. & L. Abristyn (1997). *An Introduction to Using Portfolios in the Classroom.* Alexandria, VA: Association for Supervision and Curriculum Development.

Darling-Hammond, L., & B. Falk (1995). *Authentic Assessment in Action.* New York: Teachers College Press.

Davidson, C. I. & S. A. Ambrose (1994). *The New Professor's Handbook.* Bolton, MA: Anker.

Davis, B. G. (2001). *Tools for Teaching.* San Francisco: Jossey-Bass.

Dewey, J. (1916). *Democracy and Education.* New York: Macmillan.

Diamond, R. (1998). *Designing and Assessing Courses and Curricula: A Practical Guide.* San Francisco: Jossey-Bass.

Dubson, M., ed. (2001). *Ghosts in the Classroom.* Boston: Camel's Back Books.

Duffy, D. K. & J. W. Jones (1995). *Teaching Within the Rhythms of the Semester.* San Francisco: Jossey-Bass.

Dunn, R. & K. Dunn (1999). *The Complete Guide to the Learning Styles Inservice System.* Boston: Allyn & Bacon.

Dunn, R. & S. Griggs, eds. (2000). *Practical Approaches to Using Learning Styles in Higher Education.* Westport, CT: Bergin and Garvey.

Eaton, J. (2001). "Regional Accreditation Reform." *Change,* 33, no. 2, pp. 38-45.

Ehrenberg, R. G. (2000). "Private College Trustees Must Control Costs." *Chronicle of Higher Education,* 47, no. 5 (September 29), p. B14.

Ewell, P. T. & D. P. Jones (1994). "Pointing the Way: Indicators as Policy Tools in Higher Education." In S. S. Ruppert, ed., *Charting Higher Education Accountability: A Sourcebook on State-Level Performance Indicators.* Denver: Education Commission of the States.

Fallows, S. and K. Ahmet (1999). *Inspiring Students: Case Studies in Motivating the Learner.* London: Kogan Page.

Felder, R. (1998). "How Students Learn, How Teachers Teach, and What Goes Wrong with the Process." *Tomorrow's Professor Listserv,* Stanford University, message 51, http://sll.stanford.edu/ projects/tomprof/newtomprof/postings/51.html.

Felder, R. M. & L. K. Silverman (1988). "Learning and Teaching Styles in Engineering Education," *Journal of Engineering Education,* 78, no. 7, p. 674.

Feldman, K.A. (1998). "Identifying Exemplary Teachers and Teaching: Evidence from Student Ratings." In K. A. Feldman and M. B. Paulsen, eds., *Teaching and Learning in the College Classroom,* 2nd edition, pp. 391-414. Needham Heights, MA: Simon and Schuster.

Feldman, K.A. (1987). "Research Productivity and Scholarly Accomplishment of College Teachers as Related to their Instructional Effectiveness." *Research in Higher Education,* 26, no. 3 (May), pp. 227-298.

Fink, L. D. (1995). "Evaluating Your Own Teaching." In P. Seldin, ed., *Improving College Teaching,* pp. 191-204. Bolton, MA: Anker.

Fisch, L. (1996). *The Chalk Dust Collection: Thoughts and Reflections on Teaching in Colleges and Universities.* Stillwater, OK: New Forums Press.

Fogg, P. (2002). "Some Adjuncts at Western Michigan U. Win Right to Tenure." *Chronicle of Higher Education.* 49, no. 12 (November 15), p. A15.

Gappa, J. & D. Leslie (1993). *The Invisible Faculty.* San Francisco: Jossey-Bass.

Gardner, H. (1999). *Intelligence Reframed: Multiple Intelligences for the 21st Century.* New York: Basic Books.

Gedda, G. (2002). "Powell Says Recruit More Minorities." *Associated Press Newswire* (May 17), http://wire.ap.org/APnews/center_story.html@FRONTID=ELECTIONS&STORYID=APIS7JI.

Gibbs, G. (1998). "Teaching Large Classes: Strategies for Improving Student Learning." *Tomorrow's Professor Listserv.* Stanford University, message 21. http://sll.stanford.edu/projects/tomprof/newtomprof/postings/21.html.

Golding, J. (2001). "Teaching the Large Lecture Class." In D. Royse, ed., *Teaching Tips for College and University Instructors: A Practical Guide,* pp. 95-120. Boston: Allyn & Bacon.

Goleman, D. (2002). *Primal Leadership.* Boston: Harvard Business School Press.

Grabe, M., & C. Grabe (2001). *Integrating Technology for Meaningful Learning,* 3rd ed. Boston: Houghton-Mifflin.

Gregorc, A. (1986). *Adults Guide to Style.* Columbia, CT: Gregorc Associates.

Grunert, J. (1997). *The Course Syllabus: A Learning-Centered Approa*ch. Bolton, MA: Anker.

Gose, B. (1997). "Efforts to Curb Grade Inflation Get an F from Many Critics." *Chronicle of Higher Education,* 43, no. 46 (July 25), pp. A19-A20.

Grieve, D. & C. Worden, eds. (2000). *Managing Adjunct and Part-Time Faculty for the New Millennium.* Elyria, OH: Info-Tec.

Hake, R. (1998). "Interactive-Engagement versus Traditional Methods: A Six-Thousand-Student Survey of Mechanics Test Data for Introductory Physics Courses," *American Journal of Physics,* 66, pp. 64-74, http://web.mit.edu/tll/published/new_research.htm.

Hannon, K. (2001). "Using E-Mail to Communicate with Students." *ASEE Prism: Exploring the Future of Engineering Education,* 10, no. 6 (February), pp. 34-35.

Hativa, N. (2000). *Teaching for Effective Learning in Higher Education.* Dordrecht, Netherlands: Kluwer Academic Press.

Harris, R. (2001). *The Plagiarism Handbook: Strategies for Preventing, Detecting, and Dealing with Plagiarism.* Los Angeles: Pyrczak Publications.

Harris, R. (1997). "Evaluating Internet Research Sources." *Virtual Salt,* http://www.virtualsalt.com/evalu8it.htm.

Haugen, L. (2000). "Writing a Teaching Philosophy Statement." *Tomorrow's Professor Listserv,* message 193, Stanford University Learning Laboratory, http://sll.stanford.edu/projects/tomprof/positings/193.html.

Hibbard, K. M., & the Educators of Connecticut's Pomperaug Regional School District 15 (1996). *A Teacher's Guide to Performance-Based Learning and Assessment.* Alexandria, VA: ASCD.

Hilt, D. (2001). "What Students Can Teach Professors: Reading Between the Lines of Evaluations." *Chronicle of Higher Education,* 47, no. 27 (March 16), p. B 24.

Howard, R. (2001). "Forget About Policing Plagiarism. Just Teach." *Chronicle of Higher Education,* 48, no. 12 (November 16), p. B24.

Howe, N. & W. Strauss (2000). *Millennials Rising: The Next Great Generation.* New York: Vintage.

Huba, M., & J. Freed (2000). *Learner-Centered Assessment on College Campuses.* Boston: Allyn & Bacon.

Johnson, D. W., R. T. Johnson, & K. A. Smith (1991). *Cooperative Learning: Increasing College Faculty Instructional Productivity.* ASHE-ERIC Higher Education Report, no. 4. Washington, DC: The George Washington University, Graduate School of Education and Human Development.

Johnson, S. (1999). *Who Moved My Cheese?* New York: Putnam.

Katz, R. N. & Associates. (1999). *Dancing with the Devil: Information Technology and the New Competition in Higher Education.* San Francisco: Jossey-Bass.

Kearsley, G. (2000). *Online Education: Learning and Teaching in Cyberspace.* Belmont, CA: Wadsworth.

Kelly, C. (1997). "David Kolb: The theory of experiential learning and ESL." *Internet TESL Journal,* 3, no. 9.

Kolb, D. (1983). *Experiential Learning.* Upper Saddle River, NJ: Prentice Hall.

Kors, A.C. & H. Silverglate (1999). *The Shadow University: The Betrayal of Liberty on America's Campuses.* New York: Harper Perennial.

Lacina, J. G. (2002). "Preparing International Students for a Successful Social Experience in Higher Education." In B. W. Speck and B. H. Carmical, eds., *New Directions for Higher Education,* No. 117. San Francisco: Jossey-Bass.

Leslie, D. (1998). "New Directions for Research, Policy Development, and Practice." In D. Leslie, ed., *The Growing Use of Part-Time Faculty: Understanding Causes and Effects.* New Directions for Higher Education, 104. San Francisco: Jossey-Bass.

Leslie, D. & J. Gappa (2002). "Part-Time Faculty: Competent and Committed." In C. Outcalt, ed., *Community College Faculty: Characteristics, Practices, and Challenges.* New Directions for Community Colleges, 118. San Francisco: Jossey-Bass.

Light, R. J. (2001). *Making the Most of College: Students Speak Their Minds.* Cambridge, MA: Harvard University Press.

Longmate, J. & F. Cosco (2002). "Part-Time Instructors Deserve Equal Pay for Equal Work." *Chronicle of Higher Education,* 48, no. 34 (May 3), p. B14.

Lovitts, B. & C. Nelson (2000). "The Hidden Crisis in Graduate Education: Attrition from Ph.D. Programs." *Academe,* 86, no. 6 (November/December), pp. 44-50.

Lunde, J. P. (2000). "101 Things You Can Do the First Three Weeks of Class." *Tomorrow's Professor Listserv,* Stanford University Learning Lab, message 168. http://sll.stanford.edu/projects/tomprof/newtomprof/postings/168.html.

Lyons, R. (2001). "Recognizing the Contributions of Adjunct Faculty." *Adjunct Advocate,* 8, no. 6 (July/August), pp. 12, 37-38.

Lyons, R. (1999). "Adjunct Professors: A Priceless Resource." *Community College Week,* 11, no. 13 (January 25), pp. 4, 16.

Lyons, R. (1996). *A Study of the Effects of a Mentoring Initiative on the Performance of New Adjunct Community College Faculty.* Unpublished doctoral dissertation, University of Central Florida, Orlando.

Lyons, R., M. Kysilka, & G. Pawlas (1999). *The Adjunct Professor's Guide to Success: Surviving and Thriving in the College Classroom.* Boston: Allyn & Bacon.

Lyons, R., M. McIntosh, & M. Kysilka (2003). *Teaching College in an Age of Accountability.* Boston: Allyn & Bacon.

Macmillan, J. (1997). *Classroom Assessment: Principles and Practice for Effective Instruction.* Boston: Allyn & Bacon.

Marincovich, M. (1999). "Using Student Feedback to Improve Teaching." In P. Seldin, ed., *Changing Practices in Evaluating Teaching.* Bolton, MA: Anker.

Massy, W. (2003). *Honoring the Trust: Quality and Cost Containment in Higher Education.* Bolton, MA: Anker.

Matthews, R.S. (1996). "Collaborative Learning: Creating Knowledge with Students." In R. J. Menges and M. Weimer, eds., *Teaching on Solid Ground: Using Scholarship to Improve Practice*, pp. 101-124. San Francisco: Jossey-Bass.

McCabe, D. & P. Drinan, (1999). "Toward a Culture of Academic Integrity." *Chronicle of Higher Education,* 46, no. 7 (October 15), p. A19.

McKeachie, W. (2001). *Teaching Tips: Strategies, Research, and Theory for College and University Teachers,* 11th edition. Boston: Houghton Mifflin.

Meister, J. (2001). "The Brave New World of Corporate Education." *Chronicle of Higher Education,* 47, no. 22 (February 9), p. B 24.

Middendorf, J. & A. Kalish (1996). "The 'Change-Up' in Lectures." *National Teaching and Learning Forum,* 5, p. 1+.

Millis, B. J. & P. G. Cottell, Jr. (1998). *Cooperative Learning for Higher Education Faculty.* Phoenix: Oryx Press.

Moulds, R. (1997). "An Interactive Annotations Assignment." *The Teaching Professor,* 11, no. 4 (April), p. 6.

Moxley, D., A. Najor-Durack, & C. Dumbrigue (2001). *Keeping Students in Higher Education.* London: Kogan Page.

Murray, J. P. (1997). *Successful Faculty Development and Evaluation: The Complete Teaching Portfolio.* ASHE-ERIC Higher Education Report, 8. Washington, DC: The George Washington University, Graduate School of Education and Human Development.

National Center for Educational Statistics (2001), http://www.nces.ed.gov/pubs2000/projections/chapter2.html.

Novak, G., E. Patterson, A. Gavrin, & W. Christian (1999). *Just-in-Time Teaching: Blending Active Learning with Web Technology.* Upper Saddle River, NJ: Prentice Hall.

Ohmann, R. (2000). "Historical Reflections on Accountability." *Academe,* 86, no. 1 (January/February), pp. 24-29.

Olsen, F. (2002). "Phoenix Rises." *Chronicle of Higher Education,* 49, no. 10 (November 1), pp. A29-31.

Olsen, F. (2001). "Getting Ready for a New Generation of Course-Management Systems." *Chronicle of Higher Education,* 48, no.17 (December 21), pp. A 25-27.

Palmer, P. (1998). *The Courage to Teach.* San Francisco: Jossey-Bass.

Panitz, T. (2001). "Yes Virginia There is a Big Difference between Cooperative and Collaborative Learning." *Tomorrow's Professor Listserv.* Stanford University, message 237, http://sll.stanford.edu/projects.tomprof/newtomprof/postings/237.hml.

Popham, W. J. (1999). *Classroom Assessment: What Teachers Need to Know,* 2nd edition. Boston: Allyn & Bacon.

Ratey, J. J. (2001). *A User's Guide to the Brain,* New York: Pantheon Books.

Ravitz, J., Y. Wong, & H. Becker (1999). *Teaching, Learning and Technology National Survey,* www.crito.uci.edu/tlc.

Reisberg, L. (2000). "Are Students Really Learning?" *Chronicle of Higher Education,* 47, no. 16 (November 17), pp. A67-70.

Restak, R. (2001). *The Secret Life of the Brain.* Washington, DC: Joseph Henry Press.

Rhem, J. (1998). "Problem-Based Learning: An Introduction," National Teaching and Learning Forum (December), 8, 1, http://www.ntlf.com/html/pi/9812/pbl_1.htm.

Rodriguez, S. (2002). *Giants among Us: First Generation College Students Who Lead Activist Lives.* Nashville: Vanderbilt University Press.

Roueche, J., S. Roueche, & M. Milliron (1995). *Strangers in their Own Land.* Washington, D.C.: Community College Press.

Royse, D., ed. (2001). *Teaching Tips for College and University Professors.* Boston: Allyn & Bacon.

Ruben, B. (2001). "We Need Excellence Beyond the Classroom." *Chronicle of Higher Education,* 47, no. 44 (July 13), pp. B15-16.

Sanders, W. B. (2001). *Creating Learning-Centered Courses for the World Wide Web.* Boston: Allyn & Bacon.

Schmidt, P. (2002). "Most States Tie Aid to Performance, Despite Little Proof that It Works." *Chronicle of Higher Education,* 48, no. 24 (February 22), pp. A20-21.

Schmidt, P. (2001). "State Higher-Education Leaders Want to See Improvements in Job Training." *Chronicle of Higher Education,* online daily news (August 1).

Scriven, M. (1995). *Student Ratings Offer Useful Input to Teacher Evaluations.* ERIC/AE Digest, ED398240. Washington, DC: ERIC Clearinghouse of Assessment and Evaluation.

Seldin, P. (1999). *Changing Practices in Evaluating Teaching: A Practical Guide to Improved Faculty Performance and Promotion/Tenure Decisions,* Bolton, MA: Anker.

Selingo, J. (2001). "Pennsylvania Rewards Fast Graduation, but Public Colleges Cry Foul." *Chronicle of Higher Education,* online daily news (August 3), http://www.chronicle.com/daily/2001/08/2001080301n.htm.

Silberman, M. (1996). *Active Learning: 101 Strategies to Teach Any Subject.* Boston: Allyn & Bacon.

Slaughter, S. (2001). "Professional Values and the Allure of the Market." *Academe,* 87, no. 5 (September/October), pp. 22-27.

Smallwood, S. (2002). "Faculty Union Issues Standards for Treatment of Adjuncts." *Chronicle of Higher Education,* 48, no. 47 (August 2), p. A 12.

Sousa, D. A. (2001). *How the Brain Learns: A Classroom Teacher's Guide,* Thousand Oaks, CA: Corwin.

Spence, L. (2001). "The Case against Teaching." *Change,* 33, no. 6 (November/ December), pp. 10-19.

Stark, J. & L. Lattuca (1997). *Shaping the College Curriculum.* Boston: Allyn & Bacon.

Stephens, A. & S. Wright (1999). "The Part-Time Faculty Paradox." *Community College Week,* 11, no. 13 (January 25), pp. 6-8, 14-15.

Stewart, I. & V. Joines (1987). *T A Today: A New Introduction to Transactional Analysis.* Kingston-on-Soar, UK: Lifespace.

Tapscott, D. (1998). *Growing Up Digital: The Rise of the Net Generation.* New York: McGraw-Hill.

Tatum, B.D. (1997). *"Why Are All The Black Kids Sitting Together in the Cafeteria?"* New York: Basic Books.

Tuckman, H. P. (1978). "Who Is Part-Time in Academe?" *AAUP Bulletin,* 64, pp.305-315.

U.S. Department of Education, National Center for Education Statistics, 1999–2000. *National Postsecondary Student Aid Study* (NPSAS: 2000).

U.S. News and World Report, "America's Best Colleges", (2003).

Van der Werf, M. (2002). "Many Colleges will Close or Merge, Standard & Poor's Predicts." *Chronicle of Higher Education,* 49, no. 16, p. 34.

Vargas, J. (2001). "Improving Teaching Performance." In D. Royse, ed., *Teaching Tips for College and University Instructors,* pp. 254-280. Boston: Allyn & Bacon.

Waller, C., R. Coble, J. Scharer, and S. Giamportone (2000). *Governance and Coordination of Public Higher Education in All 50 States.* Raleigh, NC: North Carolina Center for Public Policy Research.

Walvoord, B. E. & V. J. Anderson (1998). *Effective Grading: A Tool for Learning and Assessment.* San Francisco: Jossey-Bass.

Wankat, P. (2002). *The Effective, Efficient Professor.* Boston: Allyn and Bacon.

Weimer, M. (1990). "What to Do When Somebody Criticizes Your Teaching." In M. Weimer & R. A. Neff, eds., *Teaching College: Collected Readings for the New Instructor,* pp. 143-44. Madison, WI: Magna.

Wellman, J. (2001). "Assessing State Accountability Systems." *Change,* 33, no.2, pp. 46-52.

Wellman, J. (2000). "Accreditors Have to See Past Learning Outcomes." *Chronicle of Higher Education,* 47, no. 4 (September 22), p. B20.

Wiggins, G. P. (1993). *Exploring the Purpose and Limits of Teaching.* San Francisco: Jossey-Bass.

Wilson, R. (2001). "Ohio State 'Taxes' Departments to Make a Select Few Top-Notch." *Chronicle of Higher Education,* 47, no. 38 (June 1), pp. A8-A9.

Woodell, J. & E. Garofoli (2003). "Faculty Development and the Diffusion of Innovations." *Syllabus*, 16, no. 5, pp. 15-17.

Wright, W. A., P. T. Knight, & N. Pomerleau (1999). "Portfolio People: Teaching and Learning Dossiers and Innovation in Higher Education." *Innovative Higher Education*, 24, pp. 89-103.

Yamane, D. (1996). "Collaboration and Its Discontents: Steps toward Overcoming Barriers to Successful Group Projects." *Teaching Sociology*, 24 (October), pp. 378-383.

Zachary, L. (2000). *The Mentor's Guide*. San Francisco: Jossey-Bass.

http://www.nces.ed.gov/pubs2000/projections/chapter2.html

http://www.cpsr.org/cpsr/privacy/ssn/ferpa.buckley.html

■ ■ ■ ■ ■ ▬▬▬▬▬▬▬▬▬▬▬▬▬▬▬▬▬▬▬▬▬